Helping Your Child
Improve His Reading

BY RUTH STRANG

Helping Your Gifted Child
Helping Your Child Improve His Reading

The Adolescent Views Himself: A Psychology of Adolescence
The Administrator and the Improvement of Reading
(*with* Donald M. Lindquist)
Counseling Technics in College and Secondary Schools
Group Work in Education
Exploration in Reading Patterns
An Introduction to Child Study
Making Better Readers
(*with* Dorothy K. Bracken)
Role of the Teacher in Personnel Work
Teen-Age Tales
Study Type of Reading Exercises

Helping Your Child Improve His Reading

By RUTH STRANG

University of Arizona

E. P. DUTTON & CO., INC.

NEW YORK, 1962

COPYRIGHTS FROM WHICH PERMISSION TO QUOTE HAS BEEN GRANTED

Conant, James Bryant. *Recommendations for Education in the Junior High School Years*, 46 pp., Princeton, N.J.: Educational Testing Service, 20 Nassau Street.

Glasgow, Ellen. *The Woman Within*, pp. 24–25, New York: Harcourt, Brace and Company, 1954.

Strang, Ruth, and Paul J. Eagan. "Teen-Age Readers," Vol. 50 (June, 1961), *The PTA Magazine* (*National Parent-Teacher*).

Published simultaneously in Canada by Clarke, Irwin & Co., Ltd., Toronto.

Library of Congress Catalog Card Number: 62-7811

Contents

6 / 3 / 5

Preface

CAN parents change, or are they saddled with their present attitudes and habits? Does understanding of a child and his problems of growing up make any real difference in what parents actually do, or in how the child matures? Many people today take a negative, defeatist attitude toward those questions.

However, there is a positive way of thinking about child growth and development. We have sound psychological evidence that children learn under certain conditions—when they feel a need for learning, when the task is meaningful and appropriate to their ability, when they can see results, and when they experience satisfaction in the process and the product. Parents can consciously help to create these conditions.

This is especially true in helping the child learn to read. Parents not only can avoid creating situations in which the child becomes bored, frustrated, or resentful about reading; they can also create situations in which the child can succeed with reasonable effort, whatever his ability may be; situations in which he can get some satisfaction from reading, whether he reads a book of riddles, an adventure story, or fascinating facts about history or science.

In this book we have tried not to be prescriptive. We do not want to sound like the voice of authority telling parents what to do about their child's reading. Our aim is to give parents a background of understanding that will help them to determine their own role in the reading development of their child. Many specific suggestions will be given, as a reservoir of ideas from which parents may select any pattern or combination of patterns that seems appropriate to their child. Thus they will become more competent and confident in their rightful role as co-workers with teachers in the formal aspects of their child's education.

Although serious reading problems often involve the parents' at-

9

titudes toward themselves and toward their child, it is not the purpose of this book to change these deep-seated attitudes. It would be impossible for any book to do so. But it is possible to help parents perceive the child in a new light, and to change their behavior to some extent. Even small changes in the parents' attitude and behavior may give the child more comfort, confidence, incentive, or skill. By resolving certain conflicts and by correcting certain misconceptions, the book may clear the air, as it were, and lighten the parents' burden of uncertainty and doubt.

The author is especially indebted to Mr. Paul J. Eagan, Dr. Ethlyne Phelps, and other teachers who obtained from their high school students introspective and retrospective reports about their reading development as it occurred at home and in school; to Jean Archer, Diane de la Mater, Dick Gamble, Kathy Mund, Judith Peck, Margaret Prouty, Kathy Scott, John Tyler, and other high school students whose compositions we have quoted freely; and to other writers in the fields of reading and parent education.

ONE

Reading from the Parents' Point of View

PARENTS are naturally concerned about their child's reading. Reading is associated with social prestige; it affects social relations. Our principal means of communicating with one another are reading, speaking, listening, and writing. Inability to use these tools may seriously interfere with a person's social adjustment.

Reading broadens our interests and enriches our leisure hours. Despite radio and television, reading is here to stay. In 1954 the Chicago Public Library reported an average circulation of ten books for each child of elementary school age. Children's books are bestsellers; more are being published every year.

Reading is necessary for success in school, in college, and in almost every vocation. There are few jobs, if any, that do not require reading ability. To be good citizens we must understand current events by comprehending, weighing, and remembering what we read.

When our child is successful in learning to read, and comes home from school saying gleefully, "Mommy, let me read to *you*," we rejoice in his accomplishment. It is enough at this stage that the child is thrilled by the magic of getting meaning from little black marks on white paper. When, in the fifth grade, the report comes home that Bill is reading at or above grade level, we feel relieved. Later, we are proud to have him placed in the "Honors" or "Advanced" group in high school. We are pleased and reassured by any evidence that our child is successful in reading.

On the other hand, when our child has difficulty with beginning reading, when he lags behind other third graders in reading, when he has a hard time keeping up with the wide reading required in the fifth or sixth grade, when he is placed in a special reading group in junior high school, or when he gets a low score on his college entrance board examinations, we are very much concerned.

11

Our worry is aggravated by the conflicting points of view expressed in popular articles and books on reading. Many of these articles and books blame the schools: Johnny can't read because the schools do not teach him to sound out the words by certain phonic methods. Johnny can't read because the schools have gone "progressive" and no longer teach the three R's. Johnny can't read because teachers are poorly prepared and poorly paid for their work. And one high school principal, writing in *Harper's Magazine,* said in effect that one-third of all high school pupils can't read because they are stupid—incapable of mastering the chief tools of learning: reading and writing. Let us try to clear up some of these misconceptions.

ARE THE SCHOOLS TO BLAME?

The poor readers in this generation are not to be blamed entirely on the schools. The home plays an important part in making a child a good reader or a poor reader. With the best intentions in the world, some parents make reading problems of their children. Some unfavorable parental attitudes will be described later in this chapter.

Reading achievement is also affected by the times we live in. When you and I were growing up, we spent much of our time in reading. Now the average youngster spends his leisure time listening to the radio, watching television programs, going to the movies, riding in a car, and taking part in clubs and social activities. He spends little time in reading; consequently his reading skills remain undeveloped. Just as one acquires skill in sports by constant practice, so one gains fluency and vocabulary by wide reading.

Moreover, movies, radio, and television have reduced the individual's need for reading as a means of satisfying his curiosity about the world and its inhabitants. For sheer entertainment, too, children no longer need to turn to books.

All of this means that the schools are working in a whirlpool of forces that tend to reduce both the need and the desire to read. Ways must be found to make the modern media of communication the allies instead of the enemies of effective reading; they must be used to stimulate and enrich reading.

Children Are Learning To Read

Much of the popular criticism of the schools is not justified. The American schools are not turning out hordes of illiterates. Actually, pupils are reading, on the average, as well as they did a generation ago. As early as 1838, Horace Mann, then Secretary of the Board of Education for Massachusetts, reported: "More than eleven-twelfths of all the children in the reading classes in our schools do not understand the meaning of the words they read." This statement was made during a period when the phonics method was in general use. Records show that fifty years ago, in one large city, 50 per cent of almost 8,000 first graders had failed one or more times, largely because of poor reading.

Tests given recently show equal or slightly higher reading comprehension for today's children as compared with results of identical tests given more than thirty years ago.[1] This, despite the fact that there are many children in school today who would earlier have dropped out when reading and study became difficult for them. Children are now required by law to remain in school until sixteen or seventeen years of age, or until graduation from elementary school. Youngsters who are in school merely because the law says they have to be constitute the bulk of the reading problems. We used merely to report that the student had failed in history or some other subject; now we are more likely to recognize failure to comprehend a subject as a reading problem.

From a thorough study of this question, William S. Gray, an authority in the field of reading, concluded that there never was a time when so many boys and girls learned to read so well, read so many books, or read for so many purposes as they do today.

This is not to deny, of course, that many very able children are reading below their potential ability, even though they may be doing as well as average for their grade. Certainly there is room for improvement. No educator would deny this.

But blaming the schools is not the way to remedy the situation. We should take a positive approach. If our child is having trouble with reading, we should avoid making critical remarks in his hearing. Destroying any child's faith in his school and his teacher only makes it harder for him to learn. Helping a child learn to read is a joint responsibility of the home and the school.

Many Teachers Are Using Effective Methods

There is no one best method of teaching reading. Some children have profited at some times by every method that has been tried. The teacher's confidence in her special method is conveyed to the pupils. Any method that is used with faith and enthusiasm gets results. A rabbit's foot or a red flannel cloth has been known in some cases to cure certain aches and pains. If reading is nothing more than "barking at words"—merely being able to pronounce them, with no concern for their meaning—children can be taught to "read" by any systematic phonic method.

The big battles have been waged over phonics. The pendulum has swung from exclusive emphasis on phonics to the other extreme. We are now settling down to a more moderate point of view. A survey has shown that in some form, phonics is being taught in practically all our schools. For example, in the Teaching Guide for the Language Arts for the Chicago Public Schools, specific provision is made in each grade for phonic instruction. Similarly in other cities and states, phonics is being taught as an essential tool in learning to read. This is also true of the teachers' manuals of basal reader series.

The exclusive use of phonics has many dangers. Children may become interested only in pronouncing the words. This has happened. Some boys and girls have been able to read a passage aloud with great fluency, but without the slightest idea of what it meant.

Moreover, phonic drills may be so boring that children acquire a dislike for reading. Then, too, if phonics is introduced too early, some children may fail to learn to read by this method and become hopelessly lost in the process of sounding out words. Why, then, should we turn back the clock and return to the exclusive use of a method that was abandoned as the sole method of teaching reading half a century ago?

In countries where the native language is made up of a relatively few phonic units that sound the same in all words, the phonic method is far more useful than in English-speaking countries. Each of the twenty-six letters of our alphabet has more than one sound; the letter *a* has close to fifty sounds. Furthermore, what is essentially the same vowel sound is represented by different letters: for example, the short sound of ĕ is heard in *met, sweat, any, said, says, jeopardy.*

Or the letter combination remains the same but is sounded differently, as *ou* in *sour, pour, would, four*. These are just a few of the complexities encountered in teaching phonics.

On the other hand, parents may well become impatient with a teacher who uses the "whole word" or the "look-and-say" method exclusively. Children must learn the sounds that constitute the building blocks of all the words in our language; they cannot learn 25,000 different words one by one. The question is not Should teachers use phonic methods? Of course they should. They do, to some extent, in 99 per cent of our schools. To be on their own in reading, children must learn ways of recognizing unfamiliar words.

The question is, rather, When and how should phonic methods be introduced? The most approved procedure is to begin by teaching the child to associate letter sounds with printed letters in words that are thoroughly familiar and meaningful to him. More will be said about this in later chapters.

Many teachers have discovered that some children do better by one method and others do better by another method. The skillful teacher observes the child's response and uses the method or combination of methods by which he learns best.

Any method that helps a child enjoy achieving accurate comprehension is an effective method. By starting in with his need to read, one enlists his effort. Books that entice the reader by means of humor or the excitement of adventure help him to overcome difficulties that are not, for him, unsurmountable. Other factors in the effective teaching of reading include instruction that is given when it is needed, and drill on words or sounds that the individual child finds especially hard.

In appraising methods of teaching reading, we should recognize three common fallacies: (1) that learning is essentially an unpleasant experience and that the more disagreeable it is, the greater is its value; (2) that criticism is more effective than approval in stimulating a child to put forth greater effort; and (3) that the greater the difficulty of the reading material, the more it will challenge the child—this is what Gertrude Hildreth has called "the spur fallacy." To be sure, a certain degree of difficulty is challenging to most children. They reject too easy material as "baby stuff." But beyond a certain point, difficulty is a deterrent. The child gives up and withdraws from a reading task that yields him nothing but frustration. The ideal is (1) plenty of easy, interesting material to develop fluency and vocabulary painlessly—but not without effort—and (2) a progression of experience with reading material that *gradually* increases in difficulty. With a basic sight vocabulary and sufficient mastery of word-recognition skills, the child will be able to experience the excitement of having words tell him what the characters are saying and what happened next.

A child's interests are a springboard to reading. Any activity that is important to the child leads him to put forth effort in finding and reading books related to it. Any experience that arouses a child's curiosity may lead him to read more about it. A visit to the zoo led a reluctant reader to peruse book after book on monkeys. The desire to raise a prize pig for the county fair induced another boy, who called himself a "remejal reading problem," to read and comprehend a fairly difficult government bulletin on the subject. Parents, teachers, and librarians can help the child to find the book he needs when he needs it.

Reading Teachers and Consultants Are Being Employed

In more and more schools, reading teachers and consultants are being employed. They help the teachers by suggesting or demonstrating more effective methods of teaching, by supplying appropriate reading materials, and by helping with specific problems in the teaching of reading.

The reading teacher also works with small groups of pupils who need special help. He tries to understand each child and his reading difficulties, to give the instruction and practice that each one needs, to find books that each one can read with enjoyment, and to help every child increase his self-confidence by experiencing success.

When a parent wants to discuss his child's reading, he may have a conference with the reading teacher or consultant as well as with the child's regular teacher. These conferences are especially helpful to parents who have children with serious reading problems. The reading consultant may also meet with several parents in a small group where they can reveal their feelings about their children's reading difficulties and discuss what they can do to help.

Teacher Preparation Is Improving

If a child gets off to a poor start in the first grades; if the teaching of reading is neglected in subsequent years; if individual help is not given at any grade level to any child who for any reason is backward in reading, then we have allowed another reading problem to develop.

Although practically all elementary school teachers have had courses in the teaching of reading, this pre-service education may not have been entirely effective in bridging the gap between theory and actual classroom practice. It is no easy task to teach thirty-five children who have not been "school broken," and who present thirty-five different patterns of ability and background. Put yourself in the teacher's place. How fatiguing is it for the teacher to be in continuous contact with so many children for so many hours a day? Constant supervision of *three* lively children drives some parents nearly crazy. Yet, even under present school conditions, teachers not only maintain order and teach subjects; many even contrive to win the affection of their pupils. Parents should be glad when their children like the teacher; we all learn more readily from people whom we like.

Administrators often assign a young, inexperienced teacher to the first-grade class. If she is well prepared, has enthusiasm, and enjoys little children, she may do a superior job of teaching beginning reading. The children in her classes are fortunate. But what about the children who draw a teacher who is inept, insecure, and unable to apply effective methods of teaching reading? It is the principal's responsibility to do something about such a situation.

A Canadian elementary principal was asked why there were fewer reading problems in the upper grades of his schools than in our junior high schools. He said he thought it was because Canadian administrators gave careful attention to securing the best possible teachers for the first grades. If a teacher in the first grade was doing a poor job of teaching reading, the supervisor gave her special help; if that was ineffective, she was replaced by a teacher of proved competence in the teaching of reading. In this way effective instruction in beginning reading was assured.

Because of low salaries and unattractive working conditions, some of our communities cannot secure competent teachers; they have to settle for poorly prepared teachers. Even good teachers are hampered in many places by lack of suitable reading materials, an outmoded curriculum, or unenlightened administrative policies.

High Schools Present Problems

There are several causes for the pile-up of poor readers that has occurred in some of our high schools. One obvious cause is the policy of promoting pupils on the basis of age rather than on that of achievement. Children who do not catch on to reading in the first grade are promoted, but do not receive the individual help that they need in the second grade. One fourteen-year-old boy who had not learned to read during his eight years of schooling described his predicament in this way: "In the first grade I didn't like the teacher—I mean she didn't like me. And I had the same teacher for two years. In the third grade the teacher tried to help three of us who hadn't learned to read. But after that, no teacher ever bothered with me." His parents, too, were unaware of his reading problem and did not "bother with him."

Another cause of poor reading in the upper grades is lack of a developmental reading program. Reading instruction should continue throughout the school years and into college. As the poet and philosopher Goethe said: "Learning to read is a life-time process. I have been at it all my life and I cannot say yet I have reached the goal." Every teacher should give instruction in the reading of his subject.

Unfortunately, very few teachers in junior and senior high school have had any preparation in the teaching of reading. Consequently, when they are given the responsibility they feel at a loss. Many of them are now taking courses in the teaching of reading, either in connection with their subject or with the special developmental reading course that is usually offered to all pupils in the seventh and eighth grades.

In order to assist the school in building an adequate reading program, parents should know what it comprises: (1) instruction in reading as an intrinsic part of the teaching of each subject; (2) a developmental reading course, if needed, for all pupils at some strategic grade level; (3) special reading groups for pupils whose reading is so poor that they cannot profit by regular classroom instruction; and (4) work with individuals whose reading problem is too complex to be handled by the teacher in a group.

In his report on the junior high school, Dr. James Bryant Conant emphasized the need for more effective reading instruction in our high schools:

> Pupils will not succeed in high school unless they can read at least at the sixth-grade level. The ability to read is imperative in secondary school. I have been in schools in which practically no one in the ninth grade was reading as low as grade 6 and I have been in schools in which 35 to 50 per cent of the ninth graders were reading at the sixth-grade level or below. . . . Many communities . . . need to recognize the seriousness of the reading problem and to attempt to upgrade their reading programs. . . . Though instruction in the basic skills is the special responsibility of the elementary schools, it is the responsibility of the secondary schools as well.[2]

ARE POOR READERS "JUST STUPID"?

Even on group intelligence tests, the majority (69 per cent) of the children who were referred to the St. Louis language-arts centers because of failure to learn to read had normal or superior intelligence. For example, a fourteen-year-old boy in the seventh grade could barely read fourth-grade material. When he came to a difficult word, he often said silly things to make his classmates laugh and divert their attention from his poor reading. His usual attitude was one of defeat: "You can't teach me nothin'! Lots of people have tried. I'm too dumb to learn." Although his intelligence was slightly above average, he was convinced that he was stupid. Continued failure in reading and inability to learn subjects that required reading had confirmed his habit of self-disparagement. With special individual instruction in reading for two hours a week over a period of three months, he learned the basic vocabulary and word-recognition skills that he had failed to acquire earlier; with delight he began to read easy books that had interest and value for him.

Slow Learners Have Learned To Read

There are few, if any, children who cannot learn to read better if they are given time to grow and if they are provided with favorable learning conditions. Some will go ahead fast; others will proceed more slowly. A mentally deficient boy had failed to learn to read during eight years of schooling; however, he had grown enough mentally during these years so that, when he was given appropriate individual instruction, he was able to read signs, directions, and other important things in his environment. After a year of intensive teaching he could read books of about third-grade difficulty. This was sufficient reading ability to enable him to get a job and to hold it during a depression period when many college graduates were out of work. Reading, like other aspects of a child's development, is a continuous process of growth, sometimes slow, sometimes rapid; the rate varies with different children. No two children, not even children in the same family, follow exactly the same pattern of reading development.

There Are Other Causes

If a child is having trouble in reading, his teacher or principal should help the parents to find out why. The special services of a reading specialist, counselor, or psychologist may be enlisted. Many factors contribute to reading ability. No one can say a poor reader is just stupid until all other possible causes of his reading difficulty have been studied. In the majority of the cases that are brought to reading clinics, various specific causes of the reading failure are found. In other aspects of his life, the child may show interest, initiative, and other indications that he is potentially capable of learning to read. He has the mental ability, but, for some reason, he has not been able to learn to read. He is not just dumb.

To determine whether a child has the ability to learn to read better, the crucial test is to give him the best possible instruction in the most favorable environment and see how well he learns. If he does not respond to these conditions, we should accept his present performance and not expect him to do the impossible. Later, as he grows a little more mature mentally, he should be able to make corresponding progress. The role of both parent and teacher is to encourage the child's potentialities for learning.

In certain cases, inability to read is due to a combination of factors such as defective vision, hearing, or intelligence; unfavorable environmental conditions; or negative parental attitudes. If these conditions cannot be remedied we should help the child to understand his strengths and limitations, and to learn all he can in areas where reading ability is not absolutely essential.

THE PARENTS' ATTITUDES TOWARD THEIR CHILD

When a child who has been eager to learn to read ceases to have any interest in words, the parents naturally become anxious. They are likely to resent being told that they shouldn't worry about it or put pressure on the child to read. They have been told that they should not sit the child down with a book and teach him to sound out words. Yet they want to do something to help. There are many helpful things that they can do—these will be described later. But it would be well for them to make first a calm examination of their own attitudes toward their child and his reading.

Parents have mixed feelings about their child's reading. These are affected by family pride and personal ambition—and by feelings of personal inadequacy. Other operative factors include the child's personality, ability, and behavior, and the attitudes of other people in the community. The range of parental attitudes is wide.

Never Satisfied

Many parents are never satisfied with their child's achievement in reading. No matter how well he does, they say, "You could have done better." Even a bright child wants parental approval for his good work; for the slow-learning child it is a necessity. For a child who is not doing as well as he can, the parents' recognition of the progress he has achieved and their realistic hopes for his further attainment form a stimulating and helpful combination.

Embarrassingly Boastful

The child who brings home a superior report of progress in reading and other phases of schoolwork is sometimes embarrassed when his parents show his report card to friends and relatives and boast about his achievement. In some instances the child is bothered not only by the way this affects other people's attitudes toward him but also by the feeling that the parent is taking credit for *his* achievement. In other instances the child may feel that the parent cares more for his achievement than for him as a person. These feelings of resentment may lead the child to relax his academic effort.

Indifferent

Parental indifference sometimes hurts a child more than criticism. It all depends upon what the parent's behavior means to the child. Children often say they like "strict" teachers and parents. By "strict" they mean persons who care enough about them to make them do what they ought to do. One boy actually said, "I'd rather have my father punish me than not care about me."

No one likes to be ignored. A wife who seemed to be able to manage her husband very skillfully explained her success by this remark: "When my husband doesn't do what I want him to do, I ignore him, and if there's one thing he cannot stand it's *ignorance*."

A bright child who is doing well in school may slump in his work if he realizes that nobody cares. One girl felt there was no one in her life who cared whether she succeeded or failed. When she brought home a good report, no one seemed interested, no one shared her satisfaction in achievement. This wall of indifference deterred her from putting forth further effort. A child who comes from a home where school learning has little prestige lacks the very important incentive of a warm personal relationship with someone who is interested in his achievement in reading.

Impatient

Impatience on the part of the parent may make the child feel discouraged with himself. With elementary and even junior high school children, it does little good to emphasize the future importance of reading skills. They are chiefly interested in the immediate success and advantage to be gained by improved reading: their parents will be pleased, the teacher will have increased respect for them, their classmates will recognize their accomplishment, they will be able to do their homework more easily and quickly, and, most important of all, they will be able to read more interesting books.

The important question to ask about any parental move is, What does it mean to the child? Even an occasional outburst of impatience or criticism may help the child to put forth greater effort *if* he perceives the parent's behavior as an evidence of love and of concern for his best development.

Overanxious

Anxiety is catching. Anxiety on the part of the parent or the teacher is often conveyed to the child. It becomes a stumbling block in the path of reading progress. An overanxious child is not in a favorable frame of mind for learning.

Sometimes the child's anxiety is manifested in frantic efforts to cover up the fact that he does not know the words, or to conceal the fact that he is attending a special reading class. We can take a child's reading difficulty too seriously; we may make him self-conscious and worried about it.

Parents often express their anxiety in efforts to help the child by tutoring him, putting pressure on him to read at home, not allowing him to play after school until his homework is done, constantly asking him about his progress in reading, taking him to one clinic after another, or giving him something he wants only on condition that he improve his reading.

Parents are uncertain about how much pressure to put on a child. They asked anxiously, "But if I do not try to make him read, will he not get further and further behind?"

Advice to parents on this question has undergone shifts in emphasis over the years. In the 1930's parents were expected to be strict—to control if not suppress their children's impulses. "Spare the rod and spoil the child" was often taken literally. In the period from 1942 to 1945, a reaction set in. Parents were urged to be mild, nondirective, and permissive; some went to the extreme of "letting the little angels do anything they wanted to." When the bad effects of this extreme laissez-faire attitude began to be recognized, a modified approach was recommended. This was more permissive than the practices of the 1930's, but still stressed the need for maintaining control and setting limits to what children were permitted to do. It was recognized that children have to learn to consider the rights and feelings of other people and that such socially adaptive behavior does not develop spontaneously. The child requires guidance both in achieving socially acceptable behavior and in realizing his potential abilities.

There are all kinds and degrees of home pressures; they may be arranged on a continuum as follows:

Harsh, sarcastic pressure—"You're just stupid, not like your bright sister."

Unrealistic pressure—expecting more than the child is able to do.

Indirect pressure—the child is given no chance to rebel, resist, or assert himself.

Putting all the responsibility on the child—"I wash my hands of the matter. It's up to you—do what you wish." This is quite different from sharing responsibility with the child.

Indifference—the parents don't seem to care whether the child reads or not.

Interest that is confined to the child's achievement, and does not include the child himself.

Interest in the child's achievement that stems from real affection and concern. This kind of interest the child perceives as evidence that the parents want him to succeed in reading, and to be happy in his success.

Pressure must be considered with reference to:

1. The goals—realistic or unrealistic.

2. What the pressure means to the child—that the parents care about him, or that the parents are disappointed, ashamed, or anxious to change him.

3. The total parent-child relationship—if it is one of genuine understanding and love, the child will accept pressure that he would otherwise resist.

4. Sensitivity to the way the child is feeling at a given time.

In most instances we can substitute pull for push—the pull of a specific, immediate goal that the child wants to attain is far better than pressure exerted on the child to attain the parents' goal.

The parent who is overconcerned and oversympathetic about a child's reading difficulty may increase his anxiety about it. A certain degree of anxiety serves as an incentive to learning, but intense anxiety makes learning impossible.

If parents have strong feelings of frustration, disappointment, or anxiety about their child's backwardness in reading, which crop out despite their best intentions, the less they say and do about the child's reading, the better. They should leave the problem with the school, and work through the teacher, counselor, or reading specialist rather than directly with the child. The child's reading teacher will suggest concrete ways in which parents can be helpful to the child.

Openly Hostile

Some parents feel a strong hostility toward their backward child. This may be owing to a combination of circumstances in their own lives: thwarted ambition, a guilty feeling that they are somehow to blame for the child's handicap, some disturbance in the intricate marital relationship or in their relations with the other children in the family, or any number of other complicated causes. Despite their best intentions, these hostile feelings rise to the surface. Expressing them is a relief to the parents but may have a destructive influence on the child. Such parents need expert help in recognizing and handling the causes of their hostility. When they have learned to accept themselves, they will be able to accept the child as he is and as he can become.

Genuinely Pleased

The parent who is genuinely pleased about the child's progress in reading encourages his continued improvement. It is well established that, in general, praise is more effective than blame, approval than criticism. However, if praise is to be effective it must be genuine rather than artificial, spontaneous rather than studied, concrete rather than vague, deserved rather than gratuitous, accurate rather than erroneous. The right kind of praise is likely to stimulate the child to put forth more effort. It reinforces his concept of himself as an approved person, and thus increases his self-esteem and diminishes any anxiety or fear that he may have about himself.

Nothing is more effective in furthering a child's development than making the appropriate response to his daily behavior. By approving his moves in the right direction, we help to reinforce the essential steps in the reading process. By ignoring a wrong move, or quietly indicating that it is wrong, we help the child to avoid it in his future learning. Since parents are usually the most significant persons in the child's life, it is most important that they make the right response to his progress, or lack of progress, in reading.

Understanding, Accepting, Expectant and Affectionate

This is the ideal atitude. It involves understanding the child's reading development, expecting the best of him and accepting his earnest achievement, all in an atmosphere of respect for the child as a person.

Firmness and consistency are not incompatible with loving-kindness. Parents should not give in to the child against their better judgment. Children want to grow up and leave behind their baby ways. Ability to read is generally recognized by children as a sign of being grown up. Thus improvement in reading is allied to a fundamental urge of childhood. They love the person who helps them to help themselves and to succeed in the things they think are most important. Some children like to share reading experiences with their parents; for example, rereading with them one of their favorite books. Teachers should encourage this practice.

Sometimes a parent's acceptance is only on the surface. Parents who recognize and regret their disappointment or resentment about the child's reading failure often try desperately to conceal their real feelings from the child. They may not succeed. The child may sense their impatience and frustration. This is especially true when the parent attempts to help the child with his reading. As one youngster said, "When my father tries to help me with my homework, I get all puzzled up. When he becomes impatient with me, I read worse than ever."

When one of their children is a more able learner than another, parents often make invidious comparisons, without meaning to do so, or without realizing the effect they may have on the child. Reading carries so much prestige that other accomplishments cannot, as the child sees it, make up for a reading deficiency.

Unable To Face Facts

Some parents resort to wishful thinking; they have difficulty in facing reality. Even on the best possible evidence, they refuse to believe that their child is retarded in mental ability. Consequently they try anything or anyone that promises to make him a better reader.

Being dragged from one clinic to another is hard on the child. Each successive unsuccessful experience intensifies the child's feeling of hopelessness about himself and his reading.

Some special treatment will often produce a temporary spurt, only to be followed by a lapse into the former reading pattern. To give both parent and child some idea of the degree of improvement that can be expected, there must first be an accurate diagnosis. However, instead of devoting several hours to an initial diagnosis, which may frighten an already insecure child, it is usually better to proceed gradually, combining diagnosis with instruction. Thus the child is encouraged by seeing evidence of his progress, and the teacher gains a more accurate understanding of the child's ability and rate of learning. The child's early experiences in reading should be pleasant and satisfying. Paul Witty [3] has pointed out that children who discover very early that reading can be fun usually become good readers.

PARENTS' ATTITUDES TOWARD READING

Our own attitude toward reading and our own reading habits affect the child's desire to read. How much do we read? When was the last time we brought home books from the library? How much do we enjoy reading? What are our purposes in reading. Reading interests are caught as well as taught. By seeing us read, the child will learn that reading is the thing to do; that it is important; that people get satisfaction and enjoyment from it, and that it is an evidence of maturity, not childish or "sissy."

Parents should appraise their own reading:

What do you get out of your reading? *Why* do you read? *What* do you read? Are you satisfied with the way you read? Do you have a deep love of reading? Do you see reading as a part of your own program of lifelong learning, of self-understanding and self-development?

Are you an efficient reader? Can you change gears to meet the demands of the kind of material you are reading—slow, creative reading for poetry, swift reading for skimming or for getting the general idea? Or do you read everything at the same pace?

Are you a thoughtful, critical reader? Do you use both your head and your heart when you read? Do you recognize satire or irony?

It is also enlightening to keep a diary record of the way you spend your weekdays and your weekends. How much time do you spend in reading? What do you read in the time available? What do you retain from your reading? Following are two actual daily schedules. Could you suggest any improvements in the examples of reading interest that these parents present to their children?

The following is an account of a commuter's day. Note the kind and amount of reading he does:

6:45 A.M.—Alarm goes off. With some trouble I get up, wash, and dress.

7:15—Take a cup of coffee and a piece of toast.

7:30—Arrive at the railroad station at 252nd Street. Since this is a one hour and a half train ride, I start to read the book I brought with me —*The Canvas Dagger* by Helen Reilly. I usually finish about half of one of these Detective Books before I arrive at the office.

8:47—Arrived at the office. Since my work day doesn't start until 9:00 A.M., I often take up a newspaper and read the sections devoted to: (*a*) sports, (*b*) finance, (*c*) local news, (*d*) world affairs.

9:00—Start my daily schedule of work. My work has to do with the insurance world, i.e., policy granting and the compiling of all the data sent to my firm regarding claims.

10:30—Coffee Break—Spent time with other members discussing a news item. I gave my views based on what I had read and heard on the radio. It was surprising how many of my business associates did not know even the basic facts about the topic.

11:30—Return to work.

12:00—Lunch Hour—Had a good lunch at the office cafeteria then wandered out of the building to do some shopping at the many stores around our area. It's amazing to me the amount of advertising these stores do in order to get people to come in.

1:00—Returned to the office—My work for the afternoon was on a pamphlet on "Safety on the Highway." This pamphlet concerned itself with some suggestions that have been offered by authorities in the field of safety on how to stay alive on the highway. This was truly an enjoyable piece of work for I gained from this pamphlet a great deal of information about the terrible slaughter we bring on ourselves when we get behind the wheel of an automobile.

2:30—Coffee Break—I did nothing but talk about the above pamphlet. I was gratified that all were interested.

2:45—Returned to work on this pamphlet.

4:45—Finished for the day and headed for the train. Completed the book I started in the morning and then started to read the magazine which I had bought at the news stand at the station.

6:00—Arrived at the suburban station and drove home.

6:15—Ate dinner.

7:00—Watched television while I also read some of the evening papers.

10:30—Retired to bed—set alarm clock for 6:45.

When asked why he read these kinds of material, this commuter gave the following reasons: to make the train trip seem shorter, for pleasure, to find out what is going on in the world, and to be able to talk with friends about it. On Sunday he buys two Sunday papers and starts to read them after lunch, stopping often to make comments to his wife about what he is reading. He likes to read historical novels, and often reads one over the weekend. He finds it futile to try to read serious books during the weekdays because he cannot keep his mind on them.

Following is the daily schedule of a married woman with three children whose husband works six days a week. He leaves home around eight each morning and does not return until seven-thirty in the evening. This schedule is for two successive days, a Sunday and Monday:

Sunday

8:30—Up and out of bed. Got the children cleaned up for the morning.
9:00—Prepared breakfast for the family to the tune of the radio—listened to the news and the weather reports.
9:30—Gathered the clan into the kitchen for a once-a-week breakfast together.
10:00—Washed dishes. Put the kitchen in order.
10:30—Called my sister on the phone.
11:00—Started to cook lunch.
11:30—Received phone call. Started putting the house in order.
12:30—Dressed the two younger children and myself.
1:00—Set the lunch table and fed the children.
1:30—Washed the lunch dishes.
2:00—Relaxed for half an hour by just sitting down.
2:30—Watched the children play for the next hour.
4:00—Served milk and cookies to children and their friends.
4:30 to 5:30—Had a belated lunch with husband and talked about purchases he had made for the business. Cleaned the kitchen up again and put up a new knick-knack shelf.
6:30—Gave the children their supper.
7:00 to 8:00—Watched TV with the family.
8:30—Got the children washed and ready for bed.
9:00—Made myself comfortable for the evening.
10:00—Prepared a snack for hubby and myself and settled back for an enjoyable TV showing which lasted until 11:15.
11:15—To bed.

Monday

7:30—Arose. Turned the radio for news and weather. Got the family up while breakfast was in the making.

8:00—Prepared husband's lunch. Fed the children and got the two older children ready to go off to school.

9:00—Had my breakfast and got the little fellow (age 4) settled with some kind of amusement.

9:30—Got started cleaning the house; this took until 11:30.

11:30—Washed and dressed myself and the little fellow to go shopping.

12:00—Arrived home to give the big boy lunch and watch the current events program on TV.

12:30—Left for an appointment with the doctor and stopped off at the bank along the way.

1:00 to 2:00—While waiting for the doctor, I skimmed several articles in the magazines in the office.

2:30—Picked up the other children at school and had a belated lunch.

3:00—Milk and cookies for the children. Did laundry work for the rest of the afternoon. This was interrupted by some gossip with neighbors.

5:00—Started to prepare supper.

6:00—Fed the children supper.

6:30—Prepared supper for husband and myself.

7:00—Helped children with their homework.

8:00—Ate supper. Caught up with quick reading of daily newspaper.

9:00—Watched TV.

9:30—Chatted with neighbor who dropped in.

10:30—Watched TV through the news broadcasts.

11:30—To bed.

This schedule represents a typical weekday and weekend day in this person's life. As you see, her time is pretty much taken up by household and family matters. She finds that she has little time for other activities, such as reading. The reading that she did do in this period was casual and incidental, and occurred when there was an unexpected lull in her day. The reading that she did in the doctor's office was mainly in the issue of *Life* that concerned the role of the American woman in today's society. This is her dominant reading interest at this time—how to function in her home. She spent some time on a close reading of the article in *Life* that concerned the working mother who can still do her own housekeeping and entertaining. Her comment on it was that she did not believe it was completely truthful. Her regular reading is the monthly *Parents' Magazine*. She reads this because she hopes to find suggestions for becoming a more effective mother and housekeeper.

She also did some quick reading in the daily newspaper. She read the headlines, skimmed the first few pages for news high lights, read a few of the columnists, and ended with the comics. She reads these parts of the newspaper every day in an effort to keep up with world events. However, she says that time limitations prevent her from getting all she wants from this medium; she has to rely on TV and radio to supplement this information. She can use these media while doing her regular housework. She also uses TV and radio to pursue her interest in household affairs; she watches or listens to the programs that deal with these matters.

She is not satisfied with her daily routine because it does not give her a chance to do very much except what is indicated on the schedule. She would like to have time to sit down and "pick up a book to read," a thing she has not done for some time. This reading would be for entertainment or diversion. When questioned as to why she does not read instead of watching TV in the evening, she points out that when her husband is watching TV she has no place in which to read quietly. She admits that her failure to include more reading in her daily schedule is due in some measure to inertia.

Most adults do a very small amount of serious reading. "Like father, like son" often applies to reading habits. One seriously retarded reader identified himself closely with a father who boasted that he had become successful in business without knowing how to read. We can usually find time to do the things we want to do. Improving our own reading habits not only sets a good example to our children; it also enriches our lives.

CAN ATTITUDES BE CHANGED?

Parents of retarded readers are frequently invited to group meetings in which they discuss problems such as homework, lack of progress in reading, teaching methods, and summer planning. Following the group meeting, individual conferences are held with parents whose children are having serious reading difficulties.

Many parents are relieved to learn that they are not alone in their feelings of anxiety, annoyance, or discouragement. Parents of seriously retarded readers who participated in a free discussion of their feelings and behavior toward their children made such comments as these:

"At first I was rather hesitant to talk openly."

"I now feel that our problem is a common one."

"I feel a great deal more patient with my son than I did before."

"I don't think my son feels quite as badly as he did before. Now we openly discuss his progress."

"In the beginning, when I first discovered that he had a serious reading problem, I felt hopeless. I have since come to realize that this situation can be changed." [4]

That changes took place in the attitudes and behavior of these parents becomes evident when we study their comments in the order in which they occurred, from the first to the last session:

Session 1. "My son is just plain lazy. The guidance director told us he was below average in intelligence and this seemed to fit in with what we thought of him."

Session 2. "I still think it is a form of laziness, or possibly he has as much intelligence as an average child, but he's not using it."

Session 3. "I'm letting up on the pressure now and have stopped criticizing him constantly. He is actually a pleasure to live with lately."

Session 4. "I'm taking it easier on him; maybe it's working. He doesn't seem to be any worse anyway."

Session 5. "Well, I'm relaxed for the first time in a long time, sitting back and letting things go by for a little while, and believe it or not, the child seems to be much better, not so hateful to me."

"We've restored some of his privileges. We had taken away about everything."

"Now he seems to be taking a little more interest in reading. I notice he sits down and reads a book now and then—seems to be trying to improve himself."

"I've decided I'm not going to ruin my life hounding him; it makes him so disagreeable. He is better lately."

"I feel like a new person or at least a different person, more relaxed." [5]

Of course parents' verbal descriptions of their behavior and attitudes may not correspond with what actually occurs. However, there does seem to be a relation between a child's progress and his parents' participation in small group discussions and counseling.

SOURCES OF UNDERSTANDING

If parents are to cooperate with the school in a broad reading improvement program, they will need information about the nature of reading, techniques of understanding the individual child, modern methods of teaching reading, and ways in which they may share responsibility with the school people and the child himself.

Printed Sources

Parents may obtain much sound information about children's reading development from printed sources. (See Bibliography, pp. 215–219.) The school tries to communicate with the parents through notes sent home by teachers, letters to parents written by various members of their own group, form letters, articles in the school newspaper and the local newspaper, and booklets describing the school system in general or the reading program in particular. Perhaps your school system issues materials of this kind.

Large Group Meetings

Various kinds of group meetings help parents to reach a better understanding of the reading program. Meetings called for the announced purpose of discussing reading are usually the best attended of all parent-teacher meetings. These meetings may take various forms: an interpretation of the reading program by the reading specialist or principal; a discussion of a good reading film, such as "Skippy and the Three R's" (a film, 29 minutes, black and white or color, produced and distributed by the National Education Association), or a set of slides accompanied by a tape recording such as that developed by Percy Bruce at Roslyn Heights, New York.

Any group meeting for parents should be parent-centered; it should give the parents the opportunity to find out what they want to know about reading. Before the meeting or at the beginning of it, the parents should be invited to ask questions; the role of the leader is to help them find the answers. Answers allay the parents' anxiety about the teaching of reading in the school, and increase their understanding and insight.

Demonstrations

We often learn more when we are shown something than when we are merely told about it. This is the television technique. It can be used with parent groups. It is generally effective to demonstrate with a class of children how some phase of reading is taught to pupils of a certain age.

A variation of the classroom demonstration is the use of tape-recorded lessons. Janet E. Sprount [6] described a procedure of this kind that was highly successful. First, the principal discovered by talking with a number of parents that they were highly interested in phonics. They were sure phonics should be taught in their schools. To give them this understanding, the reading consultant taped a series of reading lessons in grades one through six. As the teacher in each class began her usual word-analysis part of the reading lesson, he made a recording that lasted five minutes. At the parents' meeting the consultant spent ten minutes explaining what the parents could gain from the recordings. After all the recordings had been played, there was time for the parents to comment on them; their remarks were most enthusiastic. They were amazed that "children learn so much in six years."

Visits by parents to the child's classroom are less satisfactory for several reasons: (1) the aspects of reading in which the parent is especially interested may not be taught at that particular time, (2) the teacher does not have time to interpret her teaching to the parent, and (3) the parent does not get the same perspective on the development of reading ability that he would obtain from a series of recordings or films dealing with different grade levels.

Small Discussion Groups

It is not enough to know how reading is being taught. We all need to bridge the gap between knowing and doing. Sometimes, like the old farmer, we resist getting more "knowin's till our doings catch up with our knowin's." For this reason parents' meetings should give them opportunities to apply the information they have gained to the understanding of their own child. It is helpful to prepare or solicit ways of applying specific facts to specific situations. This can be done most effectively in small discussion groups led by a trained person who will be skillful in handling any personal problems that may be brought up.

Group therapy. In some reading clinics parents are urged to attend small group meetings in which their own children are discussed. Other parents in the group often help the parent whose child is under consideration by telling about a similar experience and describing the methods they used and the solutions they found. This helps the parent to see what he is doing to the child and to discover ways in which he could change his attitude or behavior. More important, the parent comes to realize that other parents have the same problems and that there is no need to feel ashamed or humiliated. Almost all parents have some problems with their children. In a skillfully conducted therapy session, parents overcome their sense of failure, and learn to view problems as opportunities to learn.

Parent-Teacher Conferences

The individual parent-teacher conference or home visit is a positive approach to all pupils. The teacher and parent help each other to understand the child—his strengths and weaknesses, the situations in which he learns best, the difficulties he is meeting and the ways in which he is responding to them. Together teacher and parent seek ways in which the home and school can help the child develop his reading potential at this stage in his development. Of course, parent-teacher conferences vary greatly in their quality and helpfulness, but both parents and teachers are enthusiastic about their value and are learning to conduct them more effectively. The following short conference followed a classroom visit by a parent. It was satisfying to both parent and teacher. Mike had poor work habits and was doing poorly in reading when he entered Miss J.'s class. During the first two months of the present year he had improved immensely, and Mrs. R. came in to express her appreciation:

Mrs. R. I am well pleased with the work you are doing with the children.

Miss J. I am so glad.

Mrs. R. As a primary teacher myself I never felt Mike was working up to his ability. He simply did not know how to read. I decided to come in to see Mike's new teacher this year and tell her that I felt Mike had been given enough social adjustment and that he was ready for reading and writing. I have not been in because Mike said you were a new teacher, and I wanted to give you time to become acquainted with the class before I came in. Then Mike kept reporting all the things he was doing in school. I have been quite surprised at the way Mike has learned to read during this two-month period. He is happy in school this year and he likes you very much. I was anxious to come in to observe your techniques because of the fine progress Mike is making.

Miss J. I'm so glad you wanted to come in. I wish more mothers would be interested in observing in the classroom.

Mrs. R. Are you having any particular problem with Mike?

Miss J. No. Mike and I have talked over together the problems he must work on. For example, we discussed his work habits. He is working hard towards doing neater work and getting it finished. He is trying to remember not to get the games until he has finished all his work. I think Mike is doing a splendid job of solving his own problems now that he recognizes them.

Mrs. R. All the children did last year was play. We were actually worried about Mike. We had him tested and he tested very high. I knew there was no reason why he should not be reading by third grade. He is picking up books at home now and reading. He never did this before.

Miss J. I feel that Mike is progressing nicely in all his work. Would you like to have another conference this semester?

Mrs. R. No. I don't feel that it's necessary.

Miss J. Please feel free to visit me at any time you feel the need or desire. I'm so glad you were able to come in today. Good-bye.

The Librarian as a Resource

Providing the child with appropriate and interesting reading material at each stage in his reading development is a basic part of the reading-improvement program. Teachers, reading consultants, and librarians try to help parents find the right books. They prepare lists of books on different subjects for children of different ages and different levels of reading ability. They give book talks and set up exhibits of appealing books for children. They welcome inquiries from parents about books that their child will enjoy and be able to read independently. In the children's rooms of many libraries there are fine collections of books, and librarians to guide children skillfully in their choices. Especially important is a youth library with appropriate books for the slow as well as for the precocious reader. Attractive furniture that fits children of all age groups adds to their enjoyment of reading.

In addition to recommending specific books for a particular child, librarians and teachers may also help by giving parents general criteria for selecting books for children and adolescents. First among these criteria is enjoyment: it is not a good book for a child if he is unable to read it, or if he finds it deadly dull.

A second criterion involves the interests and needs of the child at his stage of development. As he grows older the span of his interest should broaden at the same time that certain of his interests become more specialized. He should not get into a reading rut. Interests can be developed.

A third criterion concerns the book itself and its effect on the child. Does it have enough action, suspense, humor, and imagination to keep the child reading eagerly? Are its heroes and heroines worthy of emulation? Does it make children feel that life is worth living? Does it help them gain insight into their own problems and their relations with all sorts of people? Does it have a distinctive style? Is it true to life, which has, as A. E. Housman said, "much of good and much of ill" in it? If it is nonfiction, is it accurate and readable? Does the book challenge the child's inquiring mind?

As a special service to parents, one library, in cooperation with the P.T.A. Council and other organizations, offered a short course for parents on children's reading.

In some communities parents have access to resources such as adult education classes and recreation centers; medical and psychological services and family counseling agencies may also be available if intensive psychotherapy seems indicated.

The parents, the teacher, and the librarian constitute an effective team. The parent knows the child's interests; the teacher knows his abilities; and the librarian knows books. In these and other ways, parents can gain understanding of their children, learn how they are being taught to read in the schools, and determine what role they should play in the child's reading development.

QUESTIONS AND ANSWERS

1. *Does home environment affect a child's reading?*

We can say that children are taught to read in school, but how well they learn depends a great deal on the home environment. The language the parents speak, the example they set, their attitude toward reading, and the general emotional atmosphere—these are only a few of the factors that interact to affect a child's reading. For example, Patty's parents spoke excellent English, and considered education very important. Moreover, she was a wanted child. For twelve years she was the only child. Then the parents adopted a boy about four years younger than Patty. Without realizing it, the parents began to give more and more attention to Tommy and less and less to Patty. Unconsciously, Patty became jealous, and this emotional ferment prevented her from concentrating on her reading.

In working with Patty the teacher took advantage of the early adolescent desire for independence and helped Patty to enjoy activities with her own age group. The parents became aware of the problem and tried to give Patty her share of their attention. When her anxiety about her status was relieved and she was happier at home and at school, she was free to give her attention to reading.

Parents should remember that no two children grow at the same rate—even children who appear to have the same experiences. The best development is likely to take place if the home provides the opportunities for learning and lets the child take the initiative.

2. *Is it true, as one popular writer said, that one-third of all high school pupils are "nonverbal" and cannot learn to read?*

In his recent survey of junior high schools, Dr. Conant found schools in which 35 to 50 per cent were reading at sixth-grade level or below. However, it is one thing to say that a third of the pupils are falling below their grade level in reading, and quite another thing to say that they are "impervious to book learning." Too often mental retardation is confused with reading retardation.

There are many causes, and combinations of causes, for poor reading. When we detect the causes and apply appropriate methods of dealing with them, children, young people, and adults improve their reading. Published accounts of reading programs furnished evidence of such improvement.

In a most intensive study of reading cases carried on at the University of Chicago, it was estimated that less than 1 per cent—not 33⅓ per cent as stated by the popular writer mentioned in the question above—were incapable of learning to reading. For these very rare cases other avenues of learning were recommended: pictures, diagrams, films, radio, records, trips, discussions, and other auditory visual aids. These pupils should have a curriculum that is tailor-made to their needs.

3. *How does a parent know whether his child is retarded in reading?*

Parents may obtain many indications that a child has the ability to read better than he does. Is he doing well in subjects that do not require much reading? Is he succeeding in school, despite his low reading achievement, because he listens well and organizes and remembers the facts he accumulates? Does he use facts in original ways? Does he have a hobby or interest on which he concentrates and in the pursuit of which he shows initiative and self-direction. Does he voluntarily go to the library? Does he do a variety of things in his free time?

Is the child's retardation in reading out of line with other aspects of his development? If the child enjoys playing with children of his own age and holds his own with them, shows appropriate independence in caring for himself and making good use of his time, and acts his age in other ways, his backwardness in reading may be overcome by appropriate instruction.

On the other hand, if the child is generally immature and seems reluctant to leave the security of dependency, he may view reading as a threat and resist it. Before he can make progress, he must want to grow up. He must also get satisfaction from any moves he makes in the direction of safely exploring his neighborhood, playing by himself or with his age group, or taking responsibility that he can handle successfully.

At the same time, the teacher can encourage any steps he takes in learning to read, starting at his present level and moving ahead from small to larger successes. Once he has experienced for himself the magic of getting meaning and enjoyment from printed words, he will no longer be so dependent upon the approval of his parents or teachers.

4. *What is the parent's role when a child is seriously behind in reading?*

It usually puts too great a strain on parent-child relationships when a parent tries to help a seriously retarded reader. The parent's patience is likely to reach a breaking point. Then he makes a remark that undermines the self-confidence and self-respect the teacher or the reading specialist has been trying to build up. It is much better to leave the instruction of such a child or adolescent to persons who are outside the family and not involved emotionally with the child, as parents naturally are.

The role of the parents is to show the child that they understand he has a tough job to do in learning to read better, that they admire his determination, initiative, and effort, and that they are ready to help in any way the reading teacher suggests. But at other times they are going to relax, forget reading, and enjoy doing many other things with the child.

5. *Shouldn't teachers give children instruction in phonics earlier?*

Perhaps the best answer is, "Tentatively try and see"—see whether phonics helps a particular child learn to recognize unfamiliar words and thus become independent in his reading. If the child becomes the least bit confused or disturbed by the instruction, use another approach at this time.

Some teachers report success in teaching children to sound out words after they have learned a few words by sight. Others say it is better for the children to recognize seventy-five or more meaningful words by sight before they begin to try to associate the letter sounds with the printed letters in these words. Others claim that children do not take much interest in phonics until they are at least ten years old, and a few believe that "phonics do the most good for children over the age of twelve and who are having particular difficulty with spelling." [7]

6. *What is the relation between reading and spelling?*

In general, good readers are good spellers. But there are exceptions. Some bright pupils are poor spellers. They get the meaning from slight clues—they do not have to look at all the letters. They would be helped by learning some of the simple spelling rules that have few exceptions, such as

> I before E
> Except after C
> Or when sounded like A
> As in "neighbor" or "weigh."

Instruction in phonics, while it is helpful in teaching pupils to spell, does not guarantee good spellers. In fact, many spelling errors stem from spelling the word the way it sounds.

7. *In what ways can parents and teachers cooperate on children's reading?*

Teachers today enlist the parents' cooperation in many ways:

(1) They may have conferences or meetings with the parents of preschool children.

(2) The kindergarten teacher may have a meeting with parents in the first few weeks of school to explain the purposes of the kindergarten activities and to suggest that parents help their child to bring something interesting to tell about or show to the other children at least once a week.

(3) One first-grade teacher showed parents the results of a reading-readiness test and explained how they could provide various readiness experiences at home.

(4) Sometimes a teacher will give a demonstration lesson at a P.T.A. meeting.

(5) An exhibit of children's readers and other schoolbooks, both old-fashioned and modern, emphasizes how superior modern books are in many respects.

(6) Parent-teacher conferences about the reading of individual children are especially helpful to parents whose children are not achieving their reading potentialities. Teachers should send notes home more often, emphasizing the progress the child is making and suggesting specific ways in which the parents may help.

(7) Teachers appreciate parents who understand their problems and give them credit for their efforts to help individual children, as well as to teach the entire class skillfully.

8. *How is reading taught today?*

The best schools increase children's desire to read, direct their attention toward meaning, and connect their reading with their experiences. They learn some words as wholes (the word method). They learn to sound out unfamiliar words (the phonic method), and to recognize familiar syllables and combinations of letters in new words. If a certain word is suggested by its context, the child may need to use only a few sound-letter associations in order to pronounce it correctly. Thus the child learns a combination of methods and uses them appropriately. His attention is focused on getting the meaning of what he is reading, not on the skill per se.

9. *If reading instruction in the schools is sound, why are there so many poor readers today?*

In the first place, we are more aware of retardation in reading than we used to be. In the second place, poor readers used to drop out of school; now they are required by law to remain in school until they are fifteen or older. In the third place, poor instruction in reading is only one cause of failure in reading. Lack of interest and unfavorable attitudes toward reading are characteristic of poor readers. These attitudes often stem from unhappy homes where parents are indifferent to reading, and either overanxious, neglectful, or overindulgent toward their children. In today's culture, other media of communication tend to supplant reading despite the increase in leisure time.

TWO

Reading from the Child's Point of View

ONE reason why *Huckleberry Finn* and *Tom Sawyer* are classics is that Mark Twain got inside his characters, and thought and felt as they did. To understand children and adolescents we, too, need to see things from their point of view rather than from ours. We need to view their world through their eyes.

Do we really know what reading means to a child? Have we any idea of the eagerness with which a six-year-old goes to school to learn to read? Can we imagine a child's joy in being able to recognize a printed word already rich in meanings that his experiences have brought to it? Can we comprehend the bewilderment some children feel when they try to make sense out of sentences? Do we have any idea of the emotional effects exerted on the child by our attempts to help him in learning to read? When he is slow in learning to read, does he sense our disappointment in him? Are we aware of other attractions that pull him away from books? Do we know how his self-concept is affected when we label him a retarded reader? Have we ever thought how a child or adolescent feels when he is subjected day after day to reading tasks that are too difficult for him? Do we have any idea of the joy or despair that great books may bring, or the ways in which they may enrich the child's life now and later?

Labels conceal rather than explain a child's behavior. What we call "laziness" may be languor, lack of vigor, or a low energy level. What we call "stubbornness" may be caused by a feeling of inadequacy, of inability to do the reading task required. What we call "stupidity" may be stupor, an unresponsiveness stemming from repeated failure and the fear of failing again. "*In*attention" may be attention to something else—some stimulus that is more insistent than the desire to learn to read. "Resistance" may be caused by anxiety—the child's unconscious fear that he will lose himself if he conforms to the pattern a parent has prescribed for him. If the child

43

perceives reading as part of the parent's imposed pattern, he may unconsciously resist learning to read. In this case interest in reading can emerge only as the child overcomes his anxiety about loss of self.

Anxious parents tend to make anxious children. If parents over-emphasize the importance of reading, or attach too much prestige to achievement in reading, they may put too heavy a burden on a child who has many other problems of growing up. Intense fear of losing parental love or of being a disgrace to the family tends to discourage rather than to spur learning. On the other hand, emphasis on progress and success facilitates learning.

LISTEN AND LEARN

There are two main ways in which we may increase our understanding of what reading means to our own child. One is to listen to what other children tell us about their attempts to read, and about the attempts of parents or teachers to help them. These reports give us a background for understanding our own child; they alert us to possible interpretations and explanations of his reading behavior. But these introspective reports by other children are only a prelude to the second approach: to observe and listen to our own child, not as we would observe an animal in the zoo, but as we would listen to and sympathize with a good friend.

All children are different. The complex web of relationships in each family is different. The only way to judge the effectiveness of any procedure is to observe its effect on the child. If we get indications of resentment, of mounting anxiety that interferes with learning, of boredom that leads to dislike of reading, we know something is wrong with the procedure, or with the relationship in which it is being used. If, on the other hand, the child enjoys the experience, puts forth more effort, gets satisfaction from the progress he is making, then the procedure has stood the test of use.

According to an old Chinese saying, a good method used by a bad person brings bad results, but a bad method used by a good person brings good results. So much depends on the personal relation between the child and the adult. The ideal, of course, is sound teaching procedure used by a person who conveys his loving concern for the child's best development.

In this chapter we shall listen to the children themselves. What do they recall about their reading development? How do they think parents helped or hindered them in learning to read? How do they feel about reading? What kinds of books interest them? What difficulties have they met? How do they think radio, television, movies, and comic books have influenced their reading? Have particular books or articles contributed to their personal development?

Evidence on these matters was obtained by reading introspective reports written by teen-agers, by listening to their discussions about reading, and by talking with them individually.

READING DEVELOPMENT

Children learn to read at different ages and at different rates. Some begin to read before entering school. Others do not begin until eight or nine years of age.

Many conditions influence a child's reading development. Bright children often learn to read of their own accord without any apparent instruction. Ellen Glasgow, looking back on her own childhood, wrote:

When or where or how I learned to read, I could never remember. When I look back, it seems to me that one day the alphabet was merely a row of black or red marks on paper, and the next day I was earnestly picking out letters in *Old Mortality*. I must have taught myself, for the doctors had warned my mother not to begin teaching me, and had prophesied that it was unlikely I should ever live to grow up. There were few things one would need less in Heaven than a command of the alphabet. "Don't push her, whatever you do. Let her take her own time about learning." But the trouble was that my own time was quick time. After hearing dear old Aunt Rebecca, my father's eldest sister and the perfect story teller, relate the plots of the *Waverley Novels,* I resolved, apparently, that as soon as possible I would read them for myself in my own way, which meant spelling out the words, letter by letter, as I went on. All that I now remember clearly is that *Old Mortality* and a little blue book called *Reading Without Tears* were the beginning of my serious education, and that, so far as I am aware, nobody ever taught me to read.[1]

Another highly gifted child, Marie Curie, learned to read before going to school by sitting beside her older sister who was struggling

with beginning reading books in her first year of school. One evening, when the family were all together in the living room, the father
asked the older sister to read to them. As she stumbled through the
first page, little Marie became impatient. She took the book and read
it fluently; misinterpreting the astonishment of her parents as rebuke,
she said quickly, "Oh, I'm sorry, I'll not do it again."

Quite different was the reading development of a third highly
gifted child—Agnes Repplier. At eight years of age she did not know
how to read. She was satisfying her desire to hear stories by getting
people to read to her. When her mother realized this, she issued the
"edict, wise, harsh and menacing"—no one was to read to her. When
Agnes saw the door closed to all the stories in her bookcase, she spent
a few days of blank despair. Then she sized up the situation, and
quickly, though not without effort, learned to read.[2]

The gifted children of today describe equally various and devious
paths of reading development. Some cannot recollect any special
instruction in reading. "I just learned to read," they say. Others say
they learned by recognizing words in books that were being read
to them. Others built a basic vocabulary before they came to school
by asking how to pronounce words on signs, packages, labels, and
other articles they were curious about. Still others said they learned
by sounding out words.

Beyond this beginning stage, the course of a child's reading development depends a great deal on home and school conditions and
on his own motivation or drive. The following reading autobiography
reproduced just as it was written [3] by a sixteen-year-old boy of higher
than average intelligence, shows high achievement–motivation as
well as favorable home and school conditions:

At first, before I started school, I was able to recognize my name and
a few simple words like *is; are; and; to*. However, this was as far as I was
able to read. Among the first books from which we started to read was
a book which contained the characters named Dick and Jane. The first
books contained simple sentences using simple words such as, "See Dick
run, he runs fast." As I improved, I progressed toward books which were
harder.

My parents bought for me books which were at my reading level or
just above it. They never forced me to read more. Today my parents pay

for about 10% of the books which I want. The remainder of the books I buy comes from the money which I get or earn.

I have always liked to read and my interests are centered around science and some adventure books (non-fiction type) as long as I can remember. My chief source of books are the books which I purchase and those which I borrow from the public library or from one of my friends.

Books have aided me to choose my career after my education is completed. It will be in the field of physics and chemistry. Now, I am working to establish the basis of my career by taking all of the science and mathematics I can in high school.

Television, radio, movies have influenced me in my reading. When a program such as the Bell Telephone Science Series was on television, I often did some research on the subject to be telecast before the program to get a more complete understanding of that subject. Often in these programs, an interesting fact, topic, or information may be given to which I sometimes try to read books on it in order to get a more complete and detailed information.

My reading is not limited only to reading books although books comprise a large part of the reading. I personally suscribe to the magazine *Time* and *Scientific American* and from January, 1961, I will get the *National Geographic Magazine*. My parents suscribe to several magazines also; among them I like to read *The Readers' Digest*. I purchase approximately 8 to 12 books per year, without counting the paperback books.

The pattern this boy established of reading serious books thoughtfully earned him high vocabulary and total comprehension scores (93 and 95 percentile) and an average rate-of-reading score (53 percentile).[4] Persons who are especially interested in mathematics and science may read relatively slowly; these subjects require a slower rate of reading than most fiction and other less technical reading.

Another boy of about the same mental ability, but two years younger and in the ninth grade, described his reading development, somewhat less felicitously, as follows:

When I was seven years old, our family moved from one school district to another. I was put in the beginning group of the first grade. Here I first learned to read. By the time the year was over, I had gone from the lowest to the highest reading group. In this group we read science books.

My parents have not tried to make me read any better than I can, or done anything to make me dislike reading or become worried about my reading.

I have always liked to read. When I was in fifth and sixth grade I always got my book reports in before anyone else. I made it a regular habit to read an average of about three or four books a week. Sometimes I read two books in a night after my homework was done. I still like to read, but I don't have as much time as I used to.

When I was in second, third, and fourth grade, I liked to read just about any kind of book, except romance and animal stories. In fifth grade, my favorite books were biographys. In sixth grade, my favorite books were science fiction and science books. I also, during this period, liked books that told of famous places around the world. In seventh and eighth grade I enjoyed myths, science fiction, and classic books. I still like these kinds of books, but now classic books are my favorite and I also enjoy sports books. Some classics I have read are the following: *A Connecticut Yankee in King Authors Court, The Human Comedy, The War of the Worlds; Five Weeks in a Baloon, The Swiss Family Robinson, Journey to the Center of the Earth, Around the World in Eighty Days,* and *Little Men.* As you can see, many of them are science fiction classics by Jules Verne.

Jules Verne is my favorite author. I read every book I can get that he wrote. I also enjoy H. G. Wells classics.

I have no difficulties with reading and I never have had any difficulties with reading.

Reading the story of Abraham Lincoln has made me dispise cheating and lying. Many books have stimulated my sense of adventure to make me enjoy science because it is an adventourous subject.

The comics have stimulated my interest in science fiction stories. Good movies have affected me by having classic stories, science fiction stories, and adventure stories that stimulate my interest in books that these movies were made from.

From reading this autobiography, I suppose you have concluded that I enjoy books. If you've come to that conclusion you're right.

The central factor here seems to be an enjoyment of reading that is a habit of long standing. It is interesting to note that this pattern —rapid reading of many interesting books—has enabled the boy to make a high score in reading rate (94 percentile) and in vocabulary (85 percentile), but has produced a lower total comprehension score (50 percentile). He might well have expanded his reading program to include some serious books, which he would have had to read more thoughtfully.

Children of good average ability who have had the advantages of favorable home and school conditions have generally reported rather smooth, uneventful progression of experiences.

Some have suggested conditions that resulted in reading below their potential ability. A boy of average ability gave this plausible explanation of his low achievement in reading (12 percentile): "I didn't care too much for reading and never thought of it being important. After reading a few books that I couldn't understand, I just didn't want to be troubled reading. . . . Now I am a freshman in senior high and I realize now what reading means to me and my subjects in school."

Less able students frequently mention a rise and fall of reading interest that seems to be quite typical. They seem to feel a kind of excitement about beginning to learn to read. This interest continues until the fourth or fifth grade. Then they undergo a slump. Interest picks up again when they have acquired sufficient skill to read the kinds of books that are of real interest to them. One boy described this early reading development as follows: "When I was in the first grade, I thought reading was all right. In second and third grade when I was understanding it, it was much better. Then farther up I didn't like it. And I don't like reading now [ninth grade] because I can't read fast enough and most of the time I don't know what I am reading." A fifteen-year-old girl described the fluctuations in her reading interest and proficiency as follows:

"My reading was real good the first part of school. Then about the fifth grade I didn't read very much, so I sort of got out of practice in reading. When I got into junior high school, I had to read library books to make book reports. . . . I guess that was when I really began reading for my own interest and enjoyment."

Slow-learning children often say they liked reading in the first and second grades, but were not interested from then on. This decline in interest may be due to the fact that they could make the simple associations between separate words and their meanings, but found it difficult to do more complex tasks—reasoning and relating ideas—that are required in fourth- and fifth-grade reading.

Some of these slow-learning youngsters, by making a truly

heroic effort, are reading better than could be expected. Regardless of intelligence test results, they should be given the best possible conditions for improving their reading. The following reading auto-biography was written by a slow-learning boy in the ninth grade:

I learnt to read a little in first grade. I could not read because I did not no that I needed glasses. So they got me glasses when I was in the third grade. My parents did not no that I could not read. Last summer I went to reading school. It helped me a lot. Last year in the eighth grade I had a spesial class in reading in school. It help me a lot. I can read better than I used to. I like to read more than before. I have tried to larn to sound out words. But I still do not like to read books because I cannot read good.

More power to him! More appreciation for his persistence; and, especially, more sympathy for his general language handicap and his struggles to overcome it! He needs praise, not criticism; we should accept the progress he has made, not press him to accomplish the impossible.

Contrasted with the reading growth made by the boy just mentioned is the record of a boy who had more ability but scored close to zero in reading. This boy had an unrealistic concept of his reading ability, and little recognition of the importance of reading. In his composition, he gave the impression that his parents shared his lack of concern about whether he read well or not.

Many more descriptions of reading development could be cited, but these suggest the wide variations in the reading patterns of children, even of children who are similar in mental ability. Home influences, early school experiences, the availability of interesting books, the degree to which reading is recognized as important, the quality of reading instruction, the individual's self-concept, goals, and purposes—these are among the many factors that affect a child's reading development.

THE ROLE OF THE PARENTS

As Viewed by Teachers of Reading

Reading specialists and teachers usually advise parents not to give instruction in reading at home. They point out that methods of teaching reading have changed since the parents' school days, and that the child may be confused by being taught by two different methods. Moreover, if the teacher refused to accept the method that the parents have been using, the parents may become annoyed with the child because he prefers the teacher's method.

There is also danger that the parents, who are more emotionally involved than the teacher, in the welfare of the child, will be more likely to show impatience and disappointment when the child learns slowly. They may express their annoyance verbally or in more subtle ways: "What's the matter with you today? I thought you knew that word; you just learned it yesterday." This kind of response sets the child back. It makes him feel inferior and dependent. It may increase his anxiety about losing his parents' love. It may give him the impression that his parents care *only* for his achievement, and not for him as a person.

As Viewed by Children and Adolescents

No matter what teachers and experts recommend, many boys and girls express appreciation of the help their parents gave them in learning to read. As they look backward from the vantage point of early adolescence, they recall many different ways in which their parents have tried to help them.

They mention the following ways most frequently: reading aloud to the child during the preschool years, asking the child to read aloud to them once he has acquired some reading ability, buying books for him, or bringing home books from the library or county bookmobile.

Reading aloud to children is frequently mentioned as a way in which parents have helped children learn to read. It is too valuable an experience to be crowded out of the child's day by radio and television. It is a means of communication between parent and child as well as an introduction, as Agnes Repplier expressed it, to "the delight that lies between the covers of books." [5] The child who has become acquainted with the language patterns of literature by hearing stories read aloud finds it easier to anticipate words and phrases when he begins to read for himself.

Adolescents recall many variations of the practice of adults' reading aloud to them as children:

"If I had to pick out one person who influenced my reading the most, it would be my grandmother. She is the one who really started me reading. She used to sit and read to me by the hour when I was little. Now that I can read by myself she just makes sure I have enough to read. She gives me four or five books a year for my birthday, Christmas, or other occasion." [6]

"My mother said that while she was expecting my younger brother and sister, she would read for hours to my older sister and me. Then after the birth of the twins she was so busy that it was impossible to read to us, and therefore the twins missed out on that early experience. However important this is, I don't know, but I do know that my older sister and I read a lot more than the twins, especially the girl twin who would rather work than read."

"When I came home from school, my mother would make me read a Dick and Jane book. My parents encouraged my reading."

"My mother read to me some when I just started to school, but not something I could learn to read myself. She didn't have much time to help me learn to read because she worked."

"I began to read in the first grade but I didn't make much headway until I tried reading stories my mother had read to me. I remembered the plot of the story and was able to guess the words I didn't know."

Reading to the parents. As soon as the child has learned to read, this may also be an enjoyable—and memorable—experience. It not only gives the child extra practice in reading; it also affords the parents opportunities to give him the approval and praise that help him along the road to better reading. In the words of several adolescents:

"It was very hard for me to learn to read. In the first grade it took me a long time to get started. My parents would sit down with me about every night and listen to me read. I know now what they must have gone through because now I listen to my brother and it is not easy to be patient with him."

"My parents helped my reading along by listening to me read. When I would stumble over a word, they wouldn't tell me what it was. They would help me find out what the word was by looking at the surrounding words and the spelling of the word. At the time I thought they were being mean, but as I grew older I learned that they did it for my own benefit."

"My parents would help me by reading one page and I would read one. This got me more interested in reading."

"My mom and dad helped by making me read the newspaper, books, and signs. They tried to teach me words and how to break them into syllables."

If reading aloud to the child or listening to him read becomes a burden or a bore to either the parent or the child, or if it interferes with other things that either party very much wants to do, then its value is lost.

Specific instruction in reading seems to have been appreciated by some youngsters. They describe the following procedures, which seem sound:

"To help me find out how a word was pronounced, Father would say, 'Sound the word out by syllables.'"

"My parents have helped me to read better by teaching me how to pronounce words and telling me the meaning of them, so I would know what they meant when I used them again."

"When I started in the first grade I was in the poorest readers' group. My mother made some reading cards to give me more practice. She would flash the cards at me every morning and night. They helped me to become a better reader fast. Since then I have been in the highest reading group."

Another child reported that a similar procedure made him dislike reading. The effect of any attempts by parents to give instruction in reading depends very largely on the parent-child relation and the spirit in which the instruction is given.

"My parents keep telling me, 'If you don't understand a word look it up in the dictionary. And do not run sentences together.'"

"My family helped me a lot in reading, not by standing over me with a broom, but by telling me what I should do and what not to do. One way my dad helped me was to look up one word a day in the dictionary and one word in the encyclopedia."

And another teen-ager made this wise comment, "A person helps you when he helps you see the best ways out, not tells you what to do."

Recommending suitable books and making them available. This is more important than giving specific instruction in reading. In their compositions teen-agers frequently mention their parents' help in this respect:

"My parents have helped me by taking me to the library and reading with me. I wish they had made me read more because now I don't care much for reading."

"Mother and Dad would both give me books to read, saying that they were too hard for me. I would read the books and they would both act real surprised. I know now that actually what they were doing was giving me challenges in reading."

A sixteen-year-old boy of average mental ability attributes his high reading score (92 percentile) to his home experiences: "I always did like reading and still do. We used to get our books from the county bookmobile. But now I buy them because it's almost a hobby and if I lose them I don't owe anybody money."

By hook or by crook, books must be made available. Teen-agers express their appreciation of parents who bring them the right books. One boy wrote: "A lot of times my mother brings home some good award-winning books from the county bookmobile, but sometimes she brings home a book that is girlish."

Thinking of his early school days, another boy said, "Almost every time my parents went shopping, they would bring a little story book for me to read or look at."

Like adults, children will often pick up a book that is lying around, when they would not bother to get it from the library. Some teen-agers would rather buy a paperback book at the corner store than go to the library. Fortunately, publishers are now issuing more and more paperback books of excellent quality that are of interest to teen-agers, such as those selected for the Scholastic magazines book clubs.

Both children and young people appreciate personal book recommendations by parents. They are proof that parents care enough to notice and remember things that they think the child would especially enjoy.

Recommending a book is quite different from nagging the child to read it. Some youngsters resent nagging. Others make comments like the following: "At first I resented being made to read a certain book, but after I got into the book, I liked it and was glad I had read it."

To make successful recommendations we must find books that are really appropriate for a particular child or adolescent. What does he really want to read about? Most of us do not read just for the sake of reading. We read to find out something we want to know or learn how to do something we want to do; we read to share ideas with our friends; we read to satisfy our curiosity about the word of nature and the world of man; we read for sheer enjoyment; we read to open new doors for the mind. These are some of the values that we should keep in mind when recommending and buying books for our children.

No parental help in reading was reported in some of the compositions. Some children regret that their parents had not helped them more:

"My parents never taught me anything besides manners. All the things I know today I was taught in school. I wish they had taught me how to read a book faster."

"If my mother and father would of got me to read a little bite mor I might of become interested in reading. They wanted me to do better in my other school work and didn't stress reading much."

Both of those ninth-grade boys had the ability to read much better than their very low reading test scores indicated. Perhaps if their parents had responded to their interest in learning to read, not by giving them boring instruction but by showing them how they could get the meaning of words they wanted to know; or if the parents had encouraged and reinforced their efforts to read and had provided them with suitable reading material at each stage of their development, they might have been reading up to their ability.

On the other hand, one fifteen-year-old boy who made an exceptionally high score in reading comprehension said: "My parents never did help me much in reading. Once in a blue moon, they might read me a short story. I have always liked to read. Sometimes I would get a book over my head. Sometimes I could read it and sometimes I couldn't." Instead of merely helping the child with his reading, these parents seem to have accomplished something still more important: they made him feel responsible for his own improvement. Parents and teachers often assume the full burden of responsibility for a child's learning. This responsibility should be shared. The child should take an increasingly larger share as he grows older. Ideally we should give the child just enough help to get him over the hurdle—enough to prevent frustration and discouragement, but not so much as to make him dependent. Timing is very important in the giving of help.

Attempts to help that backfired. Adolescents frequently recall that their parents made ill-timed or misdirected attempts to help them. Practices that some children regarded as favorable to learning had the opposite effect in other cases. This is illustrated by the following quotations:

"When I came home from school mother would say, 'Open the book,' and she would help me with the words that I had trouble with. When she would say, 'Read the book out loud,' it would make me mad because I always like to read in a quiet place by myself so I wouldn't be bothered."

"I wish my parents hadn't made me read so much, for now I have to wear glasses and can only read twenty minutes at a time."

"I was about four years old when my mother tried to teach me to read. She would take a card and write a word on it and then say it. This way took a very long time and after a while I became very tired of reading."

One poor reader in the ninth grade wrote:

There was one thing I wish they hadn't done and that was to tell me all the words instead of letting me try to pronounce them in syllables. I needed help in pronouncing the syllables and working out the pronunciation myself. Since I didn't know how to do this, I didn't like to read.

This child was ambitious; she wanted to be on her own in reading. But apparently no one at home or at school—and this was the school's responsibility—taught her word recognition skills.

A fourteen-year-old girl with a much lower reading score than would be expected of her complained of her parents' critical attitude: "When I used to read to my parents, they used to tell me I was reading too fast or too slow. If I missed a word when I was reading, they would always tell me I shouldn't have missed that word. It would always get me so mad that I wouldn't like to read and that would worry me, too."

Too often parents and teachers tell children they should read better, but do not show them just how they can improve.

Although a child may seem indifferent about his reading, he may really be concerned about it. If he lacks the ability to read better, he becomes discouraged about himself and resentful of his parents' criticism and pressure. One fifteen-year-old boy, who seemed to be reading about as well as he was able, wrote:

"I no I should improvent my reading. I never do it. I just waist time. My parents have plenty wanted me to read but I never set around to doing it. One reason is because my parents made me read and I do not like them to do it. So I do not like to read as I used to when I was back in the third grade." Reading has become increasingly difficult for this slow-learning boy, and the nagging of his parents has added resentment to his feelings of inferiority and complete confusion about all the language arts.

Other home conditions that are unfavorable to reading and study are more fully described in Chapters 7 and 13 of *The Adolescent Views Himself*.[7] Adolescents frequently mention distractions, other work or recreational activities, and worries. The first two are illustrated by these quotations:

"Sometimes I would start reading a book and my brother would come in and turn on the TV or radio. That would disturb my reading."

"After I'd learned to read I liked it, but I worked on the crops and didn't have time to read any except in school. Now, at fourteen years, I don't read much because of homework, movies and TV."

Many irrelevant thoughts may pull a child's attention away from reading—thoughts about a rival sister or brother who has Mother's exclusive attention while he is cooped up in school, memories charged with emotion that are evoked by a word or sentence in the reading selection, anticipations of a party in the near future, feelings of guilt over some real or imagined mistake, or fantasies that provide escape from a frustrating world. These irrelevant thoughts should not be confused with an imaginative response to reading material, nor with prethinking about the selection to be read.

Choosing appropriate books for a given child requires knowledge of books and understanding of the child. A skillfully chosen book may start a child on the road to reading after years of indifference:

"I never cared much for reading," one boy wrote, "until I started reading Mark Twain's books. They were very interesting to me. I have read

The Adventures of Huckleberry Finn more than ten times. When I watched *Huckleberry Finn* on TV, I found it wasn't as good as reading the book."

If we require, or even recommend, unsuitable reading material, we may cause the child to dislike reading, as in this case:

"My parents used to buy books I didn't like," one poor reader said. "That made me not like to read."

Sometimes the books we give a child are not interesting because they are too difficult; he cannot read them without frustration. Sometimes a book is intrinsically dull. Sometimes it bears no relation to the child's real interests or needs. Selecting the right book for the right child is as important as it is difficult.

Unsuitable reading material appears to have been partly responsible for this boy's dislike of reading:

When I was five or six years old, my older brother was in the first grade. My father and mother thought I should read the books he brought home to study and read. My father also bought some cards that had words on them, and he would drill me on these cards.

Whenever we went on long trips, I would try to read all the signs. . . . Now I just read for facts and when it is necessary. I hardly ever read for enjoyment unless it is comic books or comic strips.

This boy has average intelligence. Other factors behind his lack of enjoyment in reading and his relatively low score on the reading test (20 percentile at age fourteen) may be too much early pressure, followed, possibly, by a withdrawal of parental interest in his reading as he grew older.

Another boy who showed about the same mental ability and made the same reading score described home conditions and parental teaching methods that seem also to have had a poor effect on later reading proficiency:

I learned to read at home before I went to school. My mother taught me. First she taught me the alphabet and vowels, then she taught me how to say words using the alfabet. Both of my parent were good readers but they could not teach me how to read fast like them. I never have been interested in reading. I had very few books that I could concentrate on and read for meaning. Radio and TV are two things that keep me from reading becaus I have been lisening to them every time I wanted to hear a story.

Complexity of the Parents' Role

These few quotations serve to show the complexity of the parents' role in helping a child learn to read.

Even some children who speak favorably of their parents' attempts to help them reveal by their reading scores that they are still reading below their potential ability. They rush through a reading assignment with feverish haste, comprehending very little of it. Or they plod along, word by word, hating every minute of the reading period. One discouraged girl wrote, "My parents have trided to make me a better reader from little on up." Apparently they did not succeed in making her proficient in any of the language arts.

One fourteen-year-old boy of average mental ability had a speed-of-reading score at the 85 percentile, but his vocabulary score was at the 3 percentile and his comprehension at the 17 percentile. His reading history included the following unfavorable features: (1) lack of effective instruction in the first grade: "they just told me the words and that's all"; (2) parents who made him read: "they forced me to read books and I didn't like it. It was boring and it didn't help at all"; and (3) dull books: "from the first to the third grade I didn't like any book whatsoever." However, in the fourth and fifth grades this boy became interested in dog and horse stories, and in one year read ten books. This spurt of interest was followed by a lapse; it was not sufficient to counteract the previous unfavorable influences.

That some children do profit by parental help is verified by their fine subsequent achievement.

What makes the difference? The important thing is the way the child feels about the help his parents try to give. If he feels that they are spending the time to help him with his reading because they love him and want him to be happy and successful, he will usually respond to whatever methods they use. If, on the other hand, he feels they are merely performing a duty, or helping him because they don't want him to disgrace the family by becoming a "remedial reading case," he may resent their help and not profit by it.

If the parents convey to the child their own respect for reading and delight in books, he may catch their attitude. Similarly, boredom may be contagious.

Sensitivity about the way the child is feeling is all-important. Does he resent being deprived of the normal playtime for children of his age? Is he discouraged because he receives only criticism when he is doing his best? Does he get the impression from his parents' impatience that he is slow and stupid? Is he afraid of losing his parents' love if he does not measure up to their standards? Sensitivity to the child's feelings will help the parent determine the role he should play in a given situation.

The parent's help will consist mainly in providing suitable reading material—books that are interesting to a particular child, that meet his needs at a given time, that are challenging but not frustrating. By reading a great deal of varied material that is interesting but relatively easy, the child develops fluency and builds vocabulary naturally through context.

Too often parents push the child ahead too fast. Their attitude is: "He can read a first-grade book—then let's go ahead to a second-grade book." It is better for him to read and enjoy a number of the interesting trade books for beginners than to stumble through a more difficult schoolbook. It takes thought and time to provide a suitable progression of reading experiences.

It is also better for the parent not to dispute the teacher's methods. Some popular books on reading are as unsound as they are persuasive. It is disturbing and confusing for the child to be caught in a conflict of methods—and of allegiances.

All sorts of methods work for some children at some times. We should watch the child's response to the procedure we are using. If he learns successfully and happily, it is a good method for him. If he fails to learn or becomes restless, anxious, or rebellious, it is a bad method for him.

CHILDREN'S FEELINGS

It is not difficult to get clues as to how a child is feeling. He reveals this by his facial expression, by signs of fatigue or eyestrain, by twisting and squirming like an animal that wants to get out of a cage, or by subdued docility, as well as by the words he says. Of course, we cannot observe feelings directly; we have to make inferences from the clues we observe. The way a child feels about himself, his reading, and his parents' efforts to help him improve is of great importance; his feelings and attitudes govern his responses to the reading situation in which he is placed.

Children are often remarkably tolerant toward adults. As one fourteen-year-old girl said: "If I don't like reading, and if I'm worried about it, I don't believe it's my parents' fault, I believe it's my own fault."

Children often give parents the benefit of the doubt: "My parents said I was dumb (but I know they're kidding). But that doesn't worry me cause I know I am pretty dumb." One does not know to what extent this child has accepted her parents' thoughtless kidding at its face value, or how deep her feeling of failure and defeat really is. Some parents who have the best intentions will say in Johnny's presence, "Helen does well in her schoolwork, but Johnny is captain of the baseball team." Unfortunately, Johnny knows all too well that reading is important; it is not reassuring, as the parent intended, to have his skill in baseball set up against Helen's superior reading ability. If parents only knew how deeply children may suffer from their feelings of inadequacy, they would be more cautious about comparing reading accomplishments within the family circle.

The feelings of failure that develop at home are often reinforced at school. The poor reader cannot fail to observe that others read much more fluently than he does, that they finish the test questions long before he does, that they are reading books he cannot comprehend, and that he is placed in the lowest reading group, which is recognized as the "dumb group," regardless of the fancy name that may be given to it. As the child grows older, we can help him to accept his limitations, and focus on the things he can do well and on the level of reading ability he can achieve.

We probably do not know how many children worry about making mistakes when they read. Some mention it specifically in their accounts of reading aloud to their parents. Older boys and girls mention their embarrassment in reading aloud before their classmates.

Some children are discouraged from reading by the negative attitude of their classmates: "The reason I dislike reading is because my friends used to call me a bookworm and I didn't like that."

Many adolescents indicate that their attitude toward reading changed when they realized its personal importance to them: "I'm beginning to like reading now [at fifteen years] because I know reading is important to me."

Fear underlies many reading problems. The child may not recognize his fear of failure, of losing his parents' love, of being ridiculed by his classmates, of being stupid. Fears may lurk behind many façades. To the parent and teacher the child may appear to be indifferent to or content with his poor reading. He may appear stubborn, hostile, or unreasonable, or merely docile and conformable. He may refuse even to try to learn to read because his previous efforts have all met with failure; he is afraid to try again. Failure can significantly lower the child's feeling of personal worth; self-esteem is built on successful experience. A child's worry about his failure in school may be intensified by a guilty feeling that it is all his fault—he did not work hard enough. To be sure, this may be true in some cases, but in others the fault lies in circumstances that are beyond the child's control.

If we recognize the possibility that the child's ostensible attitude is a mask for underlying fears, we shall be in a better position to give him two kinds of help: to help him understand and handle his fears, and to change conditions that are beyond his control.

The way children view themselves determines to a great extent the way they approach reading. Behavior stems from attitudes. We should try to understand the child's attitudes:

1. Toward his parents and brothers and sisters. If he considers that his parents have a negative feeling toward him, his resentment may express itself in self-sabotage. Failure to learn to read hurts both the child and his parents. If he has a brother or sister who is a good reader, the child who is having reading difficulties may prefer not to try to learn; if he tries and fails, he will make his rival's superiority still more evident.

2. Toward himself as a person—dependent or independent, competent or incompetent, worthy or unworthy. One boy identified himself as "the black sheep of the family," and added, "Every family has to have a black sheep, I guess." Such an attitude often cancels effort—he's licked before he begins.

3. Toward himself in relation to reading—a child may think of himself as "a boy who can't learn to read." So, why try!

4. Toward reading—"reading isn't important," "reading is sissy," "reading is drudgery."

Attitudes in these crucial areas, whether negative or positive, determine, to a great extent, the kind of response a child makes in a reading situation. His attitudes condition the effort he puts forth and the satisfactions he gets from the reading experience. The effect of initial attitudes is cumulative; a satisfying reading experience produces an enthusiastic approach to the next experience, whereas an unpleasant recollection of past attempts to read may result in halfheartedness or out-and-out withdrawal or rebellion in the face of another reading task.

READING INTERESTS

Although interests are usually specific, there are certain kinds of books that boys and girls generally prefer at certain ages. Pre-adolescents of both sexes usually like dog and horse stories: they frequently mention *Lassie Come Home, The Black Stallion* series, and Jack London's books. Most of them also like mystery stories. More boys than girls read adventure stories such as *Twenty Thousand Leagues Under the Sea* and science fiction. As they grow older, their interests diverge. Boys continue to enjoy adventure and sport stories, and move toward historical novels and science. Girls prefer teen-age tales and become interested in love stories and careers. Both boys and girls, if they are good readers, eventually include some of the classics in their reading.

One boy of average ability, who seemed to be reading well up to capacity, described the changes in his reading interests as follows:

At the age of five to seven I liked reading very much. About nine or ten I did not like it so much. But as I got older I realized the importance of reading and grew fond of it. From then on I have liked reading very well. At the age of five to seven I liked small adventure stories. As I got older, I liked to read big and better adventure stories and some mysteries, too. Today (age fourteen) I like reading biography and *Abraham Lincoln, George Washington.*

This boy's increasing interest in reading accounts, in part, for his superior achievement in reading.

A fourteen-year-old boy in the ninth grade described his reading interests thus:

In the first grade I started reading Golden Books and had quite a collection of them. My parents helped me in various ways—by encouraging my reading and getting all the books I wanted.

When I was in grade school most of my reading was of comic books. My brother and I had over 350 comic books. Nowadays I like fiction books like Jules Verne writes. Today I want to read more and more. Just this summer I read every day, usually a book a day. The only thing that made me worry about my reading was not being able to find a book to read. I have had no reading difficulties that I could not handle by myself. So I enjoy reading more and more.

This youngster, who was about average in ability, made high scores on his reading test—90 percentile on vocabulary, 75 percentile on comprehension, and 87 percentile for total reading score. After passing through the comic-book stage, he returned to good reading with increased interest and enjoyment. Wide reading pays off.

In general, the teen-agers who said they liked to read and did read a great deal during at least part of their school life were the ones who made reading scores that were commensurate with their ability. Exceptions to this general rule were those who said they read a great deal, but apparently read superficially. They usually scored high on speed of reading but low on comprehension.

INFLUENCE OF RADIO, TV, MOVIES, AND COMIC BOOKS

Much has been written about the way in which the mass media of communication affect children. Paul Witty [8] has systematically studied this question over a period of years; he has summarized information on how many hours a week children spend viewing television, which programs they watch, what effect television has on their reading. Elementary school children spend, on the average, about twenty-seven hours a week looking at TV programs. Their parents spend about the same amount of time; teachers and high school students spend less. Except in individual cases, there is no clear evidence that watching TV decreases reading. But it will be interesting to hear what some teen-agers say about the influence TV has had on them.

Undoubtedly, TV competes with reading, as the following statements suggest:

"When I see dramatizations of stories on TV, I have no urge to read books about them."

"TV has affected my reading, because when a good television movie comes on, I stop reading."

"When my brother comes in and turns on TV, I can't read so I watch TV."

"If you can see a story on TV, why not watch it? Why read it?"

"Sometimes I begin to read and then I hear something on TV or radio. I will often stop reading to see what it is. But I'm improving in this."

In defense of television, radio, and movies other teen-agers give them credit for a number of values, some not commonly assigned. The most common comment is that these media sometimes stimulate them to read or to buy books:

"Radio and TV have helped me because when they advertised books, that made me want to read them. Watching stories on TV also made me want to buy the books."

"On TV I always listen to science fiction movies. The more I listened to them the more I would like to be a space pilot and now I read science fiction stories and like them."

"TV made me want to read more about the political debate I heard and find out the facts about it."

"Movies have influenced my reading by prompting me to read the book because the movie was interesting."

"The movies have affected my reading greatly by making me want to read some books and compare them with the movies."

"If I have missed seeing a movie that is good, I usually try to read the book."

A bright girl with excellent reading ability gave several concrete examples:

TV, the movies and comics have had some effect on my reading. For example, I saw an episode last year which was taken from the book *Pride and Prejudice*. I became so interested in the plot and characters that I got the book from the library and read it. Another time I saw the movie *Flicka* and its sequel *Thunderhead* and eventually read both books. These are just examples and have occurred many times.

Other young people mentioned more unusual values of these mass media:

I think TV, radio and movies have made things more interesting and easier to follow. I understand more of what I am reading. On the other hand, TV has kept me from reading. It didn't exactly keep me from reading; it was easier than reading.

Probably this adolescent girl is not the only one to follow the line of least resistance.

Radio and TV help me to listen better and so I can read better.

When I watch TV, I always try to pronounce words correctly and watch out for words I don't know the meaning of.

These few quotations suggest most of the pros and cons of radio, TV, and movies as they are related to reading: they do enrich the child's experience background for reading; they introduce him to new words, thus increasing his vocabulary; they may arouse his interest in reading certain books and plays; they may stimulate him to compare the book with the television, radio, or movie version. Whether TV and radio increase one's listening ability is an open question. Sometimes it seems as if continuous bombardment by insignificant sounds must cause psychological deafness, or a disinclination to listen.

Even more has been written about the effect of comics, especially on juvenile crime and mental health. The teen-agers have something to say about the values of comic books. They make three main points: reading the comics may give one the impression that reading in general might be fun; it is necessary to acquire some reading ability in order to understand the comics; and certain comics may lead one toward a better quality of reading material. They have expressed these ideas in their own words as follows:

"Comics gave me a funny point of view of reading." [If comics convey the idea that reading might be fun instead of drab drudgery, they serve one useful purpose, especially for reluctant readers.]

"TV, radio and movies have no effect on my reading ability. But comics did. You have to be able to read before you can understand what is going on. So comics have helped me in my reading."

"I think comics have also influenced my reading of funny stories, because the comics made me want to read stories the comics were about."

"When I was about eleven or twelve, I used to like comics, but now I like adventure stories which I get from the Public Library."

Reading will survive television as it has survived other competitors. The more able learners prefer to use their own imaginations rather than accept the producer's version of a story. They prefer to reflect on what they read rather than be hurried from one program to another. The interruptions for commercial messages annoy them. And they want to have access to the ancient and modern wisdom of the world.

These programs do take up a lot of children's time. But we can help them plan a balanced day, including time for reading, for outdoor activities, for being alone, and for being with friends.

Parents are pleased when children break away from TV, the modern Pied Piper, and return to reading worth-while books. A recent cartoon pictured a little boy reading a book and his mother at the telephone saying: "I'm so excited I can hardly bear it. Tommy's turned off the TV program and picked up a book!"

EXPRESSED DISSATISFACTIONS WITH READING

In their compositions, adolescents mention few difficulties or dissatisfactions with their reading, other than slow rate. When asked specifically to state their dissatisfactions, poor readers mention a great many kinds of difficulty.

Their dissatisfaction with their *rate of reading* is expressed in many ways:

"Too slow—just not fluent. My study is slowed up by my slow and faulty reading."

"I find it necessary to spend too much time reading."

"Slow reading leads to frustration."

"Desire to read more widely."

"It takes so long that interest wanes."

Faulty comprehension and poor memory give rise to these comments:

"Don't know what I am reading—what the story is all about."
"Can't remember the meanings of words."
"When I finish reading, I don't remember what I've read."
"I read inaccurately."
"Hard to get the point of my assignments."
"I can't understand most of the things I have to study, because I can't read."

Inability to concentrate:

"My father feels I don't concentrate enough."
"Unless the reading comes to the point right away, I lose interest."

Specific difficulties with the mechanics of reading include difficulty in pronouncing new words, inability to recognize their meaning, misreading words, extreme difficulty with spelling, and skipping words.

Being below grade level is of concern to many—"not being able to keep up with my grade."

"I would like to improve my reading so that I may do well in my other subjects."

These are surface descriptions of reading difficulties. Interviews with these individuals would uncover the deeper roots of their difficulties.

INFLUENCE OF READING ON PERSONAL DEVELOPMENT

Many children and adolescents assert that reading has had little or no influence on their personal development. Those who say this are mostly poor readers. The influences they do recognize are interesting and sometimes amusing:

"The books I have read that influenced me were mostly *Huck Finn* and *Tom Sawyer,* who were always getting in trouble and running away. I found out in these books that running away never gets you anywhere except the place you're going."

"I like teen-age books the best," [a teen-age girl said] "they give me more ideas on what kind of friends I want and what kind of guy I want to marry. These are both very important factors in someone's life."

After reading a book one likes, one often chooses another of the same kind: "Sometimes when I read a book I like very much, it influences me to get another book and read it."

Another kind of influence takes the form of identification: "'When I read different stories, I wonder if that would ever happen to me and what would I do. So I read on and find out what the story says."

Other books arouse specific emotions:

Some of the books that I have read made me want to go out and kill every enemy we have. Some books make you cry, like *God Is My Co-Pilot*. I saw this first on TV; that's why I had to read it. I know the book is better than the picture.

Still other books help readers increase their understanding of themselves and others: "A book about a family of eight children and their troubles made me realize that you can have a big family and still be happy."

The Trembling Years, a book about a girl stricken with polio, described her thoughts and feelings, her pain and trouble so vividly that it made one girl realize how much she had to be thankful for.

To some adolescents reading gives a deeper understanding of world problems. After reading Ernie Pyle's *Brave Men,* one boy wrote:

After reading this book I learned the truth about war. . . . I saw its horror. I saw that men in the Armed Forces were not supermen, but just ordinary people pulled into the maelstrom like needles pulled to a magnet. I learned that there is glory to a victorious army, but it comes only after many men are killed or wounded. The book gave me the viewpoint that war is evil and opened my eyes to the destruction of war.

A few adolescents mention the religious significance that they have found in certain books:

Two books have influenced my attitudes enough to mention. These are *The Robe* and *Love Is Eternal*. *The Robe* has given me a deep respect for my belief in Christ and God. *Love Is Eternal* has made me see love in a different light. Both have given me a few reasons as to why people have a purpose on this earth today—that is to love their fellow man and forgive their faults and infirmities.

One boy described how reading influenced his choice of a career:

Books have influenced my point of view toward my career—that of being a pharmacist. If I had not read books on the subject, I would probably not have decided to be a pharmacist. When I read books on the lives of other people, I see how they lived and how they treated other people. I believe those who were kind have influenced my life. They taught me to be more thoughtful of the people around me.

One perceptive sixteen-year-old girl said she believed that "when you read something, it affects you in either a negative or affirmative way."

Whether or not a book influences an individual depends on the individual as well as on the book. He may not be ready for the message that the book contains; he may not have had the life experiences that he would need to interpret it. One girl whose mother urged her to read Shakespeare prematurely, refused to do so. For a time, she called everything she especially disliked *Shakespearean*. Later she began to read Shakespeare of her own accord, with pleasure and profit. An individual's response to books is also likely to be affected by the attitudes of his friends, by his reading ability, his interests, and his needs at a given time.

CONCLUDING STATEMENT

To help a child learn to read, we must first of all be sensitive to the way he is thinking and feeling. Does he approach reading tasks with eagerness and confidence, or with reluctance and fear? Let us try to see each situation through his eyes.

Children and adolescents have given us sound advice, advice based on their firsthand experience. We may summarize it briefly: Children have happy memories of being read to by parents or grandparents. Before they go to school, they would like parents to help them read words on signs, and other words that they are curious about. They want parents to care about their reading, and to give them credit for the progress they are making.

They want parents to help them pronounce unfamiliar words and get their meanings, but not to tell them things that they are able to figure out for themselves.

If they are having difficulty and need additional practice, they are glad to have their parents cooperate with the teacher.

They appreciate having their parents bring home books that they are able to read and that are really interesting to them.

They want their parents to be sensitive to their feelings—to understand that they need much more approval than criticism; to appreciate their efforts and not become impatient when they are slow to learn; to expect the best of them; to realize that they really want to please their parents. They also want their parents to avoid doing certain things that make them angry, bored, or overanxious.

Questions and Answers

1. *How do children feel about being placed in special or remedial reading classes?*

It depends on the class, how it is introduced and how it is taught. Many students consider it an opportunity, as this boy did:

The summer after the fifth grade my mom had me go to a reading teacher to learn me how to read and that did some good, but not enough. In the eighth grade I was put in a special reading class. I learned more about reading in that class than anywhere else.

It is very important to introduce the class to the pupils as a special opportunity for those who have the ability to read better. There should be no stigma attached to being in the special reading class. In many schools the word "remedial" is not used; these classes are called Special English, Reading Improvement classes, Small English classes, or other names that avoid suggesting something is wrong with the children enrolled in them. As a matter of fact, so-called remedial classes are really developmental because instruction begins where the individual pupil is, and helps him to progress from there.

2. *In seeking special help in reading for a child, is there a danger of making him feel inferior?*

Wendell Johnson, one of the most creative thinkers in this field, emphasizes the danger of labeling a child as a stutterer or a psychiatric case. This would also apply to labels such as "retarded reader" or "remedial reading case." Some parents, in their sincere efforts to help the child read better, take him from one clinic to another, subject him to many tests, and usurp his play and recreation time for remedial work. Such strenuous efforts to improve his reading may well give the child the idea that something is very wrong with him; that his parents are dissatisfied with the way he is and are trying to change him. All of us resist being changed. Our self-concept is persistent.

The parent should first be sure that a special reading class is necessary. Under skillful instruction many children make the desired progress in their regular classes. If the child is unable to profit by regular instruction, he may then be assigned to a special reading group. This is done by the reading specialist, whose decision is based on teachers' recommendations and observations, as well as on the results of both standardized and informal tests. The feelings of the child and the point of view of the parents should also be considered before placing child or adolescent in a special reading class.

3. *How can a parent know when to accept the child's reading achievement as the best he can do, and when to put pressure on him to do better?*

This is a very complicated question. The only answer that can be given without detailed knowledge of the child is: "It depends. . . ."

It depends on the child's mental ability: Is he retarded in other ways, slow to learn, unable to profit by the best instruction?

It depends on the child's physical condition: Has he uncorrected defects of hearing or vision? Is his energy level generally low?

It depends upon his previous school history: Was he deprived of effective reading instruction in the lower grades?

It depends upon his feeling about himself: Is he afraid to grow up; afraid to learn about the world and himself through reading? Is he expressing some hostility or resentment by not learning to read?

These and many other conditions may prevent any child from

using his real ability. In any case, putting pressure on him is not likely to improve matters. It is necessary to discover the cause of his difficulty, with whatever expert help is available, and to do what the diagnosis shows to be desirable and necessary.

Children often say that they wish their parents had made them read more. They want parents to have standards and hold firmly to them. This is sound, provided the standards are ones that the child *can* live up to. The pull of a clearly recognized, realistic goal is far more effective than any amount of parental pushing and prodding.

4. *What kind of fears may underlie inability to read?*

Fears lurk behind many façades. The child who seems stubborn and refuses to read may be terribly afraid of not making a good showing. The child who seems to resent parental help may be afraid that the parents will be impatient with his slow learning. The child who is apparently compliant may go through the motions of reading without any real inner motivation because he fears losing his parents' approval and good will.

Many of these fears decrease as the child sees objective evidence of his success in reading, and as reading situations become less tense and deadly serious.

5. *Can a child read too much?*

Few parents seem to be worried about this. Probably today's world is "so full of a number of things"—besides reading—that few children read to excess. However, an occasional parent may overemphasize reading, or an occasional child may retreat into the world of books in order to escape from the real world that has been a source of bitter disappointment to him. Such was the case with Joan, who was unpopular with the other children because she was indifferent to them and because she dressed and behaved differently. Joan cultivated an intellectual aloofness and always tried to shift the conversation to books, authors, or philosophy. Here was a gifted child who used reading as an escape from a social world in which she was unhappy.

This excessive interest in books is rare; it should not be confused with intellectual curiosity. The latter finds in books an understanding of life—not a refuge from the distress of life.

THREE

What Is Reading?

Four-year-old David, holding the newspaper upside down, looked at it intently as he had seen his father do. "I'm reading," he said.

His twin sister picked up her mother's grocery list and rattled off a number of items that bore no resemblance to those on the list. Both children were merely imitating their parents, whom they had seen reading in these ways, for different purposes.

Billy was looking at a picture book and telling an authentic story about each picture. He was learning to observe details, to see relations, to get meanings, and to communicate them to others. So far he had no need for printed words. "Words are for people who can't read the pictures," his brother explained.

Jeannie liked to hear the same story over and over. Soon she could remember it exactly as Mother read it. When she picked up the book herself and repeated the story page by page, she appeared to be reading, but she was really only remembering the words she had heard.

Ted always looked at each page as his father read the words. Before long he could point to certain words and say them. He had learned to associate the printed word with its sound and with its meaning.

By the end of the second grade, Paul had been so intensively, and exclusively, drilled in phonics—associating letter sounds with their printed forms in words—that he could pronounce words like "atomic energy" and "political controversy." He could pronounce all the words in his brother's high school history text—but he did not understand a word of what he was reading.

If a child can pronounce all the words in a passage correctly, can he read? Not if he does not understand a word of it! What is more futile than merely pronouncing words without getting any meaning from them? What could be a greater waste of time! Reading is not word calling.

Yet this is the way some children read. They can give a perfect pronunciation to every word in a paragraph, but when you ask, "What is the paragraph about?" they do not know—or care.

Alfred, at ten years of age, would quickly leaf through a book, put it aside, and say, "I've read it." He did not know anything more about the book than some adults know about the Sunday papers after several hours of going through them.

Karen, in junior high school, dutifully but passively read every word in the reading assignment. When she was through, she remembered very little of what she had read.

Pamela, in the same grade, approached the reading assignment quite differently. Before beginning to read, she stopped to think what the section was about, what she already knew about it, why she was reading it, what questions it would answer. Then she read with an active mind, skimming parts that did not seem important, pausing to reread and think about sentences that answered her questions. After reading in this way, she reviewed what she had learned and then took a little more time to see how she could use the ideas in the class discussion the next day. Pamela was bringing meaning to the reading material, getting meaning from it, and putting her new synthesis of meanings into a useful form.

Paul, a college senior, represents a mature reader—the kind of reader we hope all our children will become. He constantly derives meaning from what he reads by relating it to his own background of experience. He judges an author by the way he selects and presents facts; Paul sorts out the facts from opinions and inferences. By examining the feelings and values the author has expressed or implied, he avoids being misled by the author's intentional or unconscious misuse of words. By comparing the author's point of view, inferences, and conclusions with those that he himself has arrived at, and with those of other writers in the field, he puts himself in a position to draw valid conclusions from the material. His habit of thinking critically while reading enables him to apply the knowledge he gains from reading to the solution of personal and social problems. In addition, he uses this knowledge as a means of developing deeper insights into the meaning of his experience, and thus enhances his personal development and social sensitivity.

We could continue with many other snapshots of the reading process. Make-believe reading may indicate the beginning of a desire to learn to read. Reading pictures is a prelude to reading print. Anticipating the next words in a story is a habit that is common to efficient readers. Associating the sound of words with their printed form is the first step in formal reading instruction. If a child learns to pronounce unfamiliar words in order to unlock their meanings, he has taken a big step toward becoming an independent reader. But if he merely pronounces words without concern for their meanings, he is not reading in the true sense of the word—he is not using the printed word as a tool for thinking and living. As Edgar Dale, an authority on reading, has so well said, reading is getting meaning from the printed page by putting meaning into it.

There is danger that reading may become a mere adjunct to television. A recent cartoon pictured one mother saying to another, "I think children should learn to read. Gives them something to do if the TV goes out." Is TV crowding out reading time in your home? Does the family look at television when they used to read together? Do television and motion pictures satisfy your children's curiosity and leave them with no desire to explore the world of books? The only way to combat these tendencies is to make sure that children's early years are full of satisfying and rewarding experiences with books. Then they may say, as one teen-age youngster did, "Although there are lots of things I like to do, give me a good book any time."

THE BROAD VIEW OF READING

In the broad view, reading is regarded as a manifold process that involves associating words with meanings and letter sounds with the printed symbols, thinking, feeling, acting, and becoming. Creative and thoughtful reading begins when the reader has learned how to find out what the author actually said.

The Physical Basis of Reading

If you took your child to an eye specialist, he would be concerned to discover visual defects that might make it impossible for the child to see letters and words clearly. A clear visual impression of the word is basic to reading.

If the child is farsighted, he will find it difficult to read a book if he holds it at the usual distance from the eyes. Farsightedness is more uncomfortable for the reader than a small degree of near-sightedness. The usual school eye examination, based on the old Snellen chart, often gives parents a false sense of security; this test does not detect farsightedness, nor does it detect some other eye defects that have a bearing on reading.

Another eye difficulty that may blur the child's impression of the printed word is a muscular imbalance that causes the eyes to move inward or outward, or to deviate from a parallel horizontal plane. This can sometimes be corrected by special orthoptic exercises under the supervision of a competent eye specialist.

You may find that your child has a degree of astigmatism that can be corrected by glasses.

Eye difficulties may cause so much discomfort that reading will acquire unpleasant associations for the child.

Many schools give all their pupils a visual screening test. The purpose of this test is merely to determine which children should be referred for an expert eye examination. Sometimes parents are annoyed because the optometrist or ophthalmologist finds nothing wrong with the child's eyes. The parent feels that he has paid for an unnecessary eye examination. In some cases, the visual screening test does over-refer—that is, it detects difficulties that really do not need to be corrected. In other cases, the eye doctor may give the child a superficial examination that does not detect conditions that may make reading difficult or uncomfortable for him.

If, after a careful examination, a competent eye doctor prescribes glasses, the parent should, of course, have these glasses made and see that the child wears them.

There are many reasons why some children try to avoid wearing their reading glasses. Boys may think that glasses make them look "sissy." Girls may think that glasses make them look homely. Either boys or girls may consider glasses a nuisance and forget to bring or wear them to school. If you can find out why a child or adolescent is refusing to wear the glasses that have been prescribed for him, you may be able to enter into his world of reasoning and help him change his attitude. You should also interest him in keeping the glasses clean and properly adjusted.

Hearing, too, needs to be checked. Sometimes teachers are so concerned with the psychological effects and aspects of teaching the child to read that they ignore his physical condition. One rural teacher who had tried in every way to interest one of her pupils in schoolwork, said: "No matter what I did, she sat there just like a log. On the playground, too, she didn't take part in the games with other children. Finally I went to visit her home. In the course of the conversation the mother remarked, 'I reckon Mary's doing right well, considering she can't hear.' Mary had had a severe case of scarlet fever that had resulted in loss of hearing." The mother had not reported this important information to the school, and the teacher had not thought to check on the child's hearing as a possible cause of her school difficulty. One proved characteristic of good readers is that they hear and understand conversations and stories.

Poor nutrition may also interfere with a child's learning. After World War I, George Stoddard studied educational problems in European countries and came back with a new definition of a school: "A school is a group of children who have had breakfast." Little learning takes place if the child is seriously undernourished or ill. Consideration of the child's health and physical functioning is a prerequisite to reading instruction.

Meaningful Seeing

Visual perception is as important as visual efficiency in a child's reading development. By visual perception we mean the ability to recognize figures and forms in pictures, and words or parts of words in storybooks. Good readers are usually able to recognize a form or a word from a few clues, as in the childish game of "Hangman" where several letters of a word are given, for example: — e — d — — g. The child fills in the missing letters to make the word *reading*. Some children can reconstruct the word quickly, while others have to guess letter after letter.

Reading as an Associative Process

Many teachers begin reading instruction by building up a basic sight vocabulary of fifty or one hundred words. They may present a word simultaneously with the object, picture, or action for which it stands. This process may be represented as follows:

$$\text{Printed word} \left\langle \begin{array}{l} \text{object} \\ \text{picture} \\ \text{action} \end{array} \right. = \begin{array}{l} \text{meaning of} \\ \text{printed word} \end{array}$$

One step removed from this simplest form of association is the linking of the printed word with the spoken word, which has already been invested with meaning:

$$\text{Printed word—spoken word} \left\langle \begin{array}{l} \text{meaning} \\ \text{meaning} \\ \text{meaning} \end{array} \right. = \begin{array}{c} \text{meaning of} \\ \text{the} \\ \text{printed word} \end{array}$$

For example, if the child has had many experiences with cats, the spoken word is rich in meaning for him. Consequently, when the adult points to the printed word and says "cat," the printed symbol takes on meaning.

The usual method of building sight vocabulary is through little stories that the children dictate to the teacher. These may be about the class turtle or rabbit, a little white kitten who strayed into the classroom, or the big machines at work near the school. The children read the story as a whole, and the teacher uses various devices and exercises to test their understanding of the separate words. If the children have adequate mental ability and a good basis of spoken language, and if the reading material resembles their conversation, they quickly form associations between the unknown printed symbol and the familiar spoken word and its meaning.

Independence Through Word-Recognition Skills

In learning Chinese one would have to go through this associative process with every single word; this is foolishly laborious in learning a language whose words are built of a limited number of letters. Therefore we begin to use the phonetic approach as soon as the children have acquired a small vocabulary of meaningful words. This process may be described as follows:

| Associating the letters in the printed word | with | the sound of these letters | gives | the pronunciation of the word |

If the spoken word is familiar to the child, he can get the meaning of the printed word—if he wants to, and is not interested in merely pronouncing it.

To direct the child's attention to the meaning of the word in the sentence, the teacher often asks, to begin with, "What do you think the word might mean?" Then she may ask, "Which letter does the word begin with? Do you know other words that begin this way?" As the child tries to sound out the letters he knows, he may solve the word without having to sound out all the letters. Later he will recognize familiar syllables, prefixes, suffixes, and roots. But he should always be concerned about whether his solution is correct and whether the word makes sense in the sentence.

Comprehension Unlimited

Seeing the words clearly, knowing instantly by sight those that recur frequently, and being able to puzzle out the meaning of unfamiliar words—these are all basic to reading sentences, paragraphs, and pages for meaning. When you ask a child who has just read a story, "What was the story about?" you may get any of a number of replies. These represent different levels of comprehension. He may merely repeat a few of the author's words, just as a parrot might. He may tell the story accurately in his own words; this shows he has been reading the lines well.

He may read between the lines and reconstruct the characters in his imagination from the clues the author gives; he may tell why he thinks they behaved as they did. Or he may read beyond the lines and make his own generalizations, conclusions, and inferences. These higher levels of comprehension are approached in a simple way as soon as the child begins to read independently. The teacher or parent asks questions such as these: Would you like to have Jimmy for a friend? Why or why not? Why did he give the stranger the wrong directions? Would other people have done the same thing under the same conditions? What might have happened if he had made friends instead of enemies of the natives?

Use of Reading

There is a time, perhaps, when the wonder of being able to get meaning from printed words is completely absorbing to the child. It is at this stage that he is likely to say, "Mommy, let me read to you." But as soon as reading becomes a tool rather than a toy, the child reads for a purpose. What he reads is remembered more readily when it is put to use. He reads to find out what the class is going to do that day, to follow directions, to get information, to make a play out of the story he has read, to read a letter or a notice on the bulletin board, or just to enjoy an amusing story or poem. The manifold utilization of reading constitutes another aspect of this broad view.

Feeling Responses to Reading

Would you say that a child was reading in the broadest sense of the word if he showed no pleasure, no excitement, no satisfaction, no emotional response of any kind to the material he was reading? Surely not! Children need the therapy of laughter and the therapy of tears [1] that books may give. They weep over the death of poor Charlotte the spider and laugh through their tears at silly Wilbur the pig. Reading without feeling is a mechanical process; it does not involve the child's personality as a whole. The way a book makes us feel is one of the best indications of its value.

As soon as the child has acquired a basic sight vocabulary and has mastered enough word-recognition skills to read independently, reading becomes a process of thinking, feeling, responding. As such, it lends itself very early to the purposes of character formation. In fact, that was the main aim of the McGuffey readers and similar books of a century ago. One story titled "Helping Father" concluded: "Daniel did a great many things which his father had always paid a man for doing. And he had plenty of time for play besides, and then he enjoyed his play better because there is always a satisfaction in doing good, which lends a charm to everything we undertake." [2] Such content was calculated to make the reader either congratulate himself because he was like Daniel, or feel guilty because he had not helped his father and been happy in doing so. Thus conscience is developed, especially in children whose parents love and accept them, seldom use physical punishment, and reason with them if they do something wrong.

Personality and Character Development Through Reading

Theoretically, self-development is facilitated as the child identifies himself with worthy characters. The literature that has lasted over the years has been notable for its moral influence. An individual shows his character by his way of living, which is the product of deep-seated values and ideals. These values arise from his experience, both past and present. Reading is part of this experience. Its impact may be constructive or destructive, positive or negative, slight or intense. From the earliest years, we should be alert to the possible contribution that reading may make to a child's character.

High school students have reported many instances in which some book or article has influenced their point of view, attitude, or behavior. One ninth-grade girl said, "Until I read *The Old Maid,* I never realized how a child could hurt her mother." After reading *Dear and Glorious Physician,* a ninth-grade girl wrote, "I had the feeling I should go out and do something great. Of course, this feeling did not last long, but it did get me thinking about what I could do for humanity." Many other adolescents have written about books that helped them to understand themselves, get along better with their family, maintain their good intentions, deepen their religious life, or acquire a sense of direction or destiny in their lives.[3]

Almost two-thirds of more than a thousand college students who were questioned about how reading had affected their personal development felt that books had contributed to the development of their philosophy of life. A third thought that reading had helped them to discover their ideal selves, change some of their attitudes, and develop by emulation some of the personal qualities of admirable characters.

Reading, we believe, contributes to personal development, and personal development, in turn, enriches reading.

CHILD DEVELOPMENT AND READING

The child's gains in total development contribute to his reading development. Similarly, his growth in reading contributes to his further all-round development. Reading is an important tool of learning, a source of happiness, a way of gaining understanding of oneself, the world, and other people; and a means of social and emotional adjustment. The reciprocal relation between child de-velopment and reading may be shown schematically as follows:

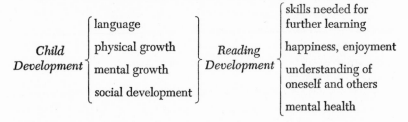

Child Development { language, physical growth, mental growth, social development } *Reading Development* { skills needed for further learning, happiness, enjoyment, understanding of oneself and others, mental health }

Multiple Immaturity

If your child seems to be retarded in physical growth, social development, word knowledge, or mental alertness, he is likely to show a similar retardation in learning to read. It may be that he just needs a little more time to grow. You might do well to follow the example of the mother bird in the children's poem. Instead of pushing the fledgling out of the nest to fly or fall, she said,

> Birdie, wait a little longer,
> Till your little wings are stronger.

Two boys both of whom started out as slow growers later made pronounced gains in reading, one with and the other without remedial instruction.

Some children have missed, for one reason or another, the kinds of "normal" experiences that seem to be indispensable to healthy, all-round development—persons to talk with, freedom from want and freedom from fear, an adequate diet, opportunities to play with other children, work they engage in wholeheartedly, and chances to rest when they are tired. If this is true of your child, then you can contribute to both his general development and his reading maturity by supplying these experiences.

Methods of Dealing with Immaturity

There are three methods of dealing with a backward or slow-learning child. The first method Willard C. Olson [4] has called *forcing*. If a child does not begin to learn to read in first grade as children are expected to do, the parent may insist that the teacher use all sorts of exercises, games, drills, and other devices calculated to make the child a good reader. In many cases, master teachers can do this. But is it worth the effort? At a later age the child will be able to make the same progress at a cost of far less effort both on his part and on the part of the teacher. In the long run, nothing is gained by premature attempts to teach beginning reading. In some cases no amount of practice will be effective; it may even make the child resistant to reading.

A better method is *pacing*. Each child is helped to progress at his own rate and on his own initiative. If he is ready to read, as many bright children are when they enter first grade, the teacher provides the instruction and the interesting reading material that he needs and lets him go ahead as fast and as far as he wishes. If the child is not ready for formal reading instruction, the teacher provides more prereading experiences of the kind that children find in good homes during the preschool years. Each child is given encouragement and individual help when he gives evidence of being ready to read.

The third method, *delaying* reading instruction for all children, does not recognize individual differences. It is a suitable method for the slow-learning child. The mentally retarded child who enters school when he is six may not be ready to read until he is eight or nine years old. But this does not justify a general delay in all children's introduction to reading.

Obviously, the best method is to recognize individual differences, provide the most effective instruction, offer encouragement and opportunity to learn, and be guided by the results. Once a child has shown interest and responsiveness, he is likely to profit by specific guidance and instruction in reading.

Principles Underlying Child Development

Certain principles underlie both child development and reading. The first is that affection is a basic need of children. A parent may express affection in various ways. In early infancy, the mother shows her love for the child by holding him warmly in her arms, fondling him, and meeting his needs. Later, praise and approval are seen by the child as signs of affection. As the child grows older he may realize that the parent is showing love when he sets firm limits that reinforce his self-control and help him to realize his most acceptable self. That is why children and adolescents often describe their favorite teacher as one who is "strict," and approve parents who, as they say, "make them mind" or are "not too strict and not too easy." But love is not enough. To affection must be added understanding— an understanding of how children learn and grow—and an expectation that the child will do his best.

A second principle is that every individual has resources within himself—growth potentials and an inner urge to grow in his own best way. Although certain developmental sequences are common to all children, each child has his own unique pattern and rate of development. All we need to do is to provide conditions that are favorable to that development, very much as a gardener tends his growing plants. Sometimes physical defects, emotional disturbances, or poor schooling may deflect the child's normal course of development in reading. When these blocks are removed, the child is freed to grow according to his natural growth pattern.

If we accept this principle of growth, we shall expect our children to take more responsibility for their development. When they are confronted with a difficulty, we shall not rush in to solve their problem for them. Instead, we shall offer a suggestion, raise a pertinent question, and unobtrusively help them to succeed through their own efforts. In 1775 a father wrote to his daughter, "I do not want to *make* you do anything; I want to know what Nature has made you, and to perfect you on her plan." Don Marquis emphasized the same principle when he said, in his humorous way, that someday parents would no longer bring up their children, but provide the right conditions and let them bring themselves up. Our task is to provide a favorable environment and to guide our children in all the related aspects of their growth.[5]

Closely allied to this principle of growth is the principle of readiness. There is, to paraphrase Shakespeare, a tide in the process of learning, which, taken at the flood, leads to optimum achievement. In the life of every child there are "teachable moments," moments and periods when he is most eager and able to learn. By taking advantage of a child's readiness to learn, we help him to avoid the experience of failure, both in beginning reading and also in later stages of his schooling.

A fourth principle is that a child's development and progress in learning are affected by his concept of himself. Inferiority feelings and lack of self-esteem have an unfavorable influence on the child's behavior and accomplishment. Some reading problems stem from fear of competing with a more competent brother or sister. Occasionally a child fails in school in order to "get even with" a parent who seems to care only for his achievement and not for him as a person. We need to cultivate a keener awareness of the child's feelings about himself and his situation.

Two additional principles of learning are very important in the teaching of reading. One is the principle of meaningfulness—children should seek meaning in the words and sentences they are reading, not memorize them blindly. The second is the principle of use—children should enjoy or put to use the ideas they gain from reading. Excursions, pictures, discussions of similar experiences—all help to invest the printed material with meaning. If they need to obtain information or learn a reading skill in order to carry on a vital and interesting activity, they will make use at once of whatever they have learned.

These principles are interrelated. Meeting the child's basic need for affection and response from his earliest years has a favorable effect on his total development. The way a child develops also depends on his inner resources and the impetus supplied by his unique development pattern. His readiness for new experiences depends on the nature of his previous experiences and on his present stage of physical and psychological development. If conditions have been favorable, the child will have developed a positive, confident view of himself; he will have no emotional need to sabotage his own best development. If the learning task is meaningful and immediately useful to the child, it may help him to pull himself together and cope with any emotional problems that have arisen.

If we can translate these principles into productive relationships with our children and use them as a basis for making the right responses to their day-by-day behavior, we shall help each child to realize his best potentialities.

THE READING PROCESS

In describing the reading process, the best place to start is with the child. The child meets a reading situation to which he makes a certain response, which leaves some memory in his nervous system to influence the way in which he views the next situation where similar reading is involved.

Individual Differences in the Reading Process

Let us observe the process in the case of Jimmy. Jimmy is outgoing, curious, confident, and eager to read as he has seen members of his family do. He also wants to experience for himself the adventures in all those books Mommy does not have time to read to him. His eyesight and hearing are good, as is his general health. He is mentally alert and has profited by a home environment that has afforded him many opportunities to talk about his interesting experiences, learn the meaning of many spoken words, ask questions and receive answers, and associate letters with their sounds in spoken words. When he hears a story read to him, he listens carefully and can tell what the story is about. Although he has not been to kindergarten or nursery school, he has learned to play with other children of his own age. Since he is curious about the signs and labels that he sees, he has asked their meaning and has learned what these printed words say. Jimmy is ready to read.

What about the reading situation? This, too, is favorable. He likes the teacher, and she likes children and enjoys watching them grow. The other children, too, are friendly and have come to school in the expectation of learning how to read. The teacher starts with their interests. As they tell her about things that are important to them, she prints their stories on the board or on a chart; she uses their simple vocabulary and sentence patterns. Jimmy quickly learns to read these stories, and, after a little varied drill, he recognizes the separate words. All these conditions are conducive to learning to read—a friendly, encouraging atmosphere; reading material that is both suitable and appealing; skillful teaching that gives the child success and satisfaction in each step of the process; rewards for putting forth effort.

Jimmy's response to this reading situation has already been described. He feels confident about his ability to learn, likes reading and school, and can say with pride, "Daddy, I'm learning to read."

Although he sometimes forgets some of the words, he remembers many of them from day to day. Soon he will be associating the letter sounds with the printed letters in the meaningful words that he has already learned. These associations will gradually become more numerous and increasingly useful in unlocking the meaning of the new words he meets.

Having met these first reading experiences successfully, Jimmy will look forward to the next day's lesson. He will perceive the reading situation as one in which he can succeed with reasonable effort, one in which he can win the approval of people who are important to him, and, even more important, one that gives him that wonderful feeling of competence, of learning and growing.

For Billy, who is naturally slow in learning and has missed the preschool experiences that contributed to Johnny's readiness to read, the reading process was quite different. The situation presented to Billy was too difficult for him. He felt that the teacher did not like him; at least she was impatient with his inability to learn and remember the words. He felt discouraged and stupid. Instead of welcoming the reading period as Jimmy did, he dreaded it.

It will be noted that Jimmy and Billy brought different intellectual capacities and language abilities to the reading situation. All the specific abilities of this sort bear complex relationships to one another. Instruction that develops one of them may have a favorable influence on others.

Possible Influence of Personality

Self-confidence, self-reliance, emotional stability, and outgoingness seem also to be characteristic of the good readers in the primary and elementary grades. If these personality traits are missing to begin with, they may develop as the child meets success in his first attempts to learn to read.

In a study of good and poor readers of high school age, Holmes [6] found that the ratings that mothers gave fast-reading daughters on certain personality traits were remarkably similar to the ratings the daughters gave themselves. However, the ratings that mothers gave to slow readers were not only different from the girls' self-ratings; they were more disparaging. Mothers regarded their slow-reading daughters as more nervous, moody, quiet, unresponsive, hard-boiled, submissive, critical, or impulsive than the daughters regarded themselves.

Although we have no clear-cut scientific evidence of the importance of personality factors in reading, work with individual reading cases has repeatedly shown a circular response that begins either with an emotional difficulty or with failure to learn to read. This circular response may be represented as follows:

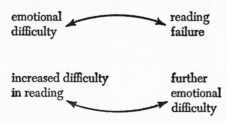

Role of Incentives in the Reading Process

Certain underlying desires, needs, values, and convictions may be more important than personality factors. These, too, may be built in part by means of reading, and may, in turn, promote further reading development. Intelligence, language ability, visual and auditory perception—these and other specific abilities are all important. However, none of them, singly or in combination, entirely accounts for an individual's reading performance. The search continues for some "psycho-catalytic mobilizers" that marshal all the available skills on a particular reading task.[7] Reading should be its own reward. Learning per se is satisfying to a child. Especially in the early years, the child finds joy in any activity that brings pleasant, tangible results. Punching the keys on a typewriter and seeing letters appear on the clean white sheet of paper, scribbling on a piece of paper or a blackboard, copying the letter forms that one sees, supplying the rhyming word in a jingle—all these and many other activities have intrinsic interest for the young child.

The child also wants a certain amount of praise, affection, and recognition. If these rewards are given when he makes some genuine progress in reading, they tend to reinforce the behavior that evoked them. If they are withheld up to a certain point, their absence may motivate the child to try harder. If they are given too frequently and indiscriminately, they carry less value, and therefore less power to influence the child's reading.

If the child is emotionally sturdy, punishment or criticism may lead him to put forth more effort. But if he is sensitive and insecure, these negative responses may cause him to withdraw from the situation and refuse to put forth any effort at all.

Popular children who read well may stimulate a poor reader to do better. For example, one popular boy laughed aloud at the amusing parts of the story he was reading and showed an intense absorption in the exciting parts; his behavior interested the reluctant readers in the class. A girl who was admired by the other members of the class for her unusually expressive and dramatic reading stimulated many of them to abandon their monotonous word-by-word reading. Similarly, children are impressed by seeing their parents reading for enjoyment and information. One boy said: "I remember lying in my bed and gazing at my mother across the room, eating cherry chocolates and reading. I recall thinking, 'Boy, when I get older, I'm going to read every chance I get.'"

These and many other subtle aspects of the total reading situation determine whether one greets the next reading opportunity with enthusiasm and interest, as Jimmy did, or with dread and fear of failure, as in Billy's case.

QUESTIONS AND ANSWERS

1. *What are the characteristics of a mature reader?*

He enjoys reading and finds time for it, no matter how crowded his schedule is.

He has a purpose in reading—for relaxation, inspiration, or information. His purpose may be personal or social, practical or theoretical; to stir his imagination or spur him to action.

He adjusts his rate and method of reading to the nature of the material and to his purpose. For some purposes he will skim quickly; for other purposes he will associate ideas he has already acquired with the key words he catches as he runs his eye down the page. For still other purposes, he will read to get the main idea of every paragraph and relate it to the other ideas, noting the supporting details if he needs them.

He reads widely. Though he may read intensely in one field, he does not neglect other kinds of reading.

He applies the ideas he gains from reading to his own development and to social problems.

2. *What do intelligence tests tell about a child's ability to learn to read?*

What an intelligence test tells you about a child's ability to learn to read depends on the nature of the test, the conditions under which it was given, and the characteristics of the child. It also depends on the way in which the school interprets the test results to parents.

Most group intelligence tests, which are given to a class as a whole, require a good deal of reading. Naturally, the poor reader will not do well on these tests. They tell more about his present reading achievement than about his reading potential. Some tests tell more than others because they show whether a child is relatively skillful (1) in comprehending words and using them fluently, (2) in remembering specific facts and past experiences, (3) in doing arithmetic, or (4) in reasoning about certain things. If he ranks high in the verbal parts of the test, we should expect him to do well in reading. If he ranks low in verbal ability but high in other mental abilities, we feel that he will be able, with practice, to improve his word comprehension and fluency.

The individual intelligence test, when it is given by a specially trained person, tells much more about the child's potential reading ability.

The child's personality affects the test results. If a child is curious, independent, self-confident, and interested in solving intellectual problems, he is likely to do his best on an intelligence test. However, if he has the opposite qualities, he may not demonstrate his true mental ability. Beween the ages of six and twelve, if he gains self-reliance and experience in meeting the challenges of a good school, his intelligence score is likely to increase.

Intelligence test scores and IQs should be interpreted to parents, not given to them without explanation. The IQ alone means little. It does not tell the parent what kinds of mental ability his child has—whether he ranks very high in some abilities and low in others, or whether he stands on about the same level in each ability. A single intelligence test score may be very misleading; a child's IQ can change considerably between the early preschool years and the high school years. In fact, in one study one-fourth of the children, who were tested at regular intervals from age two and a half to age twelve, increased their scores by eighteen to fifty-seven IQ points.[8]

3. *Do modern children read? What evidence do we have on this question?*

Your own observation will give you an answer in the local situation. How much does your own child read? What place does reading have among his competing interests? What are the reading habits of his friends?

Going further afield, take a look at the sales of children's books. They have increased tremendously in recent years, and now exceed the sales of most of the best-sellers. For example, from 1942 to 1954 nearly 320 million Little Golden Books were sold. Many parents have a hard time getting their children out of the supermarket without buying a book.

Juvenile book clubs have flourished. More than ten million children and young people are members. Outstanding books are selected by judges of children's books. Juvenile book clubs include the following:

Arrow Book Club, Scholastic Magazines, 33 West Forty-second Street, New York 36, N.Y.

Catholic Children's Book Club, 260 Summit Ave., St. Paul, Minnesota.

Catholic Youth Book Club, Garden City, N.Y.

Junior Literary Guild, Garden City, N.Y.

Parents' Magazine Book Club for Beginning Readers, Bergenfield, New Jersey.

Parents' Magazine Book Club for Children, Bergenfield, New Jersey.

Teen-Age Book Club, 33 West Forty-second Street, New York 36, N.Y.

Weekly Reader Children's Book Club, Education Center, Columbus 16, Ohio.

Young People's Book Club, Spence Press, Inc., 153 N. Michigan Ave., Chicago 1, Ill. (story biographies and stories of historical events).

Young Readers of America, 345 Hudson St., New York 14, N.Y. (nonfiction).

Circulation lists of public libraries show that large numbers of children's books are being checked out. These include the children's classics as well as many modern books of fine quality.

4. *What makes a book easy or difficult to read?*

Children say a book is easy if it is interesting. And it is interesting if it appeals to the child's imagination or reflects his firsthand experience, and thus meets a need in his life here and now.

A book is difficult if it is packed with new ideas that are stated but not illustrated, if it is poorly organized or contains long, involved sentences and many unfamiliar words.

5. How can a person who has formed lazy habits of reading learn to read faster?

If the person has acquired basic vocabulary and word-recognition skills, he may jog himself out of unnecessarily slow reading habits by using mechanical devices such as a reading-rate controller or by setting time limits for himself. Some students have increased their speed without loss in comprehension by forcing themselves to read, from five to thirty minutes a day, a little faster than is comfortable. They note a daily increase in the number of pages read in the time allotted.

Other students have set an arbitrary but reasonable time limit for reading a given amount of material. For example, one alert person picked up a magazine in a doctor's office where she had to wait ten minutes. She found an article that interested her and decided to see what she could get out of it in ten minutes. She read the introductory paragraph carefully, to become acquainted with the author's point of view. Then she skimmed, reading the first one or two sentences of each paragraph. She read more details in the paragraphs that contained information of special significance to her. She had just enough time to read the summary paragraph before the ten minutes were up. A friend who was with her asked, "What did you get out of that article?" and was surprised at the amount of accurate information she had gained in such a short time.

6. What is the relation between speed of reading and comprehension?

In general, the rapid reader comprehends what he reads. He reads rapidly because he grasps large units of thought.

But there are exceptions. The student who reads everything rapidly will not comprehend the more difficult reading material. One cannot skim unfamiliar or difficult science or mathematics texts. The relation between rate of reading and comprehension is determined by the difficulty of the material and the reader's familiarity with it.

You have heard of people who can read a page at a glance. They could not do so with material with which they were unfamiliar.

When the subject matter is familiar to them, what they probably do is to catch a few key words as they sweep their eyes down the page. Their minds do the rest. From their background of knowledge, they reconstruct the meaning from the few words or phrases that their eyes have caught.

7. *How fast should a person read a page?*
The figure 350 words per minute is sometimes given as the average rate of reading for adults.

Actually, no average figures can be given. The rate of reading varies with the difficulty of the material, the reader's familiarity with it, and his purpose in reading it. Frivolous fiction should be read at the speed of light, and serious books at a pedestrian pace. I. A. Richards has written a book describing "how to read a page."

The important thing for children and young people to learn is that they need several rates and that they should choose the rate that is appropriate to the material and to their purpose in reading it. It may take only a split second to spot the information one needs —a date, an answer to a specific question—much as one spots a four-leaf clover. It takes a little longer to get the main ideas from topic sentences, headings, captions, and pictures or diagrams. It takes still longer to support these main ideas with significant details. And the reader must be prepared to spend additional time if he wants to see relations among the ideas, and draw sound inferences and conclusions. Sometimes he may read slowly just to enjoy the author's style or follow carefully the development of a train of thought. For the latter purposes, speed is a dubious advantage.

8. *What is strethosymbolia?*
The word itself simply means "twisted symbols." A child with strethosymbolia does not see letters and words as most people see them. He sees them reversed or upside down, or both. He may mistake *b* for a *d*, and read *ton* as *not*. The child may write a whole word backward so that it can be read only in the mirror.

This difficulty stems from a kind of mental immaturity—neither side of the brain has become clearly dominant; the individual is ambidextrous, as he was in infancy. A right-handed person's center for language skills is usually on the left side of the brain. Children with strethosymbolia may use either side of the brain for perceiving and interpreting words and letters. The result is that their perceptions are confused. Children with a mild degree of strethosymbolia often overcome or outgrow it in the course of good reading instruction.

A child who makes occasional reversals in reading and writing letters does not necessarily have this problem of brain dominance; he may merely have failed to acquire the habit of reading and writing from left to right. If the tendency is severe and persists beyond the third grade, special reading instruction is indicated.

9. *Why are boys more commonly referred to reading clinics than girls?*

A number of explanations have been suggested, among them the following:

There may be a hereditary factor of specific language disability in males. Certainly girls exceed boys in the total number of words spoken and the number of different words known at a given chronological age. Someone has remarked that girls talk more than boys but boys know more about what they are saying!

Certain cultural conditions may favor girls' superiority in reading —they engage in games that are less active than boys' games and require more talking; they are likely to have closer daily contact with their mothers; teachers often prefer "nice little girls" to "rough, noisy boys."

Girls mature earlier than boys and are therefore more ready than boys to begin reading in the first grade.

Boy babies are usually bigger than girls; they are therefore more likely to have a difficult birth, with the possibility that oxygen deprivation may injure some of the brain cells associated with reading.

It should be borne in mind that though sex differences in speech and reading development appear early, they become less apparent as children grow older. Moreover, differences in reading ability are greater within each sex than between boys and girls.

FOUR

Preschool Prelude to Success in Reading

PRESCHOOL experiences pave the way for successful reading in school. From early infancy the child is building attitudes toward himself and his world. First of all, he is learning to look. Out of a vague blur of light and darkness, certain objects take on meaning—perhaps the first of these is his mother's face. Practice in seeing objects is prerequisite to later perception of printed words. The baby is also learning to listen, to babble in his own way, and to imitate the speech he hears. Thus he builds up the oral vocabulary that is essential to beginning reading. As he approaches school age, the preschool child enjoys many prereading experiences.

PERVASIVE ATTITUDES

Patterns of personality begin to emerge soon after birth. These patterns and attitudes may affect the child's reading later on. Many of the older boys and girls who come to reading clinics seem unable to put forth the effort that learning to read requires. They are pleasant but passive. They go through the motions and do the reading exercises, but make no progress. They never take the initiative.

It is not too farfetched to suggest that a passive attitude toward reading may stem from the experiences of infancy; it may have been reinforced by subsequent preschool experiences. For example, if a baby is repeatedly left alone to cry without relief, he may acquire a general feeling that it is futile to put forth effort. He does not gain a sense of confidence in the world into which he has been thrust.

The child who has been successful much of the time in meeting daily experiences and overcoming obstacles is likely to approach each new developmental task with self-confidence. On the other hand, the child who has been pushed and prodded beyond his real capacity, who has been urged to be "a little man" when it is hard enough for him to be a four-year-old, may develop a resistance to learning of any kind.

Thus parents' attitudes and relations with the child may help or hinder his future reading development. Among the parental attitudes that seem to have the most unfavorable influence are hostility toward the child and persistent attempts to coerce him into learning things that he is not ready to learn. The child of whom an impossible perfection is expected is likely to become anxious; he may try to withdraw from a hostile world, or may passively resist attempts to change him. In all phases of their growth children need the appreciation, understanding, and attentive response of other people.

We may go to the other extreme and expect too little of the child. It often happens that the parents of a bright child who is a poor reader have been excessively indulgent and protective; they may also have been inconsistent in their discipline of the child during his early years.

The pervasive attitudes that children have are not the result of occasional lapses in parental patience or child care; they are the cumulative product of repeated experiences.

LEARNING TO LOOK

The baby gradually learns to see details against an otherwise vague background; this paves the way to seeing words as wholes, and distinctive letters in words. As his experience widens, the preschool child learns to discriminate more closely. He will point out the doggie in the picture book and not confuse it with the kittie or with Mary's little lamb. He will select certain colors for his painting and certain toys for his playhouse. More precise perceptions also lead to more precise speech and communication.

DEVELOPMENT OF SPEECH

During the preschool period, children make remarkable progress in talking. Out of their babbling sounds they begin to shape a few words of their native language. Without any formal instruction they learn to recognize language sounds, to furnish them with meanings that are suggested by their experiences, and to use many words in conversation. They recognize the meanings of many words that they hear but do not yet use. This oral vocabulary will serve the child well when he begins to learn to read; the first step in reading is to associate the printed word with an experience or with a spoken word around which many meanings have clustered.

Reading is dependent on several interrelated aspects of language development, which seldom occur singly or in isolation. Speech normally develops during the second year of life, depending on the child's physical and motor development. By his second birthday, the average child usually knows a few hundred words.

Basic to all the aspects of the child's development is the mother-child relationship. The child whose mother meets his needs affectionately and cheerfully and talks to him as she goes about her tasks or takes him for an airing, learns to listen and talk sooner and better than another child of equal ability who has been cared for in a hurried, impersonal, disinterested, or preoccupied way. If a baby is happy, he will seldom cry. The less he cries, the more time he has to babble about things that are of concern to him, though incomprehensible to us.

Children brought up in loving homes have a definite advantage over children reared in impersonal institutions. They learn to speak earlier. They talk more. They have a larger preschool vocabulary. In fact, they tend to be superior in all aspects of the language arts. However, this is not true of those who are overprotected—those whose mothers anticipate every need and give them no incentive to speak, no need to ask for what they want. These children tend to develop forms of immature or infantile speech such as lisping and baby talk.

Only children, especially girls, who enjoy a large share of their mother's attention from infancy, are usually more accelerated in language development than children who have brothers and sisters, other things being equal. Twins, who have to share their mother's love and attention, from earliest infancy, often show a lag in language development. The kind of attention and the length of time that a parent or parent substitute can give children has a real bearing on their speech and reading proficiency.

As the child grows older, his language development is facilitated in many ways—by opportunities to ask questions and obtain fairly adequate answers, to have meals with his parents, to talk with them before and after school, and to discuss with them why certain of his actions were considered either "good" or "naughty."

Varied experiences such as picnics, camping, tea parties, new things to see and hear and do, new places to visit, stimulate the child's interest in the world and increase his store of firsthand experience with it. A trip to the seashore adds a cluster of ocean words. Going to the airport or taking a plane trip acquaints the child with air travel. The zoo introduces the child to animal friends that he will meet again and again in his reading.

Just going for a walk ranks high on a child's list of pleasures. Preschool children, who are normally on the go from morning till night, will not get tired on a walk if they are allowed to stop and look when they feel like it. They may meet a friendly dog or cat, find leaves and seed pods to collect. They may walk silently, absorbed in all they see and hear. Or they may chatter incessantly. Rainy days, when there are enticing puddles that they can swish through in their waterproof galoshes, are particularly enchanting to preschool children. If the child is free to flit here and there wherever it is safe for him to venture, if he is not dragged along or hurried, he will respond eagerly when we suggest, "Let's take a walk."

TV, with all its problems, does make meaningful certain words that the child hears over and over again. However, it is not a substitute for personal contact with parents. In fact, the child whose parents allow him to look at TV hour after hour, just to keep him out of the way, gets little practice in using the words he picks up from this modern Pied Piper.

Sharing family experiences not only broadens the child's understanding but also contributes to his emotional stability. By participating and contributing as an accepted member of the family group, the child gains a sense of belonging.

Firsthand experiences make their maximum contribution to the child's speech if parents take time to listen to his adventures, encourage him to dramatize them, discuss them, and ask questions about them. Pictures or picture stories often stimulate the child to tell realistic or fanciful stories of his own. The child may like to tell stories about the pictures he has drawn himself. One boy drew a motorcycle with swirling lines all around it, which, he explained, represented the noise it made.

In encouraging verbal expression the adult should be as spontaneous and interested as the child himself. We lose the beneficial effect if we turn the child's eager account of things that have interested him into a formal recitation, or if our inquiries degenerate into nagging.

The preschool experience most frequently recalled by older children is that of listening to stories or poems read aloud by Father, Mother, Grandmother, or some other member of the family. By this means, preschool children become acquainted with the vocabulary and language patterns of literature. They like to hear favorite stories told over and over until they know them by heart. They like to supply the missing words or lines in jingles. These memories make subsequent reading easier.

To give children practice in anticipating words in sentences some parents play a game of sentence completion. They say: "Teddy, I'm going to say something to you and leave off the last word. See if you can guess what it is." Then they give sentences like:

"It's time to give Fido his _____."

The child may say, "bone," "dinner," "water," or whatever makes sense. Any sensible answer should be accepted, whether or not it was the answer you had in mind. Played as a game, this exercise is fun; it is also a direct preparation for learning how to get the meaning of a word from its context—a basic word-recognition skill that the child must learn when he begins to read.

All home situations are favorable that lead children to want to acquire language skills, and help them day by day to invest spoken words with meanings.[1] Some precocious children show a spontaneous interest in learning letters, reading signs and labels, writing their names. There is no reason why they should not have a chance to explore these as well as other new experiences. They are part of a developmental process that takes different forms with different children. Interest in all the language arts is natural to children who grow up in a literate environment.

PREREADING EXPERIENCES

Before they are two years old, children enjoy turning the pages of a book or magazine. Soon they enjoy looking at the pictures and hearing simple rhymes. They begin to look at books by themselves and to add the endings to rhyming lines that they have frequently heard. By three years of age they can sit still long enough to listen to an entire story—and to complain if the reader leaves out any parts of it.

The child should see persons who are important in his life enjoying reading; he should have books and magazines of his own to handle; he should enjoy having stories read to him; he should relate his exciting, everyday experiences to reading material; and he should have an interested listener to whom he may tell his own stories. All these experiences contribute to the child's readiness to learn to read. In addition to having a stockpile of about five thousand words, it is an advantage for him to have learned to anticipate meaning in sentences, to recognize similar sounds in spoken words, and to identify and name letter forms.

Many preschool experiences are directly related to learning to read. There are experiences that arouse the child's interest in reading, experiences that familiarize him with books and with the language of books, and experiences that constitute the first steps in acquiring word-recognition skills.

Enjoying these experiences with the child is far different from setting out to teach him to read. There are no formal reading lessons during the preschool years; no pressure to learn certain words; no overanxiety on the part of the parent, which may communicate itself to the child. His interest in books, his curiosity about printed words, and his increasing sensitivity to the letter sounds in words grow naturally, just as his oral speech does.

"I Want To Read, Too"

When a child sees Daddy reading the evening paper, Big Sister reading a letter from her boy friend, Mother consulting her cookbook, Brother reading the road signs as he drives the family car; when he hears people read aloud some passage of interest at home, in Sunday school, or in church, he begins to realize how important and pleasant it must be to read.

A tenth-grade girl accounted for her keen interest in reading by saying, "The person I have to thank for most of my reading background is my mother. Even as a harried housewife with two young children, she managed to read two or three novels and innumerable magazines a week. I used to watch her and beg her to teach me some words, and by first grade I knew enough to be thoroughly bored by Dick, Jane, Sally and their going, coming, seeing, and running!"

Parents who enjoy reading convey their enjoyment to the child long before he becomes of school age. And the desire to read is basic to all further reading development.

The role of reading in the home is described by Bonaro Overstreet,[2] who emphasizes the emotional overtones that make reading a vital, unforgettable experience. By means of personal experiences, she shows how books bridge the gaps between the individual as he is and as he wants to become, and between his immediate environment and the wider world of people, places, and ideas.

In speaking of books as property, Bonaro Overstreet emphasizes the joy of possession of cherished books, and one's responsibility for the care of borrowed books. She mentions the value that books have in creating an atmosphere in the home; they are "allies of silence." A family engaged in reading experiences a peace of mind that is impossible in a home in which the silence is continually shattered by the blare of radio and television and the bickering of children and adults. Finally, Mrs. Overstreet gives illustrations of the ways in which the memory of fictional incidents and lines of poetry may enhance and deepen the significance of the present moment.

Books as Friends

Love of books begins in babyhood. Long before babies can walk, they can handle linen picture books. If Tommy grabs the magazine Daddy is reading, Daddy can help him find the pictures in it and let him turn the pages, one at a time, very gently.

We can help children acquire a love of books just as we help them learn to love animals; we must take time, over and over, to guide them in the gentle handling of books. Teachers have noted that children who have learned to love books at home handle their schoolbooks carefully.

Books should be lying around in every room of the house, including the child's room. Picture books and attractively illustrated stories that the child has enjoyed hearing invite him to have a look for himself. This is a prelude to independent reading.

Reading Aloud

Reading aloud to children has many values. It introduces them to the delights that lie between the covers of books; it acquaints them with the vocabulary and language patterns of printed materials; it arouses their curiosity and desire to unlock for themselves the stories and characters imprisoned in the pages of print. Sharing a loved book also brings parent and child closer together emotionally.

As a father reading to his own small children, Leonard Wibberley [3] cautions parents not to read aloud from a sense of duty just because reading aloud is good for children. Adults should read to children only books that they themselves enjoy. Reading should be fun for both child and parent. As the parent reads some part of the book that he has enjoyed tremendously and sees the same delight on the face of his child, in that moment he is one with the child.

Parents should also be sure that the child is ready for the book. They should not be in a hurry to share their favorite stories or poems. At five or seven years a child is not likely to respond to *The Wind in the Willows* or *Treasure Island*, but at eight or nine he may listen enthralled.

If the books the parents select are boring or otherwise unsuitable, reading aloud may do more harm than good. It may create a dislike of reading. One child, at bedtime in his upstairs room, expressed his protest in this masterpiece of mixed-up prepositions: "What did you bring that book I didn't want to be read to out of up for?"

The following are some criteria for selecting books to read to children:

Books that give enjoyment of imagery and rhythm as well as of character and plot.

Books that contribute to the child's understanding of himself and confirm and extend his everyday experience. An anonymous writer put it this way:

"A good book has grass and earth and familiar things on a level with the child's eyes; but it also has treetops and wind and stars to draw his gaze upward."

Books that go beyond the real world into the realm of imagination.

Books that cover a wide variety of interests—contemporary works and children's classics, fiction and nonfiction, prose and poetry.

Books that are of interest to both the child and the adult who is reading to him.

Adhering too rigidly to a reading schedule may take some of the joyful surprise out of the experience. However, the best time for reading aloud is usually before bedtime in the evening. Then the children gather around, sit on the floor, or curl up in a chair to listen expectantly as Father or Mother announces the title and the chapter. One chapter a night is usually enough.

There should be some rules, too. Children may wiggle as little children must wiggle. They may look at the pictures while Father or Mother reads. This may result in comments and questions at the end of the chapter. But they may not play with trains or planes or do other things that distract attention from the reading. If they do, they are warned; if they persist, they are sent to bed.

As the children grow older and have learned to read well enough to hold the attention of an audience, they may take turns reading their favorite stories during the family reading hour.

Being read aloud to is an experience that children cherish. Older children have set down their recollections of listening to parents or grandparents reading aloud to them, and have speculated about the influence this may have had on their love of reading:

I am quite an avid reader now and I think my grandmother, who read aloud to me is largely responsible for it. Each month I read about one novel and two or three short stories.

My little brothers are very poor readers. They have no interest in it at all. I think this is partly due to the fact that my grandmother was ill and could not pay much attention to their reading interests and habits.

There are really two main factors which encouraged my reading. One was my home environment, and the other equally important factor was my nursery, kindergarten, and elementary school experiences.

The first book I ever owned was a linen book at a very early age. From that time on every evening either my mother or grandmother would read me a story before I went to bed. Later when I was older and could read, I would read parts of the story and my mother or grandmother other parts. Reading before going to bed became a habit, so much so, that I still feel I have to read a little while before going to bed. It seems strange, but I can still remember large parts of the stories that were read to me out of Golden Books, Fairy Tale Books, and the Book-house.

At the age of two I started to nursery school where my love of reading was enhanced.

Story time was always a wonderful magic time for me at school, and I could hardly wait for the time when I could do my own reading. So, when I was old enough to start school, I was as eager as a beaver. Learning to read, so far as I can remember, was always pleasant. I can't remember ever being pushed or scolded in my reading.

I am glad I had such a pleasant introduction to reading and learned to really like to read. It must be terrible not to like to read; I can't imagine it!

ROOTS OF WORD RECOGNITION

There are many steps to becoming an independent reader—one who can pronounce an unfamiliar printed word or get its meaning in other ways. Some of these steps can be taken during the preschool years. Children who have had these prereading experiences are usually ready for the teacher's regular instruction in reading.

Some preschool children learn of their own accord to recognize a number of words before they come to school. They recognize certain words in the storybooks as Mother reads to them. "What is this word? How do you say it?" they ask. They may ask Mother or the nursery-school teacher to point out on the page where it says "little black sheep." They want to know "what that sign says." They hear and see the name of their favorite cereal in a TV commercial, and see it on the cereal box in the kitchen. Incidentally, some trade names are so firmly impressed on children that they later insist that "does" is spelled "Duz." One mother said, "We never taught Donald the alphabet; he just picked it up by himself." This learning seemed less mysterious when we found out that Donald often played with alphabet blocks—usually in the presence of some obliging adult who was ready to name the letters for him.

The child may be given some practice in searching for the meaning of spoken words, recognizing similar sounds in the words he hears and speaks, and learning the names of the letters, not necessarily in their alphabetical order. Reading experts disagree about whether parents should give the child systematic practice in these important word-recognition skills. But they do agree that if such practice is given at all, it should be in the spirit of play.

Some definite suggestions for parents have been given by Paul McKee.[4] These, he insists should be carried out in a game atmosphere —no pushing, no shoving, no staying at it until the child becomes bored or restless or inattentive.

1. Practice in guessing the word from the sentence in which it occurs. The mother would say, "Teddy, I'm going to say something to you and leave off the last word. See if you can tell me what the word might be." Then, keeping busy with her housework, she would give him sentences such as:

"I'm washing the dishes with hot _____."

"Let's put the clothes out in the sun to _____."

"It's time to give Spot his _____."

She would accept any word that makes sense—not require him to give the exact word she was thinking of. In the last sentence, she may have been thinking of "dinner," but if Teddy said "bone," that was a sensible answer, too.

This game directs the child's attention to the meaning of a word in a sentence. Later, in school, his first step in getting the meaning of a printed word he does not know will be to inquire what the context seems to demand.

2. Practice in distinguishing the initial sounds of words. During the preschool years there is plenty of time to learn them gradually, one at a time. Key words for each sound help the child to remember them:

b	as in ball	j —	jump, etc.
c —	come	ch —	chilly
d —	daddy	sh —	show
f —	fun	wh —	what
g —	go	th —	thumb, and so on.
h —	help		

This exercise is oral. No printed words or letters are shown. The child sees small objects or pictures of things. Those that begin with the same consonant sound may be grouped for practice: *m* for man, milk, mailman, etc. Several groups of objects or pictures may be put in a box, and the child may be asked to take out all those that begin with an *m* sound or an *f* sound. We must be sure that the picture or object represents the word intended; for example, we should not confuse *wheel* with *bicycle*.

The child may recognize sounds in words but not know what we mean by "begin with the same sound." This he learns as we repeatedly show him, orally, that *ship* and *shop* and *shoe* begin with the same sound.

3. Practice in distinguishing letter forms from one another. The child needs to know the letter names so that he can talk about them. He can learn the names of letters as easily as he can learn the names of objects. A is the name we give to this shape: *A*, and also to this shape, *a*. At this stage it is not necessary to teach the alphabet in sequence. Later, as an aid to looking up words in the dictionary, he will learn the alphabet in segments—the letters he will find in the first quarter of the dictionary, then the second, third, and fourth.

To check on his ability to name the different letter forms, you may print the letters in squares on a piece of cardboard such as you get from the laundry:

A a	B b	C c	D d
E e	F f	G g	H h
I i	J j	K k	L l
M m	N n	O o	P p
Q q	R r	S s	T t
U u	V v	W w	x
Y y	Z z		

As you name a letter, the child can cover it up with a small cardboard square.

Slow-learning children should learn letter names one or two at a time; they should be absolutely sure of them before they are introduced to a new letter. When we move too fast, children become confused and uncertain about their ability to identify any letters correctly. As Shakespeare said, "Wisely and slow; they stumble who go fast."

4. Practice in associating letter forms with their sounds. This is phonics. Parents may well leave this step to teachers, and merely reinforce the child's school learning by means of games like this:

"I'll say three words: *toy, tell, ten.* Do they all begin alike? Yes, they begin with the letter *t*." After the *t* sound has been thoroughly learned, as it occurs in familiar words, you can say, "Now see if I can catch you. Do these words all begin with the *T* sound: *top, toy, boy?* Which begin with *t;* which begin with another letter sound?"

For another type of game, print a letter on a large card and say, "I'm going to say a word that begins with this letter. What letter is it?"

You might start with one or two letters, such as *b* or *m,* and see if the child can (1) pick out objects or pictures that begin with the *b* sound, (2) recognize the letter form of *b* or *B* when he sees it as one of several letters, and (3) associate the letter *b* with the sound of *b* in familiar words. Thus each of these three kinds of practice would be applied to the same letter.

Some children will learn very quickly to distinguish similar sounds in words, to give the correct names of letters, and to associate the letter sound with its printed symbols. Don't hold them back. Let them go ahead as fast as they want to, provided they are making the associations accurately.

On the other hand, we must be careful not to make a child feel that he must hurry up and do these exercises and get them right.

A UNIQUE EXPERIMENT

An experiment at Yale University [5] demonstrated that preschool children could learn to read, write, and take dictation. They learned these skills for themselves; they did not have to be taught. Learning was fun for them. The role of the adult was to provide opportunities and respond appropriately to the child's spontaneous actions.

This experiment involved thirty-five children aged two to five. Each child was allowed to play with an electric typewriter. At first he just pounded several keys at once. Then, as he began to strike separate keys, the adult beside him would say the letter or number he had struck. Soon he began to associate a particular key with a particular response. He also noticed the letter as it appeared on the sheet of paper. Eventually he was saying the letter he had struck before the adult did.

After playing with the typewriter for a while, the child was allowed to scribble as he pleased on the blackboard. Before long he was making letters like the ones he had typewritten.

After he had learned the letters he was able to read and copy simple sentences, or hear and copy them from his own dictation on a recording machine.

If it were definitely proved that children aged two to five could learn to read by this or any other method, would it be desirable for them to do so? What idea of reading would they get? How would this idea be different from the idea they would get by observing persons who loved to read, hearing a wide variety of literature read to them, and handling books and looking at them? Moreover, what parent would have the time and patience to respond to each letter the child typed as the experimenter did? Even if these responses could be made automatically by a machine, what would be the loss in personal contact between parent and child?

If the news of this experiment should send many parents out to buy electric typewriters for their three-year-old children, what might happen? Would most parents permit the child to take the initiative all the time, or would they, at least occasionally, feel impelled to teach? If they did, they would be defeating the main purpose of the procedure, which was to develop the little child's initiative and curiosity, and give him delight in his own competence.

During the preschool period it is more important to establish pleasant associations with reading, to foster " 'satiable curtiosities," as Kipling's elephant's child expressed it, and to stimulate a desire to learn to read, than to strive for any specific accomplishments.

SUMMARY: PREREADING ACHIEVEMENTS AND HOW THEY ARE ACQUIRED

Desire to read	Seeing others enjoy reading Being read to Handling and looking at books
Varied experiences that give meaning to words	New things to see, hear, and handle Trips to farm, seashore, airport, etc. Play activities alone or with friends or pets
A good speaking vocabulary and ability to speak in simple sentences	Being listened to Opportunities to talk with family and others Having questions answered Hearing clear, simple, precise speech

Ability to identify similarities and differences of sounds in words	{	Listening to carefully pronounced words, and repeating them Games to identify words that begin alike and that rhyme
Knowledge of the names of the letters	{	A B C blocks and books Games to recognize letters when they are named

In a composition on "How I Would Help My Children Become Good Readers," a high school boy gave this excellent advice:

If I wanted to get my child to be a good reader I would start him the way I was started. First I would take him for walks and teach him about nature. I think this would make him more inquisitive, which is very important to being a good reader.

Next when he was old enough to understand a few words I would start reading to him. I think this would interest him in books.

When he was older and knew how to read, I would encourage him as much as possible. I would keep him supplied with as much reading material as he needed.

I would also show him the library and how to use it. Then he would be able to get all the reading material he wanted.

This teen-ager, with the insight characteristic of so many young adolescents, emphasized the three essentials: a curious mind, a desire to read, and available reading material.

Equally sound suggestions to parents for preparing the preschool child for success in beginning reading were given by a gifted high school girl:

I think about the only way to encourage a young reader is to make reading pleasant. Any child who enjoys being read to will want to learn how to read for himself. I think it is very important that a child is introduced at an early preschool age to books so that reading becomes a part of him. This really is not a bit hard in this day and age as there are so many inexpensive books that can be bought for preschool children.

I think also it's important that the book should be suitable to the age of the child. A child will not want to sit still to listen to a story he does not understand, nor will a book that is suitable for a much younger child captivate his interest.

I think his early school experience has an important effect on a child's reading habits. A child, regardless of his actual chronological age, who is not ready for school will not learn reading as easily or as well as the child who is prepared to fit into the routine of school and hold a span of attention. The child who is not ready to sit still in a classroom may only associate reading with having to sit still. I do not think a child should ever be pushed too hard or scolded. Some children will naturally learn to read quicker and easier than others.

Given preschool preparation of this kind, children should be ready to continue their growth in reading and respond to school instruction.

QUESTIONS AND ANSWERS

1. *Should parents ever talk "baby talk" to their children?*

When the baby is just beginning to fumble with speech, baby-talk games may encourage him to make sounds. Refusing to speak the child's language at this stage may slow down his speech development. However, he must soon begin to learn to make the sounds of the language we all speak. To this end, we must speak to him slowly and clearly, accurately and intelligently.

2. *Are children who try to learn two languages during the pre-school years handicapped in learning to read?*

Preschool children who try to learn two languages are usually somewhat retarded in both. There are, of course, exceptions. It has been suggested that the retardation may be due to a reluctance to abandon the mother's language rather than to lack of intelligence or verbal ability. The language heard in infancy, Dorothea McCarthy [6] has said, "has deep emotional roots." The child may become emotionally disturbed if he is forbidden to use the language he has associated with his parents from the earliest years. Therefore, children who need to learn two languages should learn to use both languages correctly in the situations in which each is appropriate.

3. *Should I teach my child the alphabet?*

A child is better prepared for beginning reading if he knows the names of the letters. You can teach him to write each letter large as soon as he learns to name it. You teach the *name* of the letter *B,* not the *sound,* "Buh." Later he will group the letters as follows:

A B C D E F G —	letters near the beginning of the dictionary
H I J K L M —	letters in the middle, after the beginning group
N O P Q R S T —	letters in the middle, toward the end
U V W X Y Z —	letters near the end of the dictionary.

This grouping will help the child to find words quickly in the dictionary.

4. *Are prereading experiences a disadvantage under certain conditions?*

Two children, both of whom were above average in mental ability, came from very different home backgrounds. One, whom we shall call Joanne, could identify letters and small words when she came to school. She said her grandmother had helped her and showed her how. When she entered school she was already achieving at a first-grade level in reading and arithmetic. At the end of the year she had all A's on her report card and her measured achievement was average for the group. However, this apparently did not represent much specific additional learning for her. She appeared to be underachieving academically. She was eager to learn, enjoyed school, and was a leader in her class. Others depended on her. The A's probably represented social usefulness rather than actual achievement in reading and spelling and arithmetic. Academically, she was marking time in the first grade. The teacher had not built on her preschool achievement.

The other child, whom we shall call Jane, had a poor family background. She could not identify any of the letters when she came to school. She was not a leader and did not take part in discussions. At the end of the year her marks were all C's, but the Wide Range Achievement Test showed that she had made gains of more than a year in reading and arithmetic.

What does this comparison mean? Not that children should not have prereading experiences during the preschool years, but that teachers should not allow the child who comes to school with a good background of reading experience to languish in idleness or devote all his energy to social activities.

With effective teaching, prereading experience should help a child to make more rapid progress in the first grade than he otherwise would. Teaching that focuses on the average or below-average learner does not help the initially better reader to make commensurate progress; he may get into the habit of underachieving.

5. *Why is reading aloud to children sometimes unsuccessful?*

There are many possible reasons. If the adult dislikes reading aloud, or reads from a sense of duty, his attitude is communicated to the child. Adult and child should both enjoy the story. The child may not be quite ready for the story the parent is reading—though the parent remembers that he loved it when he was the child's age. Times change, and children's interests shift somewhat from generation to generation. Sometimes the child's unreadiness to listen may be merely temporary; something else had absorbed his attention for the moment. It is better to recognize this immediate interest than to try to override it. Older children, especially those in early adolescence, sometimes prefer an unshared reading experience. At such times they guard their private world with fierce jealousy, and resent any adult intrusion into it.

6. *How can parents foster a child's love of reading?*

"Liking to read just comes naturally to my child," you may say. Probably it doesn't. Without being aware of it, you have done, and are still doing, many things that cause your child to love reading and to want to read. As we said in the last chapter, he has seen you reading and has gathered that reading gives you pleasure and profit. He has listened to the enchanting stories that you have read him, and he wants to hear more than you have time to read to him. This stimulates him to want to learn to read for himself. As he looks at the books while you read to him, he begins to recognize certain words, and realizes that those black marks on white paper have meaning. Even after he has started school, you should continue to read him books that are beyond his own present reading ability; this will create further interest in the world of books that he will someday be able to explore himself.

Reading in the Primary Grades

Just as the preschool years are a prelude to a successful beginning in reading, so success in the primary grades builds a firm foundation for effective reading in years to come.

Starting with a desire to read and the ability to differentiate objects by observing their distinctive details, the child learns to recognize a number of words at sight. By the end of the third grade he should be able to identify instantly the basic Dolch vocabulary [1] of 220 words, which make up at least 50 per cent of the running words in his elementary school books. He will know other words, too, whose meaning he does not have to stop and puzzle out.

Having acquired an ample speaking vocabulary of meaningful words, the ability to identify sounds in words, and a knowledge of letter names, the child is in a position to begin mastering word-recognition skills. He first thinks what the word might mean in the sentence. Then he uses his stock of sound-letter associations and his knowledge of familiar syllables and other structural word parts to arrive at its pronunciation and, possibly, its meaning. Thus he becomes an independent reader, able to enjoy the many stories and other books appropriate for children of his age and reading ability.

Parents should not be disappointed if their child does not come home with a book the first day of school. Most children need pre-reading experiences before they are ready to read.

Having heard or read about the importance of phonics, many parents want to be sure their child is being taught by this magic method. We shall therefore go to some lengths to put phonics in its place, as one of several important word-recognition skills, each of which plays its part in the total reading program.

To counteract the tendency to think of reading as word calling —mere ability to pronounce printed words—reading should be presented from the beginning as a thought-getting process. Parents can help reinforce the teacher's accent on meaning.

Since reading is such an important tool of learning, parents become concerned when their child does not make the progress they expect. What can they do to help? First, they need to know what progress to expect from a particular child. No two children are exactly alike. Second, they should treat the child as a child—their loved and loving child—not as a reading problem. Third, they should confer with the teacher about specific ways in which they can help.

READINESS FOR READING

You have probably heard teachers mention lack of "readiness" in explaining why a child was not reading a first-grade book as soon as he started school. The following excerpts from a parent-teacher interview illustrate the dissatisfaction that many parents feel with the readiness program in the beginning of the first grade.

Parent: As a teacher myself, I just wanted to tell you I feel Paul has been given enough word and picture games and that he is ready for reading and writing.

Teacher: I'm so glad you came in. I wish more parents would be interested in talking over their child's readiness for reading.

Parent: That's just the trouble. My husband and I are tired of hearing about readiness for reading. We want Paul to begin to *read*. All the children seem to do in school is play. We are concerned about Paul. According to tests he's a bright boy. He wants to learn to read and we think he should begin learning to read.

Teacher: Many children need to get used to the change from home to school. They need to settle down a bit before beginning instruction in reading. I also need some time to observe which children seem ready to read and which need more of the prereading games that prepare them for successful reading. My impression of Paul thus far agrees with yours, and I am planning to put him in the group who will begin systematic instruction in reading.

As a matter of fact, Paul did not need any more of the prereading experiences that are so important to prevent initial failure. Bright children learn to read quickly and better without going through the readiness exercises that are needed by children who have been less fortunate in their preschool experiences and are less mature mentally.

To ascertain which children need the readiness experiences and which do not, teachers often give a reading readiness test,[2] near the beginning of the first grade. Sometimes, instead of testing, they systematically observe signs of readiness such as the following:

Readiness to learn: Ability to sit still long enough to learn to pay attention and listen, to resist being distracted or bothered by the other children.

Desire to learn to read: Most children come to school eager to learn to read. This desire can be fostered during the preschool years; it is basic to all further reading development.

Personal characteristics: Curiosity about signs and words, self-confidence, outgoingness, cooperation, independence, resourcefulness in finding work to do.

Physical readiness: Normal vision and hearing, good health and freedom from cumulative fatigue and illness, good motor coordination—hands and eyes work together in bouncing a ball, and so on.

Mental maturity: Ability to follow several simple directions, use words appropriately, see relationships, remember a short poem, tell story in sequence, and predict what may happen next.

Language readiness: Ability to speak clearly in sentences; to understand relationship words such as *up* and *down, big* and *little;* to correct errors in speech when they are pointed out.

Auditory and visual discrimination: Ability to distinguish differences in sounds and forms; to interpret pictures.

Prereading skills: Ability to supply a missing word in a sentence if it is suggested by the context; to recognize words beginning with the same sound; to say and recognize the names of the letters; to start associating each letter with its sound in words; to look at a line of print from left to right.

When the teacher has obtained and tabulated information of this kind about every child, she can see which experiences each one needs in order to be ready for systematic instruction in reading. Those who have high instruction-readiness scores can begin basal reading instruction. Those who are below par in oral speech, in ability to fill in the missing words at the ends of sentences, to recognize similar sounds in words, and in knowledge of the names of letters should be given these prereading experiences. Then they will be much more likely to succeed in their first attempts to read.

It would be helpful if every parent could talk with the first-grade teacher several weeks after school has begun. By then the teacher would know what experiences each child needs to give him the best chance for success in beginning reading.

Perhaps the teacher has noted some signs of difficulty in hearing or seeing. If these signs are confirmed by the school nurse or doctor, a more thorough examination is indicated. In fact, every child should have an eye examination by a specialist before he starts school.

Parents, too, can note signs of faulty hearing: Does the child pay no attention when his head is turned away from the speaker? Does he speak in an unnatural tone of voice? Does he mispronounce many words? Scarlet fever, as well as frequent colds and earaches, may impair a child's hearing.

You can foster the child's desire to read by continuing to read him stories and poems that he thoroughly enjoys. When time is limited and he wants more, you can say, "Soon you will learn to read stories yourself, when Mother is busy." Introduce him to the joys of the library. There he may browse among books and wonder what the people in the pictures are saying and what is happening in those enchanted lands.

When you are cooking, give him opportunities to bring you the flour or the sugar in its labeled can. When you are driving, ask him to read the road signs—*Go, Stop, Slow, Curve*—for you. Write simple messages on his blackboard or bulletin board, not for him to read, but to arouse his curiosity and make him feel a need for reading.

When the child is engaging in some activity, you can talk about it: "How nicely you are stringing those beads!" "It's time to put the toy engine in your toy box." "Alice wants another ride in your automobile." In this way the child associates the clearly spoken word with the object or action that is of immediate interest to him. This is a natural way to build a meaningful vocabulary.

When we are hurried and worried about many things, we cannot always reward the child by showing our interest or giving him a smile when he displays the characteristics that we want him to develop. But our interest is most important. Instead of being annoyed by his questions, we should commend his curiosity even though we cannot satisfy it. When he has taken initiative or shown resourcefulness, it does take thought, but very little time, to smile and say, "You did that all by yourself," or, "You found some-

thing interesting to do without my telling you." Children will repeat behavior that is approved by the persons they love.

If a child, for any of a number of reasons, is slow in his language
development, the home can do more than the school to build his
vocabulary and ability to communicate. Listening and speaking are
both involved. We can give him directions to carry out: "Billy,
please bring me my hat, my gloves, and my pocketbook." After
reading him a story that he wanted to hear, encourage him to talk
about it, or make another ending, or tell a story of his own. Let him
play "waiter"—let him take your order and repeat it when he comes
back: "Here is your chicken soup," "Did you enjoy the baked po-
tato?" "Was ice cream the dessert you ordered?"

A toy telephone is an excellent means of encouraging correct and
fluent speech. If the child mumbles, say, "Sorry, you'll have to
speak more clearly. This is a very poor connection." Playing "radio
announcer" also gives him an incentive to improve his oral speech.

Playing with children who speak clearly is even more effective.
The other children will not try to understand the child who mumbles or talks incoherently. Consequently, they will not do what he
wants. Often they will refuse to play with him.

One child had a mother who was overprotective and always gave
the child what she imagined he was asking for. This child would
rush up to other children and shout something they couldn't possibly
comprehend. Soon they began to avoid him. The teacher was able
to help this child in two ways: through the regular prereading exercises in recognizing similar and different sounds in words, and by
acting out playground situations with him. For example, she would
play his role and he would play the role of another child. Then they
would reverse roles and he would try a better approach. This role
playing improved both his speech and his social adjustment.

We have described games that develop ability to recognize similar
beginning sounds and concluding sounds in spoken words. Others
may be played on auto trips, or at other times when there doesn't
seem to be anything interesting to talk about. "I packed my trunk"
with things that begin with a particular consonant sound or blend,
like *ball* or *dress*. Or, "I went to the supermarket to buy . . ." innumerable articles that have the same beginning sounds. As he looks
at magazines with you, the child will enjoy finding objects that end

alike, such as *boy* and *toy,* or that begin alike, such as *cake* and *cup.* You may help him to select, cut out, and paste in a book ten or more picture cards for each initial consonant sound, to give him practice in recognizing these sounds in spoken words.

To encourage the child to think as well as to distinguish differences in words that begin alike, you can make pairs of words:

chickens   children

puppy   puddle

Then ask him: Which have wings—chickens or children? Which is an animal—puppy or puddle?

These special games and devices are not offered as substitutes for all the natural, spontaneous ways in which children in a family or a play group develop interest in reading, ability to speak effectively, and ability to discriminate among the things they see and the words they hear. The special games may be used if the teacher or parent thinks the child needs more experience along a certain line.

Readiness for reading is a complex state involving many factors. Some are part of the process of growing up and are little influenced by teaching. We have often referred to differences in rate of learning. Other factors have to do with distinct abilities that may be taught. Still others are a by-product of the child's experiences from early years. We have given special emphasis to conditions in the child's environment because those are the factors over which we have the most control.

LAUNCHED INTO READING

If your child does not need prereading experiences, or has had a sufficient number of them, the teacher will begin basal reading instruction. During this period it is wise to let the teacher give the instruction in reading. The parents' role is to learn as much as possible, through visits to the classroom, occasional talks with the teacher, or parent meetings in which the reading program and procedures are explained and described. The teacher will suggest many ways in which parents can cooperate. Here are some of the most helpful:

Share the child's enthusiasm over his first successes in recognizing new words and reading a few pages of the primer. There *is* a magic in getting meaning from those hitherto meaningless marks in books.

Whenever opportunity offers, help him confirm the habit of starting at the left and moving from left to right across the page.

Confirm his impression that printed words are talk—they tell you what the characters are saying and doing. They always have meaning. By giving him printed directions to follow, some of which lead to a pleasant surprise, you can strengthen his impression that printed words have meaning for him. For example, he may read: "Look on the table. Find the surprise there for you." A piece of candy or a little toy rewards his successful comprehension of the direction. Similarly, simple notices on the family bulletin board encourage the child to read for meaning.

If possible, become acquainted with the word-recognition skills that the teacher is helping the child to learn. Instead of telling him the unfamiliar words, let him practice his newly acquired skills. When he reads you a story, reward him by saying, "Fine, you puzzled that word out all by yourself; you didn't need anyone to help you." That is the kind of praise he likes; he wants to feel as competent and as grown up as a first-grade child can be.

When he wants to read to you, give him your full attention. Even though you cannot muster much enthusiasm for the preprimer stories, he will know that your interest in his progress is genuine.

Be judicious in your praise. Show pleasure and approval at each real evidence of the child's progress. But do not praise indiscriminately. To praise him when his performance shows indifference or lack of effort would tend to reinforce bad tendencies such as word calling or monotonous word-by-word reading. When he makes the lines sound as if he were saying them, as though he were talking to you rather than reading to you, then is the time to say, "That's fine." Undeserved praise tends to lower the child's level of aspiration. Praise decreases in value when it is given too lavishly. If the child prizes your approval, because he knows he has to deserve it, then you can spur him to do his best by occasionally withholding it.

Praise should also be specific. Instead of saying vaguely, "Good," or "All right," point out exactly what he did especially well. Then he will be more likely to do the same thing next time. In this way, too, you will be focusing his attention more on what he is reading than on your response to his performance. This will teach him to set his own standards of performance and take pride in living up to them, and thus prevent him from becoming too dependent on the approval of others.

Criticism should be used sparingly, if at all. Thinking back over their early experiences, some adolescents recall the unfavorable effects of criticism:

"When I read to my parents I would get very nervous because I was afraid I would make a mistake, so being afraid, I made the mistakes. They would say I 'should try harder' or 'you're reading too fast.' This would bother me so I began to dislike reading."

Criticism should also be specific. Vague criticism gives the child no indication of how he may cope with his difficulty, no real help in learning to read better. If your child has reading difficulties, be careful not to discuss them with friends or with other members of the family; these things are almost certain to get around—and to be repeated to the child. Even the most casual comment may make the child feel that you are disappointed in him.

Be patient. It is much easier to rush in and do something about a difficulty than to be sensitive to the child's needs. We can get some clues about this delicate matter from adolescents' recollections of their early reading experiences (see Chapter Two). Some express appreciation of their parents' help. Some youngsters wish that their parents had used another method. Others feel that their parents were not very sensitive to their feelings and moods:

Sometimes my parents would make me read when I just didn't feel in the mood for reading. I wish they hadn't done this.

WHAT ABOUT PHONICS?

Parents have an amazing interest in phonics. This is a word to conjure with. Neglect of phonics has been alleged to be the cause of children's failure in reading; it has been associated with "progressive education," and even with communism. Phonics, some parents think, is the method by which reading was taught in the "good old days" when they and their contemporaries learned to read. They think that the "look-and-say" method is the only one being used in today's teaching of reading—with such dire results. These points of view, as we have shown in Chapter One, are quite erroneous. They need to be corrected.

Many people do not even have a clear idea of what *phonics* is or how it is different from *phonetics*. *Phonetics* is the science of speech sounds. It uses a technical alphabet of its own, quite different from our alphabet. *Phonics* is simplified phonetics; used in teaching reading and spelling. It consists essentially of associating sounds with letters in words. The process of sounding out a word helps the child to pronounce it. If he pronounces the word correctly, and if it is in his speaking vocabulary, then he gets the meaning—the sound of the word recalls the meaning. By sounding *t* he gets a clue to the word *tell*. By sounding *thi*, which is familiar to him in the word *this*, he has a good start on the pronunciation of *thing, think, thick*.

Letters may also be grouped into syllables, prefixes, suffixes, and roots. If the reader recognizes these larger groupings, he can get the meaning of the word without pronouncing each letter sound separately.

Teaching speech sounds is complicated; it should be done only by persons who have specific training for it. Otherwise, for many children reading will become, in William James's words, "a great big bloomin' buzzing confusion."

If the child is taught the sounds of separate letters, he will have to unlearn the sound of $\breve{oo}$ which he learned in *g$\breve{oo}$d* when he meets the same letters in *n$\bar{oo}$n* or *t$\bar{oo}$th*. He will be confused when the sound he has learned as long *$\bar{\imath}$* is heard in words spelled quite differently, such as *eye, high, buy, cried, aisle*. The best way to avoid this confusion is to teach the child how to recognize unfamiliar words as they occur, in his reading. This approach gives the child an immediate motive for learning word-recognition skills; he can check his results by asking whether the meaning he has derived makes sense in the context, or by looking it up in the dictionary. Thus his attention is focused on *meaning*.

Some Facts About Phonics

The facts about phonics can be clearly and briefly stated:

1. Phonics should be an intrinsic part, *but only a part,* of the reading program. Neither the look-and-say method nor the phonic method is wrong; each is incomplete without the other. Some bright

children learn to read without any special instruction in phonics, and it is obvious that sound-letter associations cannot be taught to deaf and mute children who have not learned to speak. However, any child who cannot sound out new words or get their meaning by using other word-recognition skills is greatly handicapped in becoming an independent reader.

2. Phonics is only one aid to word recognition. Other aids include: getting the meaning from the context; recognizing prefixes, suffixes, roots, and other familiar parts of compound words; dividing a word into syllables; and looking it up in the dictionary. Phonics is to some extent used in conjunction with these other aids to word recognition; it should not be taught in isolation.

3. Before he begins to be instructed in phonics, it is probably desirable that the child have: a genuine interest in learning to read as a thought-getting process, a small stock of words that he can recognize at sight, ability to distinguish differences and similarities in the sounds of words, and knowledge of the names of the letters. Systematic instruction in phonics is usually introduced in the second half of the first grade; it continues to be taught throughout the grades as long as there is a need for it. It is most valuable in the second and third grades. However, the time for beginning phonic instruction will vary with individual children.

4. Instruction in phonics should be analytic rather than synthetic: that is, it should deduce sound-letter associations from familiar words rather than start with letter sounds and build words from them.

5. Instruction in phonics is best given when the child is engaged in reading, and needs to know the meaning of an unfamiliar word in order to understand the story. The child should gradually arrive at generalizations about the sounds of letters in words. This approach differs from the common practice of teaching lists of words that begin with the same letter sounds; it is more like the way the child learned to talk.

6. Before trying to associate sounds with letters in words, the child should know by sight a number of words whose meaning is familiar to him. Different authorities place this number at anywhere from 50 to 500.

7. It is also generally agreed that initial consonants are the easiest sound-letter relationships to learn. However, the order in which the

relationships are learned should be governed by the child's need for knowing them. If certain sound-letter combinations give a particular child difficulty, he may be given special practice on them.

The problem is not whether phonics should be taught but when it should be taught; to whom it should be taught—only to those who can profit by it, for some children, it seems, cannot learn by this method—what phonetic elements should be taught; in what order these elements should be taught; and how they should be taught.

Values and Dangers of Phonics

The phonic method of word analysis has definite values. It encourages correct word recognition, it counteracts the tendency to guess, and it gives children one key to the meaning of unfamiliar words.

But there are dangers in overemphasizing phonics. One is the danger of creating "word callers," children who are interested only in pronouncing words, and are indifferent to their meanings. One boy read, "This is a worm; do not step on it," as "This is a warm doughnut, step on it."

There is also the danger that children will become bored by phonic drills, which lack the intrinsic meaning of an interesting story. Moreover, if a child continues for a considerable time to sound out every letter in every word, he cannot help becoming a slow reader.

Examine your own reading. How did you get the meaning of this paragraph? How often did you stop to sound out a word? It is certainly more efficient to recognize a word by perceiving its shape, plus one or two letter clues, and by anticipating its meaning. It is unnecessary to stop and consider every letter-sound association in every word.

Difficulties and Problems

Linguists are often embarrassed by the problems of teaching English. It is not a completely phonetic language; there is not a one-to-one relation between letter and sounds. There are 26 letters, but at least 44 separate sounds. This means that some letters have two or more sounds. It would be simple if each letter always had the same sound. But obviously this is not the case. The letter *a* carries at least 22 sounds.

Moreover, the same sound is spelled in different ways. George Bernard Shaw once observed that one could spell fish, *ghoti*—

gh as in enou*gh*
o as in w*o*men
ti as in mo*ti*on.

Take long *ā* for example, as pronounced in *ate, late,* and *date.* This sound is spelled:

ea as in *bear*
ei " " *their*
ai " " *pair*
ay " " *play*
ey " " *they*
e " " *there*

If a child learns *ea* as pronounced in *bear,* how will he pronounce *beard* or *heard* or *hearth* or *tear?*

Many other examples could be cited to show how futile it is to teach lists of sounds separately. Letter–sound associations should be taught in familiar words. The child should check his pronunciation of the unknown word by seeing whether it makes sense in the sentence; this is an essential part of the phonetic approach.

When Should Phonics Be Taught?

Letter-sound associations can be formed as soon as children have learned to recognize a few familiar words. The teacher helps them to know the word by its form or shape, just as they recognize objects or note letter clues. The tall *f* in *father* distinguishes the word from *mother.*

The teacher usually begins systematic phonic instruction with the consonants that always—or almost always—have the same sound: b, d, f, h, j, k, l, m, n, p, r, t, v, w, z. These are the easiest to learn when they are the beginning sounds of familiar words. Since the consonants are always combined with vowel sounds, the long and short sounds of vowels—a, e, i, o, u, y—are often taught early.

Next, the pupils may learn the common endings: *s, ed, ing.* Practice in learning these endings may be given by means of various games. Prepare sets of cards, on each of which is printed a different form of one word: want, wants, wanted. Shuffle, and distribute four or five cards to each player. The teacher gives a sentence that contains one form of a word. The child who has the corresponding card holds it up for all to see, and then keeps it to make a set.

A similar game may be played with cards that have nouns on them, some singular, some plural. The child tells which words mean more than one. A repertory of letter-sound associations is gradually built up during the first year.

During the second year children usually learn the more difficult blends: tr, fr, fl, bl, cl, sl, st, ch, sh, th; the vowel combinations—oi, ay, oa, ea, ai, ie, ee; hard and soft *g* and *c;* and the variant sounds of *o* when it is followed by *w* or *o.*

In the third year, the pupils constantly use all the letter-sound associations that they have learned, and pay special attention to blends and speech sounds, and vowel combinations. At this stage the children may begin deriving rules of their own for pronunciation and spelling. From a great many examples such as

rid	ride
cut	cute
pan	pane, etc.,

they may derive the rule that "adding a silent *e* to a single-syllable word makes the first vowel say its name."

Or, after studying many words where two vowels come together, like *feet, maid, coat,* they may conclude that "when two vowels go walking the first does the talking." The trouble with most of these rules is that there are so many exceptions to them.

Practice in sound-letter associations can be combined with reading for meaning, as in the following games:

Phonogram Riddles
Make a set of cards containing words that have the same phonograms, such as *pan, fan, man, Dan, can.* On heavy paper write a series of riddles:

My word is *can.* Change one letter and make it something we use on a hot day.

Change one letter again and make it something we use in cooking.

Build on the Last Letter
I am something you sit on: chai*r*.

I have long ears: rabbi*t*.

I say "gobble, gobble": turke*y*.

Guess Who I Am

The leader shows the letters and pronounces them distinctly:

"I end with *ook,* can you guess who I am?"

"I end with *all,* can you guess how I look?"

Find the Rhymes

Select a number of familiar words that rhyme, and print each on a separate card. The child then finds and puts together the words that rhyme.

How Is Phonics Taught?

Many parents ask this question. In one school, the reading consultant planned a parents' meeting to answer it (see p. 34).

A parent who visits a first-grade classroom early in the school year is likely to see this kind of instruction being given:

Teacher (with a small group of children): This is the way the chalk says *Bill.* (Writes *Bill* on board.) Will the boy whose name is Bill come up and erase his name? There's another boy we call *Billy.* Billy, you come up and erase your name. There is a girl whose name is *Betty.* Betty, will you erase your name from the board?

Look at the three words on the chart. The first is *Bill.* The second is *Billy.* The third is *Betty.* Do Bill and Billy and Betty look alike? Of course not. You know Bill from Billy. Bill and Billy look different. They have different faces and figures. (As the teacher prints each word on the board, the children trace it in the air with their fingers.) You can tell one word from another in the same way—by looking at them.

Look at the words *Bill, Billy, Betty.* How is the word *Bill* different from *Billy?* How are the words just alike? What makes *Bill* different from other words? Yes, the big B at the beginning and the two tall letters at the end. Will you know the word *Bill* when you see it again? How do you know the word *Billy* when you see it? Yes, by the big B, the two tall letters, and the letter with a tail at the end of the word.

Look at the word *Betty.* In what way is the word *Betty* different from *Bill?* Yes, it has a different small letter; its taller letters are different. It has a letter with a tail at the end—the letter *y.*

Find Bill among the other words on this chart:

Bill	cat
John	Bill
cake	Bill
tell	boat
Bill	bell

Find Billy among the other words on this chart:

Bill	Billy
brown	book
Billy	bell
tell	Teddy
Bill	Betty
Billy	silly

Bill, Billy, Betty, come to the board. Erase your names as fast as you find them on the board.

(Teacher writes the three words along with many other words similar to those on the chart.)

Teacher: Let us write a story about Bill.

(Teacher writes story on board as children dictate it.)

Child: We all like Bill.

Child: Bill laughs a lot.

Child: Bill has a black dog. Its name is Blackie. Blackie came to school one day.

Teacher: Is this a true story, Bill?

Bill: Yes, I have a dog Blackie and he came to school one day.

Teacher: You have learned all the words in this story except *laughs* and *Blackie*. Let's be sure to learn them now. Look at *laughs*. What other words have you learned that begin with the same letter as *laughs?*

(Teacher writes words that children say on the board. *Blackie* is taught in the same way.)

Now read the whole story about Bill:

We all like Bill.
Bill laughs a lot.
Bill has a black dog.
Its name is Blackie.
Blackie came to school one day.

Look at the board and read the word or words I draw a line under. (Teacher moves her finger from the beginning of each line to the word she underlines.)

In these lessons, the teacher first helps the children to look at and recognize a few familiar words. Then, as the children learn new words, she introduces phonics by associating the initial consonants *l* and *b* with the same sounds in words the children already know. In this way the children begin to build up the store of letter-sound associations that they will use in solving the new words they meet in their stories.

Later, usually, the teacher may give systematic instruction in the vowel sounds to the children who need it. One teacher began the more formal study of vowels in this way:

Teacher: Each vowel has several sounds, two of which we will study now. One of these we call the long sound and we show it by this little sign—a straight line over the letter, as in ā. The short sound we show by a curved line over the letter, like this, ă. The long sound is the same as the name of the letter. What is the name of this letter? (Writes *A a.*)

Ann: A.

Teacher: And what is the long vowel sound of the letter? (pause) Remember, it is just the same as the name of the letter. What is the name of this letter?

Ted: A.

Teacher: And what is the long vowel sound of this letter?

Jean: ā.

Teacher (presents each of the long vowel sounds in this way): Now you understand that the long vowel sound of each letter is just the same as its name. Now, these vowels also have short sounds, and this is the code or sign we use to show the short vowel sound of ă. This is the sound you say in *ăpple*. Close your eyes just a minute. Can you hear the first letter sound—the short sound of *a* when I say *apple?* What do you hear?

Children: ă—*apple*.

Teacher: Good. What other words do you know that have this same short sound of *a?*

Marian: ăt, ăbsent.

Tom (the second-grade scientist): ăcid.

Ted: ăct.

Bill: ăsk.

Teacher: The *a* in *ask* has a somewhat different sound when the word is pronounced correctly. Listen—can you hear the difference: ăsk and ȧsk? The second is the correct pronunciation. I'm glad you mentioned this word, Bill, because we often give it the wrong sound.

Mary: ăt?

Teacher: Yes, that's another word with the short sound of ă.

Jim: căt, răt, hăt, săt.

Teacher (laughing): That was a whole family of short ă sounds.

In this way, slowly and with many illustrations, the children become acquainted with the long and short vowel sounds. Some of
the brightest children may discover some pronunciation rules for
themselves. For example, notice that in such words as gō, shē, hellō,
and buffalō, the single vowel that appears at the end of the word
or syllable is usually long. Children make these associations and
discoveries about sound-letter relations all during the primary grades.
At the end of the third grade, by using a combination of context
clues, letter-sounds, and familiar syllables like ly and tion, that they
have frequently met, they are able to pronounce many new words
and thus get the meaning of the story they are reading.

At home, when the child is reading aloud to you and comes across
a new word, instead of pronouncing it for him, help him to use the
word-analysis skills he is learning in school by asking:

What do you think the word might mean in that sentence?

Do you know any other words that begin with the same letter or
letters?

What parts of this word have you seen in other words you've
learned?

If the teacher has noted that your child is having special difficulty
with certain sounds, she may suggest some phonic games you can
play with him (see pages 106–107, 146–148). The word wheel is a
familiar type of practice material. The following is a typical home-
made practice exercise that can be used for any sounds or parts of
words that are causing difficulty:

    t   ell
    b
    w
    f
    s
    sh

The column of letters on the left is printed on a separate piece of
thin cardboard folded so that it can be moved up and down to form
the various words ending in ell, en, ad, or other combinations. You

will know you have been successful if your child says, "Mommy, let's play those word games together." You will play only as long as his interest is high and he asks for more.

OTHER WORD-RECOGNITION SKILLS

Building up a bank of sound-letter associations in meaningful words is an important accomplishment for children in the primary grades. They are also using other word-recognition skills. Before sounding out a word, they have learned to ask, "What might it mean in this sentence?" After they have tried to sound it out, they ask, "Does this word, as I have pronounced it, make sense?" Sometimes they recognize familiar syllables or word parts such as common phonograms as in *look* and *took, how* and *now;* endings; and prefixes. They will sometimes use a picture dictionary.

Perhaps you have noticed that children are sometimes advised to look for little words in big words. This is not recommended. Unless the little words are parts of a compound word such as *schoolhouse* or *homework,* this method is likely to be confusing. For example, it is no help to see the little word *fat* in *father,* or the two words *so* and *me,* in *some,* or *so* and *on,* in *soon.* It is much better for children to use the knowledge of phonics and of syllables and structural parts that they have already acquired.

During the primary grades your child is taught:

to read from left to right across the page.

to anticipate the meaningful words in sentences.

to recognize instantly many words at sight by their form and shape and by certain distinctive details.

to recognize rhyming words such as *can* and *man, bright* and *night.*

to form and use many sound-letter associations—single consonants, common consonant blends such as *st, sh, ch, pl.*

to identify common phonograms such as in *teach, each, book, cook.*

to see the smaller word units in compound words such as *headache* or *schoolhouse.*

to recognize familiar syllables such as *be, gin, un, der.*

In short, by the end of the third grade, your child will be able

to recognize many printed words instantly by sight, and will have
learned to puzzle out the pronunciation and meaning of unfamiliar
words. These are important accomplishments. But there is much
more to reading than word recognition. Reading must make sense.

ACCENT ON MEANING

Using phonics to pronounce a new word is only a first step to the
important goal—getting its meaning. Getting the meaning, in turn,
is a necessary preliminary to thinking and feeling about what we
read. Consequently, from the very beginning, teachers direct children's attention to the meaning and use of what they read.

To get meaning out of printed words, children have to bring
meaning to them. The meaning they bring to their reading comes
from their experiences. Experience comes before reading. A child
who brings his experience to his reading would never read the sentence "The children went into the house" as "The children went into
the horse"—it just wouldn't make sense.

Children are not really reading if they do not understand what
they read. They do not understand what they read unless they have
a background of experience that helps them to interpret the words.
The word *hen* is simply a word and nothing more to a child who
has had no experience with chickens. It calls up no images; it conveys
no meaning. In one of his plays, Pirandello said that a fact is like a
sack; it will not stand up by itself; it has to be filled with the meaning
that was originally in it. So it is with the words we read.

Teachers use many methods to direct children's attention to meaning. They ask questions before the child begins to read rather than
afterward. These encourage him to read with a purpose in mind. The
teacher may print notices on the bulletin board about what to bring
for the picnic or how to get copies of the snapshots taken on the
trip; these have personal meaning for the children. Or she may use
the blackboard to write directions for the day's activities. In the
course of a story, teachers often encourage children to speculate
about what is going to happen, and then read to see whether they
were right.

In the best schools, reading is taught as a thinking process.[3] From

the beginning the children learn that printed words are saying something to them and that the story characters are saying something to
one another.

Books remind them of similar events in their own lives—the funny
things *their* little sister did, the time *their* dog ran away. They tell
the teacher these stories; she prints them on the board or on a chart.
Since they know many of the words, they can read their own stories
along with their basal reader. This gives them meaningful practice
on the vocabulary they are learning. They make the most interesting
stories into little books—their own books. As second graders, they
often like to reread these "volumes" and remember the funny things
that happened last year.

The class as a whole often takes a trip—to a farm, to a dairy, to
the zoo. Before they go, they prepare charts on what they want or
expect to see. Following the trip, they write "thank you" letters and
dictate stories about the funny things they saw, how they felt about
the baby animals, and what they learned that was new to them.
Then they read supplementary books about farms and dairies and
zoos.

Activities of this kind involve relating experience to reading and
using reading to solve problems as they arise. The children discover
that reading is a tool. It helps them to understand and also to extend
their experience. They learn, too, that reading is a source of information about what they see and hear. They can learn how to do something, follow an interest, or acquire a new interest.

As soon as the children acquire ability to read independently, time
is scheduled for "free reading." This is sometimes done in the library,
sometimes in their homerooms where there are many sets of supplementary readers, trade books, and junior encyclopedias and dictionaries. In some schools children may take books home to read over
and over.

In a thirty-minute developmental reading period for second and
third graders, the children may be divided into groups that read
aloud on the level at which they are able to read comfortably. They
are concerned with the meaning of what they read—"what does it
say" and "what does it mean."

Bulletin boards give children additional opportunities to read.

There they may find a bit of information that is of personal concern to them, such as the day's luncheon menu, a riddle, a funny story, a bit of science news that is within their comprehension—something new to look at each day. Later a committee may use the items that are of permanent interest for a riddle book, a science book, or an animal book.

Parents, too, can encourage children to think and wonder about the stories they read. First graders can understand questions such as "How do you think this story will begin?" "What do you think will happen to Sally?" "Is this a true story—could it really have happened?" As children grow more mature they can answer more searching questions: "Why do you think Jane acted as she did?" "If you had been Mary's mother, what would you have done?" "Which part of the story seemed the most important to you?"

In a first-grade class reading a story, "Newspaper Helps" in the basal text *Away We Go* by R. G. Stauffer and others, the teacher continually encouraged the children to think while reading: [4]

The class read the name of the story in the Table of Contents and located the page on which it began.

Teacher: What do you think will happen in the story?
Pupil: Perhaps a newspaper is used to train a dog.
Pupil: Maybe a family finds a place to live by using a newspaper.
Pupil: The paper may be used to wrap some toys.
Pupil: Maybe the paper is folded and used as a fly swatter.

After turning to the story and studying the picture for possible clues, the pupils speculated further:

Pupil: The boys looked worried because this is a strange dog.
Pupil: The boys are wondering whose dog this is.
Pupil: They want to play ball and the dog gets in the way.

This speculation made the children eager to find out whose ideas were right. So the teacher told them to read the first page and then close their books. After they had read the page the teacher asked, "Who was right?"

The teacher used a similar procedure for the next two pages of print and pictures. Then, in the light of the evidence they had obtained, the children predicted what would happen next and how the story would end.

This kind of procedure helps children to enjoy a story by following its development, leads them to read with active minds, and gives them an immediate purpose—to find out if their predictions were correct. Thus reading and thinking are interwoven.

Of course, one should not read every story in this way. But going through this process of speculation and prediction a number of times in class will help children form the habits of reading with an inquiring mind and anticipating meaning.

At home, parents can encourage meaningful reading in somewhat similar ways. They can express interest in the outcome of the story: Did Janie find Blackie? Did Jack run away from home? What would be the brave thing to do in the situation described? This kind of questioning should be done informally, in an offhand manner. It is the teacher's responsibility to teach the process, and the parent's responsibility to reinforce it.

ORAL READING

In the good old days, the reading lesson often consisted in hearing each child in turn read aloud from the same book. This is exceedingly boring to able readers. In the interesting story, they read ahead, lose their place, and are scolded when the teacher calls on them. If the story is boring, they sit idly, wasting their time or thinking up some mischief that gets them into trouble. Poor readers are embarrassed, especially when their classmates shout out a difficult word before they have had time to puzzle it out for themselves. Fortunately, this method of teaching reading has now been discarded in most schools.

But oral reading has not been discarded. There is a real place for reading aloud in school, even though outside school most people read silently far more than they read orally.

In beginning reading, teacher and pupils pronounce the words, phrases, and sentences that are written on the board, on charts, on flash cards, or are printed in the preprimers. This helps the children build associations between word sounds and the letter sounds.

Soon after the children have begun to read, the teacher listens while they read a paragraph or two; this helps her to check their word-recognition skills.

When the children have learned to read independently, and can choose the books they want to read, there are many opportunities for them to share the high lights of their reading in an audience situation. Mary reads an amusing scene from her book and invites her classmates to read the whole book. David reads the class some information about dinosaurs that they wanted to know. At home, Jimmy reads the morning newspaper to find a paragraph that he hopes he will be chosen to read aloud as "Today's News Item." Four friends select a short story, read it silently, and make it into a play that they present to the class after they have practiced reading their parts.

These and many other audience situations give children an incentive to improve their oral reading. They also give children practice in being a courteous and attentive audience.

This kind of oral reading is a far cry from the outmoded method of reading-a-page-in-turn, which may embarrass the poor reader and bore the able.[5]

PLENTY OF BOOKS

At each stage in the child's development, it is desirable that he read widely, ranging far beyond the books that are required in school. Wide reading builds vocabulary, increases fluency, and exercises skills as the child acquires them.

These values are achieved only if the books are wisely chosen. The print in books for six- and seven-year-olds should be fairly large, for most children of this age are still farsighted. They will not enjoy reading if it entails the physical discomfort of eyestrain. The books should be easy enough so that the child can read and comprehend them independently. If a book is too difficult, it may disrupt good reading habits. Some children are challenged by a degree of difficulty that may discourage others. We tend to give children books that are too difficult; publishers' estimates of difficulty are often misleading. Some books designated as "Beginners' Books" are more suitable for nine-year-olds than for beginners. However, if a child is given a book that is in general too difficult, he may be able to read parts of it with enjoyment, and we can read the hard parts to him.

Some youngsters will read books that seem much too advanced for them, and get something out of them, even though there is much that they do not comprehend. Children need challenge as well as competency.

The book should also make some connection with the child's experience and interest; it should give the child some reward in addition to entertainment. You can usually judge the suitability of the book by the child's response to it. The right books develop the child's love of reading; the wrong books may produce or confirm an unfavorable attitude.

Several good readers, now in their teens, describe how suitable books helped them develop a favorable attitude toward reading:

"In my home we have many books that were written for beginners, and we also used to take *Jack and Jill*, a magazine for children. Maybe it was that, after learning to read reasonably well, I became curious about books and decided to read one. Or maybe on a cold winter afternoon I was bored, and to have something to do I read a book. It could have been many things that influenced my reading."

"I was very proud the day my father took me to the library to get my own library card. He picked out some biographies for me, because I wasn't sure what I wanted to read. For quite awhile after that all I read was biographies. My girl friends and I would go to the library once a week, and we would check out four or five books apiece."

"My school librarian read to us the last part of our library period each week. The whole class thoroughly enjoyed it, because she had tricky ways to get us to listen."

To foster personal development through reading in the primary grades, May Hill Arbuthnot [6] suggests books that give reassurance to young children: young Billy Goat Gruff isn't afraid because his big brothers are with him; Peter Rabbit is punished for his disobedience, but is later tucked safely into bed by his mother. In the series by Carolyn Haywood, the reader meets some loving parents who stand firmly behind their children, even when they make mistakes for which they must pay.

As children grow older, they need less reassurance. In their stories more emphasis should be put on achievement, as in the classic "Dick Whittington and His Cat" and the modern *The Courage of Sarah*

Noble by Alice Dalgliesh. Before long these older children will begin to glimpse wider social relationships and responsibilities in books such as Ellis Credle's *Down, Down the Mountain* and the Carrolls' stories about *Beanie*. Stories such as the picture stories about wild animals by Mary and Conrad Buff, the cat stories of Clare Newberry, C. W. Anderson's the *Billy and Blaze* stories, Robert McCloskey's *Make Way for the Ducklings,* and Robert Lawson's *Rabbit Hill* evoke feelings of tenderness, and give children a desire to love and protect as well as to be loved and protected.

Laughter, fun, and fantasy are also important in childhood. Children enjoy the gay make-believe of *The Happy Lion* or *Curious George,* and the droll hilarity of the books by Theodore Seuss Geisel (Dr. Seuss).

To develop a sense of beauty, it is most effective to read poetry aloud, beginning with nonsense verse and gradually moving to ballads and lyrics. Poetry helps to counteract the violence and brutality so often shown on the screen and brought into the home through television.

The teacher or the school librarian will be glad to recommend suitable books on subjects in which your child is interested. If the child is a poor reader and is sensitive about it, the adult should be careful not to dwell on the fact that a particular book is easy. Almost any child likes to have a special shelf for his growing collection of books that he can read independently.

It is wise to have a regular time for reading each day, though such a schedule defeats its own purpose if it is followed too rigidly. Ten or fifteen minutes a day is enough for a beginning reader. We shall foster nothing but dislike of reading if we ignore signs of restlessness or boredom.

Before the child begins to read a book, we should encourage him to discuss its title and illustrations. This is to arouse his interest in what he is reading and prevent him from focusing his attention on how he is reading. If reading aloud becomes tiresome to him, we may let him read a few pages silently, take turns with him in reading a few lines aloud, or read the part of the narrator while he reads the parts of the characters. If he reads the story fluently, it is a good idea to ask him to help you by reading it aloud to his little brother or sister.

HELP OVER THE HUMPS

As long as I can remember my mother has been a tremendous help to me. She never was too busy to stop and aid me with any difficulty I might have had. I feel this is invaluable and I know it was a great help to me.[7]

Ordinarily a parent's role with respect to a child's first three years of reading instruction in school is to be pleased with the child's progress, share his interest in reading, and provide him with many books for independent reading. As has already been suggested, we may also continue the practice of reading aloud books that surpass in ideas and artistry those that the child can read for himself.

"But, suppose my child is having real difficulty in learning to read? Suppose he is lagging behind the other children of his age? Is there anything I can do about it?" Of course there is, but before doing anything you need a thorough understanding of your child's reading difficulty.

There are many possible causes of difficulty. The child may find it hard to see or hear. He may be under par physically. Something in his relationships at home or at school may be disturbing him. He may have lost out on beginning reading instruction because of frequent absences from school or an inexperienced teacher, or he may not have been ready to read when formal instruction was begun. Perhaps he needs more practice in reading. Fatigue is another factor. In this modern age of television and city life, it is one of the commonest enemies of childhood. According to Dr. Benjamin Spock, children aged six to nine need eleven hours of sleep.

One thing seems quite certain: acute anxiety does not help. If the child, by comparing his reading with that of other children in the class, realizes that he is not doing well, he may develop a good deal of anxiety about it. His parents' anxiety, added to his own, may be the last straw. A state of intense anxiety prevents further learning.

The effect of parental anxiety and pressure was shown in the case of David. His parents were upset when David did not learn to read as quickly as his older sister did. They thought of him as "a reading problem." By nature David was brighter than his sister, but lacked her steady work habits. The teacher helped the parents to see that the pressure they were putting on David to get as good marks as his sister was hindering rather than helping him.

If the child is generally immature, it may be best to pay attention to his all-round growth; this may be the best way of helping him gradually to grow into reading. Helen, for example, was small for her age and a little below par in health. She was above average in intelligence, but had a speech defect that apparently had no physical basis. In beginning reading, a speech defect interferes with the process of associating the printed word with the spoken word, which has already acquired a cluster of meanings.

The teacher avoided calling attention to Helen's speech defect. She created a classroom atmosphere in which the child felt free to talk. The other children, too, accepted her and understood her trouble. The teacher encouraged the parents to take the same attitude in the home and to give Helen a few speech exercises as a game. As a result of this concerted action, Helen's speech improved. Her shyness decreased, she spoke more clearly, and began to take part in programs and plays. All concerned were proud of her progress.

Bobby, the youngest of three children, had been babied at home. His immaturity was more general than Helen's. His parents expected too little of him. Fortunately, he enjoyed school. The reading experiences stimulated him to put forth effort and work harder than he ever had before. Both Bobby and his parents were pleased with the progress he had made by the end of the second grade.

Some five-year-olds expressed rather amusing views about what parents and teachers should do if a child does not learn to read:

"I'd keep on trying to help her and when she got a little older she would learn."

"I would teach and teach her. I would ask mother to help. She would learn if she had that kind of help."

"I wouldn't tell anyone. I'd leave him alone and say that's pretty good 'cause little kids should be treated like humans and not like ants or something."

"I wouldn't stop. I'd keep teaching him to read until he was able to learn."

"I'd cry and be very sad."

"I'd say if you can't do it you'll just have to learn by yourself."

"I'd be mad."

"I'd say she'll never know much. She'll never be rich."

"I would take up all of her time teaching her."

"I would punish him."

What a range of adult attitudes toward children's learning is reflected in the comments of these observant five-year-olds!

Patience with Progress

Parents may expect too much of a child. They may not realize that the rate of his growth in reading is governed by his over-all rate of growth. Some children are slow growers. Some have less verbal ability than others. Putting pressure on such children to hurry up and read hinders more than it helps.

It is often hard for a parent to accept a slow rate of development. In our genuine desire to help, we give the child word drills and keep telling him to read at home. We get schoolbooks and workbooks for him to study. It might be far more effective to give him opportunities to read simple instructions for a new game he wants to play, or to read a simple recipe for a dish he is eager to have for dinner.

On the other hand, some able learners are discouraged because their parents have too low a level of aspiration for him. They do not insist on reasonable standards of excellence. The home contains few books or magazines to give them intellectual stimulation. The adults seem to have no time for reading and no interest in reading. Unless they find encouragement elsewhere, these children tend to copy their parents' apathetic attitude toward what goes on around them.

REINFORCEMENT OF READINESS

The child whose desire to read has never been aroused is handicapped when the teacher begins to give formal instruction in reading. Sometimes this lack of desire persists. Even by the end of the third grade, Sammy had made little progress in reading, despite— or perhaps because of—his mother's concern and a good deal of special tutoring. He was seven years old, large for his age, neatly dressed. He made a good first impression. He talked well, but was immature socially. He said the other boys did not like him. He seemed to have little desire to learn. During the first grade he was tutored at home and had special help in school. He made little progress, but seemed to like the special attention given him, and objected to having the tutoring discontinued. During the second year he became increasingly dependent on this special help. Much

of its potential value was neutralized by his mother's insistence that
he read the same books that the other children were reading.

For some reason, this boy seemed to have no desire to learn to
read. We can only speculate about the reasons. It may be that his
reading immaturity was associated with his inability to get along
with boys of his own age. His passive resistance to reading may
have stemmed from an unconscious hostility toward his mother, who
never allowed him to act his age and who openly favored his sister.
He may have feared that if he learned to read, the special attention
he craved would be withdrawn. At this point reading seemed to
have no meaning, use, or purpose for him.

Additional Practice

If a well-adjusted child is having difficulty in associating certain
sounds with certain letters, the teacher may suggest that the parent
play phonic games with him. Note that we say phonic *games,* not
phonic *exercises.* Some children need no practice of this kind; others
need a great deal. If the latter are given the additional practice at
the time they need it, it may prevent their experiencing confusion
and failure. Certainty gives the child reassurance and makes him
willing to take the next step.

Approval of Progress

The parent, as we have said before, should reward any step in the
right direction rather than wait to praise the end result. If a child
shows any interest or enthusiasm, it should be approved. Then he
will be more likely to repeat the desired behavior. If the child correctly identifies the sounds in a few simple words with which he
once had difficulty, we should be pleased, and should show our
pleasure.

But we should be equally careful not to reward error. If the child
repeatedly gives the wrong sound, we should correct it, ask him to
give a similar sound in other familiar words, test him again, and reward his learning with a smile or a word of approval: "That's exactly right now."

We should also take care not to make him too dependent on praise.
The pleasure and profit of reading per se should gradually come to
yield him sufficient satisfaction.

METHODS OF TEACHING

Exclusive use of any one method of teaching reading is likely to yield poor results. In the following composition a fourteen-year-old boy of average ability, whose reading scores almost touched the bottom of the scale, describes his unsatisfactory instruction, and states his present attitude toward reading:

In grade school the teachers always wrote words on the board and told us the word. They would tell us how it sounded, and would have you say the word a couple of days, until we knew the word. They didn't, until fourth grade, start to tell why the words sounded the way they did.

My parents tried to help by telling me to look up the word to see how it sounded, but I didn't know how to use the diacritical markings in the dictionary. I first became worried about my reading when I discovered that you had to be able to read to become a scientist. So I started to get on the ball and started working on my reading.

Reading has always been difficult for me up to the present day. I didn't like to read books except the ones on science and the different fields of science, especially on raising tropical fish, like *Exotic Aquarium Fishes* by Inns for example, from seventh grade on up to now. I still don't like to read too much but I do once in a while. I still like to read in the field of science and that's about the only reading I do.

There's no telling where I'd be if I hadn't had some field of interest like science. In some cases radio, television, and newspapers have taught me more than reading fifteen books devoted to the subject.

Apparently this boy's teachers put too much emphasis on the look-and-say method, and delayed the teaching of phonics too long. Of course, other conditions may have contributed to his failure to read up to his ability.

Exclusive use of a phonic method brought equally poor results, as described by another boy of fourteen:

After I had finished a book I would bring it home and read it to my mother. She was a big help to me. One summer when I was about fourth grade I spent an hour a day with her and a book she had about teaching a child to read [Flesch, *Why Johnny Can't Read*].

At fourteen, this boy is still reading far below his potential ability. He writes, "When I first learned to read, I liked to read, but now it is not much fun. It is much easier to watch TV or lisone to the radio or even go to a movi. Reading the comics is easy so I read them quite often."

Overstrictness on the part of primary teachers may cause children to feel extreme anxiety. A fifteen-year-old girl describes the effect that this tension had on her reading development:

I learned how to read in first grade. My teacher was strict and most of the time we read and learned new words. My parents made me read a lot and read aloud and I read to myself. When I read I'm scared because I'm going to pronounce the word wrong and that's the same way when I answer a question: I'm afraid I'm going to say the wrong thing.

When I first learned to read I didn't think I was ever going to learn. It wasn't bad when you know how to read. But truthfully I don't like to read because I can't read good enough.

When I read fast I can't get the meaning of the paragraphs.

When I read Civics I can't understand what I read but sometimes when I read a story I can tell you what I read and answer questions about it. Reading is what pulls me down in school work. If I knew how to read better I could have better school grades, too.

Bright children usually appreciate teachers who give them instruction when they need it, and encourage them to display initiative and independence. This method worked well in the case of Judy, who describes her primary reading experience as follows:

I have always loved to read, and my first grade teacher, Mrs. F———, had quite a bit to do with my feeling toward reading. As I was learning to read she was always ready and willing to help us pronounce words we had not come across before. We had three reading groups, the one each child was in depending on his reading ability. This in itself helped to stimulate my interest in reading, because I was always in the fastest group. Also, those in the fastest group were left on their own quite a bit while the teacher helped the other groups and this led me to depend on my own ability for figuring out new words.

I have usually always read books beyond my grade. I have done this because I find them more interesting and just as easy to read. Also, because they presented a challenge to my reading ability.

By having a television my reading time has been reduced somewhat. However, my like for reading has made me take time out for reading.

SUMMARY OF READING ACHIEVEMENTS IN THE PRIMARY GRADES AND HOW THEY ARE ACQUIRED

Continued interest in reading	Success in learning to read; approval of people who are important to the child Suitable, interesting books
Basic vocabulary of words instantly recognized at sight	Associating word with object, picture, or spoken word Experience reading Reading words in simple stories Word games
Well-established left-right movement	Well-established habit of starting at left side of page

Word-recognition skills:
  Looking for meaning in context
  Associating sounds with letters in words:
    initial consonants and familiar endings
  Recognizing other familiar parts of words
	Solving unfamiliar words in stories
	Relating beginning sounds of unfamiliar words with those of familiar words
	Phonic games and exercises, if needed
	Success in solving new words for oneself

Increasing vocabulary	Repetition of words already learned Wide reading of interesting material on present level of ability Learning new words in connection with activities
Increasing fluency	Wide reading of interesting material that is not too difficult
Reading for meaning and thinking while reading	Anticipating meaning by asking questions Relating reading to present purpose and previous experiences

The role of the parent during the first three years of school is to contribute in pleasant, casual ways to the child's readiness to read, to share his excitement in his first successful attempts to read, to help him over specific learning difficulties in any ways that the teacher may suggest, to provide him with plenty of books on his present level of reading ability, and to encourage but not force him to read at home.

QUESTIONS AND ANSWERS

1. *Have you any drills we could do with the child at home?*

There are many word games that parents and children may enjoy playing together. Some have already been described in this chapter. The following were suggested to parents by teachers in an elementary school:

Pick a Slip Game

Purpose: Increase vocabulary by words and phrases.

Materials: Print single words and phrases on slips of heavy paper. Write a numerical value from 1 to 3 in the upper-right-hand corner of each slip.

Procedure: Two or more people may play. The slips are placed face down on the table. The players take turns selecting a slip and reading it. If the player reads it correctly, he keeps the slip. If not, he replaces it on the table. Add the numbers on each player's slips, and the highest score wins.

Rhyming Game

Purpose: To develop associations with familiar letter groups at the end of words.

Material: Print single words on the slips of heavy paper 1½″ x ¾″. Have twelve sets of six cards, each set having a particular ending such as:

pan	wing	harm
man	sing	farm
can	thing	charm
ran	ring	alarm
fan	sling	arm
tan	string	disarm

Procedure: two or more people may play. The cards are dealt out to the players. The word slips are placed face down in the center of the table.

should. The child senses their anxiety and impatience, and this may make him anxious or restive, or resistant to reading.

The parents may use one method, and the teacher tends to confuse the child by using another. This sometimes creates conflicts in loyalty. If the child does not accept the parent's method in preference to the teacher's, the parent sometimes becomes annoyed with the child.

There are many helpful things that parents can do, as described in this and the previous chapter. They need not feel obliged to take on the teacher's responsibility, too.

3. *How can a parent learn about his own child's reading?*

Through daily observation and conversation parents can learn about:

The child's general interests—these often develop into reading interests.

The child's reading interests: To which stories and parts of stories does he listen with keenest interest? In which parts does his interest flag?

When he reads aloud does he have difficulty with the little common words, or only with longer words?

How does he go about getting the meaning of an unfamiliar word? If you don't tell him, does he first try to get the meaning from the context and then use letter-sound associations? Does he try to divide the word into syllables, recognize familiar parts, or look it up in the dictionary?

Does he like to talk about the books he has read?

When he has free time what does he prefer to do?

4. *What is the parent's role in listening to a child read?*

Listen wholeheartedly. Try not to allow your attention to be distracted, by grownups or by other children. Do not try to listen to the radio or look at television at the same time. Select some simple household task, such as sewing or knitting, that does not require your attention.

Listen to appreciate. As far as possible enjoy the content of the story and make some comment on it.

Do not give the impression that you are listening for mistakes. It may make the child nervous if he thinks you are paying attention to *how* he reads rather than to *what* he reads. It also distracts his attention from the content. Be a good audience.

Do not expect your child to bring home his basal reader. That is the book the teacher uses to give him basic instruction in reading. It is usually better for him to bring home supplementary books on about the same level of difficulty. These are often more interesting to you and to the child; they are meant to encourage wide voluntary reading.

If a child takes his reader home, he should read to his parents only those stories the teacher has already taught in class. He will be able to read these fluently, and will enjoy reading them.

5. *Why is my bright child not learning to read?*

Some parents who ask this question have tried too hard to help the child learn. If the child is being pushed and prodded to do something he is not ready to do, the initial problem is complicated. In a more relaxed atmosphere, suitable reading material will usually stimulate the bright child to develop interest and skill in reading— when he is ready. Once he is started, no one should hold him back; let him progress as far and as fast as he can.

It is not always so simple as this, however. When there is real incompetence, the parent needs help in determining its causes and in doing what is necessary to correct them.

6. *What kinds of experiences are helpful to children who are slow in developing visual and auditory discrimination?*

The following experiences are often used by kindergarten and first-grade teachers with groups or with individual children:

Listening to recordings of rhymes.

Having the children close their eyes and try to identify different sounds: the tearing of paper, a high note, a low note, a pencil being sharpened, a familiar song, and so on.

Noticing likenesses and differences in shapes—a chicken and a duck, a goat and a lamb, a plant as it was a few days ago and as it is today.

Finding details in a picture that tell what might happen next.

Seeing how many objects a child can remember after looking at a picture for one minute. Do this again after he has learned to remember objects in groups—for example, all the things associated with the stove in the picture.

Pointing out parts of sentences that are alike:

We went fishing.

We caught one little fish.

7. *Why are children grouped for reading?*

There are a number of different kinds of grouping that may help children learn to read better.

In large schools, whole classes may be formed on the basis of the children's reading ability as determined by standardized tests, informal tests, the teacher's judgment, and the student's own appraisal of his reading needs. The advantage of this kind of grouping is that it is easier to find a teacher who can work with a limited range of reading ability than one who can deal successfully with a wide range. Moreover, suitable reading materials may be obtained for each class. In such a program the poor reader is less likely to feel inferior and the good reader is less likely to be neglected. On the other hand, some poor readers might be stimulated if they were with better readers, and could take part in their discussions and activities.

Flexible grouping within a class is a very good thing when it is handled wisely. Students with specific difficulties come together to receive the type of practice and instruction that they need. Both good and poor readers work together on topics that are of special interest to them, and thereby learn to appreciate one another and accept their differences.

Widening Horizons in the Intermediate Grades

By THE end of the third grade, children should have acquired sufficient basic reading skills to be reading widely and independently. But reading difficulties often begin to show up during the fourth grade. Children who have not acquired a real interest in reading, a desire to learn from books, a basic sight vocabulary, word-recognition skills, or techniques of reading for meaning, find themselves all at sea in the new subjects. They have to shift from the story type of reading to the study type of reading; the intermediate grades require special skills.

Beginning with the fourth grade, teachers usually expect pupils to read extensively—not just to read. If a child has not learned to read, he feels at a loss. Rather than admit his reading deficiency, he may try to distract the teacher's attention and that of his classmates. One boy, when he was called upon to read aloud, made up his own words if he couldn't figure out what the book said: "And then King Arthur . . . ran round and round the barn." The class laughed and the teacher told him to sit down. Baffled by the boy's behavior, the teacher sought the help of the school social worker. After visiting his home, the social worker understood better why he was behaving as he did. She helped the parents and the boy himself to understand his reading difficulty. Several months of teamwork on the part of the social worker, the teacher, the parents, and the boy improved his reading. One day he said with a grin, "I guess I'm not such a pain in the neck as I used to be."

INFLUENCES ON READING DEVELOPMENT

Lack of suitable instruction in reading may also be a contributing cause of failure during these years. Reading instruction, which should be continuous throughout the school years, is often neglected after the primary grades. However, this fault is rapidly being corrected. Basal reader series are being used through the eighth grade, and intermediate and upper-grade teachers have become alert to the need for instruction in reading.

The characteristics that are common to children of this age have a bearing on their reading development. On the favorable side is increased maturity of eyes and brain. Eyes reach adult size and functioning by about ten years of age. This enables children to spend more time with books without suffering physical discomfort. Especially in brighter children, there is some evidence of a slight spurt in mental growth between the ages of eight and ten. During these years ability to see likenesses and differences undergoes rapid growth. This is an obvious aid to associating sounds and letters, and to distinguishing between words of similar form.

Children acquire a large amount of knowledge during these years. This increases their capacity for learning through reading. The more background they bring to a book, the more meaning they will get from it. The more meaning they get, the greater the rewards they find in reading. They become able to read increasingly complex content.

These should be years of rapid progress in reading—expanding interests, more mature attitudes, a faster rate of silent reading, more accomplished skills, and more dependable habits.

With boys, progress in reading may be hampered in several ways. They are physically very active, and want to spend much time in sports. They tend to resist adult authority. Their unruliness in school, which reaches a peak at about nine or ten, does not endear them to the teacher. She may spend more class time disciplining them than teaching them. Parents, too, are likely to react to their rambunctiousness with some degree of hostility. Since children of this age are not really as independent as they try to appear, they may feel rejected by their parents, whom they still need. This may produce emotional disturbances that further interfere with effective reading.

Girls of these ages are usually more successful than boys in reading and in most other school subjects. Some preadolescent boys may let their natural antagonism to girls carry over to their attitudes toward reading: "Reading is sissy," and therefore to be rejected.

READING INTERESTS

Despite these unfavorable conditions, preadolescence is usually the time when voluntary reading reaches a peak. Many children of this age still like animal stories; most of them especially enjoy adventure and mystery stories. Boys prefer sports stories, factual material on mechanics, scientific books that range all the way from prehistoric animals and earth changes to excursions into outer space and other futuristic ventures. Although some modern girls are more science-minded than those of a century ago, many still prefer fairy tales, poetry, and stories about girls of their own age living here and now or in other times and lands. In their reading autobiographies adolescents recall liking, at this stage, books about magic, humorous books, novels about treasure-hunting boys who are captured by pirates, biographies, books about "girls my age or older," modern fantasies, and books dealing with real people and families.

According to the findings of psychoanalysis, successful children's books are those that deal with universal daydreams such as the reversal of roles described in *The Prince and the Pauper*, the theme of loss and restoration as it is found in many fairy tales, the tale of the bad boy exemplified in *Tom Sawyer* and *Huckleberry Finn*, and the folk hero as he appears in pioneer stories about Davey Crockett and Daniel Boone.

ACCENT ON VOLUNTARY READING

Ways of Encouraging Reading

During the intermediate grades—four, five, and six—children should do a great deal of reading. Wide reading during these years builds vocabulary, develops fluency, and adds to the child's store of knowledge.

Parents can create a home atmosphere that is friendly to reading, and encourage the child's reading in many other ways. The custom of reading aloud should be continued or revived, if it has been permitted to lapse. For some families the television program "Reading Out Loud" may have served as a stimulus to this end. When there are children of different ages to be read to, a book aimed at the middle child will usually interest both the younger and the older ones. Since some of us are not such skillful readers as we'd like to be, we can sometimes make use of the available recordings of such children's classics as *Pinocchio, Alice in Wonderland,* and *Treasure Island.* Your library may have a number of these long-playing records. Enjoyment of books is contagious. Even a reluctant reader may be carried away by the enthusiasm of other members of the family group. One gifted adolescent girl described her home experience as follows:

From the time I was a little girl until my homework became such a terrible burden, my mother always read aloud to me, and she chose books which were well up to, if not a little beyond my interests. This as well as the fact that she has always read a lot herself and gotten a great deal of pleasure from it, is really the only strong incentive I have ever had to read.

At this age, the child may become resistant to reading if the parents insist that he read. One boy gave this warning: "In creating an interest in reading, I think it is important for adults to stay in the background. If they constantly badger the child by saying, 'Why don't you read a book?' they will build up an opposition to reading. On the other hand, they should set a goal for the child to strive toward."

It is better to recommend to the child a book in which we think he would be particularly interested, or give him a selected list from which he may choose, than to force him to read certain books. We should not overlook the fact that some children lack the physical, social, or emotional readiness to read the books that we think would be good for them. Books that are either too easy or too difficult may prejudice a child against reading.

Competing and Reinforcing Interests

During these preadolescent years there is time for independent reading—more time than the child will ever have again. Outdoor play, sports, and scouting should, of course, have their place in his daily schedule. But music lessons, dancing lessons, excessive home-work, household duties, and television should not be allowed to usurp time for reading and contemplation. Much of the homework that is required during these years might well take the form of individualized reading; this would permit the child to engage in guided reading as part of his home-school program. If reading aloud at bedtime has been an important part of the child's routine, he may want to continue seeking the companionship of books by himself at this time of day.

The development of hobbies and interests may serve as a spur to reading. Jimmy was making a rock collection; he needed books to help him label them and tell him more about them. This interest led him to read about prehistoric times and the way our mountains, canyons, and rivers were formed. Donald became interested in conservation, and was an authority on this subject by the end of the sixth grade. Tommy was interested in reading everything he could find about his baseball heroes. Ted, who liked to make and build things more than he liked to read, got his father to help him start building a boat. With a little encouragement, this interest led him to read about boats—a fascinating subject in which his buddies, too, became interested. Betty read recipes as ravenously as her active brothers ate the treats that she concocted. To build and operate her puppet theater, Karen not only read books on how to make puppets but also searched out stories that could be rewritten as puppet plays. We can help children to develop interests and to find reading material that fits their interests.

Availability of Books

A child's interest in reading may be stimulated by contact with a library. When we have an errand to do, we can drop the child off at the library and leave him free to browse and pick out some books that he wants to read. If we take out a library card in his name, he will feel grown up; now he can take books out on his own. If the local library has a book fair, he will see all sorts of colorful new books, in company with other children who are looking at them and talking about them.

Instead of depending upon adults to answer his questions, the older child can begin to seek the answers in books. Sometimes we can suggest a specific book in which he can find the answer. More often we will be able to suggest that he look for it in his own reference library, which we have helped him to build up. The picture dictionary of earlier years is now supplemented by a simple children's encyclopedia; every child should have access to a good dictionary, an atlas, and books on prehistoric and modern animals, stars, birds, flowers, trees, airplanes, ships, automobiles, and other subjects that are of interest to preadolescents. These reference books form a part of the personal library that he will gradually build.

Birthdays and holidays offer us opportunities to give the child books or subscriptions to magazines or book clubs. The child will look forward to receiving a new book in the mail each month—a hard-cover book or a paperback that is suited to his age and interests.

Teachers' Methods

Teachers, too, may do much to widen and intensify children's reading interests during these years. They should introduce books skillfully, and also see to it that pupils have time for reading and discussing them. One adolescent described her experience as follows:

In the fourth, fifth, and sixth grades, we had to read a book each week and give an oral report on it to the class. Thus I read more and more simple but interesting books and enjoyed it. In the eighth grade I began to explore more widely. That is when we had to read a classic novel and later on give a short summary of it and the author. I chose to read *David Copperfield,* and I still consider it my favorite.

Older children are intrigued by stories from the great epics: Beowulf, King Arthur, the Iliad, the Odyssey. When their interests are beginning to reach out far beyond the family circle, the lives of great heroes and heroines exert a strong appeal. These stories contribute to character development, and contain high adventure, drama, and excitement as well.

A gifted adolescent approved the practice of providing school time for reading, but criticized the quality of the books that were available:

In the elementary grades, we were always given some school time for free reading and were permitted to choose our material from the school library. But the books from which we were allowed to make a selection were usually about three years behind our interest level. This was probably due to an effort to offer material with a simple vocabulary, but it certainly didn't provide very challenging reading. Also, at each grade level, the type of books all seemed to be along one line.

In eighth grade we were assigned some really good books to read, but by that time most of us had so much other homework that we plowed through *Huckleberry Finn* and *Uncle Tom's Cabin* when we were half asleep and couldn't get any pleasure at all from them.

Teachers have to be careful not to carry the analysis of literature too far, as an adolescent girl pointed out: "I remember having to read a part of a story at a time, and then being tested on it. This took the fun out of reading the story for me. I like to read for enjoyment—and I certainly don't care how many pirates there were in the landing party in *Treasure Island*."

The Comic-Book Problem

This is a comic-book age. We shall probably have to live with them for a while. If the child's friends are reading and exchanging comic books, no mere parent can stem the tide. If he confiscates them he will only earn the children's hostility. To make a rule, "No comic books," is to invite rebellion. One fifth-grade girl who disliked reading very much summed up the attitude of many children: "When I have some spare time I read the kind of books I enjoy and the only kind I enjoy are comic books." We should not be discouraged, however, for most children eventually outgrow this interest or, at least, its addictive phase.

In the meantime we can help the child to be more or less selective about the comic books he reads. What is "comic" about those that present lurid pictures of crime and violence? Some comic books are, at least, relatively true to life. Some deal quite accurately with current events, science, and geography. Some are well drawn and pleasing in color. To choose the better comics is one step in the right direction.

The next step is to make the transition from comics to books that have some of the qualities of action, adventure, suspense, and humor that attract children to the comics. Parents, teachers, and librarians can find books that are not too long and contain many illustrations, fast-moving action, and much conversation; these may lure children away from the comics.

The problem of comics would be more easily solved if the books we suggest as substitutes were as easily obtained and as cheap as the comics. Good children's books in paperback editions are giving the comics some stiff competition. They are on sale in supermarkets and toy stores. It might even pay a parent to turn her child loose in a bookstore occasionally, with permission to buy a book or two that he particularly wants.

Parents sometimes ask, "Is it better to let my child read comics than not to have him read at all?" Diverse answers are given to this question. Is it wise under any circumstances to fill a child's mind with crime, violence, and ugliness? Is it wise to lead him to think that unreal consequences, or no consequences at all, flow from certain very real acts? This is too high a price to pay for whatever reading interest or skill he may develop by reading comics.

However, if we can protect him from the worst of the comics, the better comics may serve a useful purpose. We have to start where the child is. He may learn from comics that printed words are talk. That is all to the good. If he reads the words and not just the pictures, he will build up a vocabulary of words he can recognize at sight. Since the qualities he enjoys in the comics are also to be found in books, the comics may lead him on to better reading matter.

READING GOALS FOR INTERMEDIATE GRADES

The reading skills that children acquired during the primary grades are further developed in the intermediate grades. Sight vocabulary increases, and mastery of word-recognition skills makes independent reading possible. More and more often, older children recognize unfamiliar words by dividing them into syllables rather than by sounding them out letter by letter. As they become more expert in using context clues, they find they need fewer phonic clues to arrive at the correct meaning. They find ways of increasing their efficiency.

They learn the special vocabulary of the new subjects they are studying and acquire the special skills that are needed in reading the graphs, tables, charts, and symbols that are peculiar to certain fields of study.

They become more expert in getting the main ideas of paragraphs and noting the supporting details and illustrations. The next step is to relate these main ideas to the topic as a whole by putting them in outline or summary form. When they are learning to see relationships, pupils need instruction and practice. They should receive approval when they arrange ideas in sequence rather than leaving them scattered and isolated. Teachers have to be careful to encourage children to form the habit of seeing relationships among the ideas they gain from reading. This they can do by means of approval and by means of examination questions that call for this ability. They should not rely on multiple-choice questions alone but should encourage pupils to communicate ideas in essay replies, written summaries, and oral reports.

During these years children begin to write reports in which they use information gathered from several sources. For this purpose they need to become acquainted with the use of the table of contents, the index, the card catalogue, and reference books such as the encyclopedia. The teacher gives them instruction as well as practice in the location of information. The pupils read many kinds of materials for different purposes; they are also learning to use appropriate reading methods and rates.

Within the range of their experience, they begin to make sound inferences and generalizations from their reading, and to apply them to the solution of practical problems. They also begin to pay attention to the author's purpose, and the ways in which he may be trying to influence the reader. Since the preadolescent is practical-minded, he uses the ideas he gains from reading in his activities—in making and doing things, entertaining his friends, and acquiring all sorts of information. Reading helps him to develop his own ideas by clarifying and organizing his vague and random thoughts. Thus reading becomes ever more exciting and useful.

Children who do not make the expected progress in reading need special instruction. These children are too often neglected until their cumulative reading difficulties become serious.

This is an age in which personal standards of excellence have gone far in serving as arbiters of conduct. There is no excuse for letting able learners lapse into mediocre reading methods or read mediocre books.

SPEAKING AND LISTENING

In today's school, children are encouraged to talk. By trying to communicate their ideas to someone else, they often clarify them.

Children have a natural gift for vivid expression. This we can cultivate. We should be alert to respond to the original idea, the poetic phase. As Hughes Mearnes said in his fascinating book *Creative Power*,[1] children are seldom aware that they are "talking poetry" unless their particularly felicitous phrases are called to their attention, or jotted down from time to time.

There should still be time, as in the primary grades, for the oral sharing of experiences. When children tell about the same event, they can compare their accounts and discuss why one was clearer, more precise, and more interesting to the listeners than another. Adults can be too patient with children whose speech is mumbled, indistinct, or incoherent—too patient in the sense of accepting it without showing the child how he can communicate his thoughts more clearly.

Fluency in speaking is evoked by having something important to communicate. We cannot expect a child to speak clearly about a subject that is vague and unclear to him. Monotonous, weak, barely intelligible voices are not characteristic of children who have something that they want to communicate and that they think others would want to hear. Parents can help by listening attentively when the child has seen or heard something that he wants to tell about. This kind of practice is all to the good.

Naturally shy children with weak voices may gain confidence by acting as leaders in a game described by Van Riper.[2] The children form two lines facing each other. The leader, bent over, says in a small voice, "I'm a little fairy." Then he partly straightens up and says in a louder voice, "I'm a bigger fairy." Finally, he stands tall and says in a big voice, "I'm as big as Daddy." The second time all the children repeat the action-play with the leader. The wording can be changed to make the game acceptable to older children.

In school, some teachers are encouraging children to think aloud as they solve a problem or carry on an activity. At first the teacher may demonstrate the process by vocalizing what she is doing and thinking at each step. Then all the children think aloud in like manner. This helps them to talk intelligently, to perceive accurately, and to carry out a process more purposively.

Both children and adults learn to speak better by listening to their own voices. On hearing a playback of their speech, they often exclaim, "Do I really talk like that!" After analyzing their dissatisfactions with this first recording and learning how to correct the faults it so clearly revealed, they are usually pleased with the improvement shown in the second recording.

Speech is related to reading in several ways. The child whose speech is clear and distinct finds it easier to form sound-letter associations. Fluent speech helps him to anticipate meaning in the material he is reading. The child who achieves success in speech and wins approval for it gains a general self-confidence that improves his approach to reading.

CREATIVE WRITING

Reading may stimulate children to listen more carefully and record what they hear in creative writing. After reading poems like Stevenson's "Windy Nights," Amy Lowell's "Sea Shell," and Dorothy Baruch's "Riding in a Motor Boat," a fourth-grade class went on to write poems about sounds they enjoyed: the ripple of water, the swish of the sea, the rush of the wind, an echo in the woods, the footsteps of Father coming home.

Children are often shy about the poetry they write; they hesitate to share it with adults. We should respect their reticence. If they do take us into their confidence, about all we can do is to show appreciation of the parts that are fresh and vivid and perceptive. Effective writing stems from an attempt to clarify our thoughts and feelings for ourselves and others; it is the product of general sensitivity and mental alertness.

DEVELOPING THE CHILD'S READING VOCABULARY

You recognize thousands of printed words by sight. How did you learn them? Wasn't it mostly by wide reading? Each new author, each new field introduced you to words you had not known before. Some of these you may have looked up in the dictionary, but in most instances you sensed their meaning from the context—with the aid of some letter-sound associations and familiar parts. You probably tried to pronounce the word by syllables more often than you tried to sound it out letter by letter. These skills that you have used so often are the word-building skills that your child is perfecting during the intermediate grades.

Firsthand experience is still important in building word meanings. Teachers conduct experiments in general science, and plan excursions that are preceded and followed by discussions. In addition, they maintain bulletin boards on which pupils find important notices and clippings on a variety of subjects; they build up a file of clippings on topics in which the children may be interested, and encourage children to use both classroom and school libraries. At home, children should have similar experiences; they can also watch current-events programs and travel films on television. All these experiences extend and enrich their stock of meaningful words.

A study of the ways in which sixth-grade pupils acquired word meanings [3] throws some light on the actual outcomes of our attempts to teach word meanings in the classroom. Most of the associations that these children reported involved experiences, persons, and things. For example:

Defiant. "There was a moving picture, *The Defiant Ones.* They wanted to get away from the camp and then from each other."

Tussle. "When I have a hard time getting my rain boots on, I have a *tussle* with them."

Stationary. I talk to my friend, Phyllis, who sits beside me, and when I talk to her I just twist my neck, but she's *stationary*—she doesn't have to move."

Unanimous. "We voted for a new class president last month. Everybody was in agreement on one person, and the teacher said, 'It's *unanimous;* he's elected.' "

Livelihood. "The teacher said, 'Teaching is my *livelihood.* It's the way I earn my living.' "

The most frequent word association involved a person who was familiar to the pupil. Of all the methods used by the teacher, the pupils thought dramatization of the word was the most effective. For example, *tussle* was dramatized by having two boys engage in a tussle; and *scowl,* by the teacher's scowling.

Associations involving similarities of letters or sounds were thought to be less effective. For example:

Tedious begins with the same letter as *tiresome.*
Wary begins in the same way as *watchful.*

The most memorable meanings were those which were personalized—which were related to the child as a person and to his ego needs. For example, one word that was known by a class of very poor readers was *confiscate.* When the children were asked how they happened to know this word so well, they said: "Our teacher often uses it. She says, 'If you bring that yo-yo to school again, I'll confiscate it,' or 'I'm going to confiscate Tommy's water pistol.'"

Words that are vitalized by intimate association with children's real interests and actual daily experiences are most quickly learned and easily remembered. The difficulty of a given word is governed by the child's background of experience. For example, *fertile* was an easier word to learn than *futile* for children who had been studying about *fertile soil*.

It is also helpful to direct children's attention to a word's peculiarity of structure or any other unique feature that it may possess.

These are important facts to remember if your child has difficulty in learning certain words. Any new word will be learned more quickly if it is associated with something that is personal and meaningful to the child. Using the new word frequently in conversation also helps the child to fix it in mind. The more use a person makes of a word, the more readily it becomes part of his sight vocabulary.

Children should also be encouraged to memorize poems and sayings that have particular appeal for them. Most of us have had the experience of gaining a better understanding of an unfamiliar word by noticing the way it was skillfully used in a phrase or in a line of poetry. For example, the phrase "myriad stars" in the hymn may clarify the meaning of *myriad*, and a line from Keats, "Their branches ne'er remember their green felicity," may bring meaning to the word *felicity* in a new context.

Many books and practice exercises have been published as aids to building bigger and better vocabulary. Many of them are boring to children. Moreover, if the words are learned out of context, such books may have little influence on the use of words in meaningful reading. Most words have more than one meaning; for some, more than a hundred meanings can be found in an unabridged dictionary. A definition or synonym from a dictionary may give a clue to the meaning of a word, but the reader must still test the meaning in the context. In addition, they should learn, as need arises, the new words in the material they are currently reading. They will incidentally learn some of the prefixes, suffixes, and roots that they frequently meet in their reading, and thus become aware of word parts.

WORD-RECOGNITION SKILLS

The growing edge of a child's vocabulary is extended by his ability to get the meaning of words in context. The stronger the context clues, the fewer sound-letter associations are needed; the weaker the context clues, the more letter sounds the child needs to know. A child who uses context clues alone makes many mistakes. The one who makes poor use of context clues belabors the word unnecessarily. He needs to know just enough of the sound-letter associations to call to mind the word that makes sense in the sentence.

Consequently when your child in the fourth, fifth, or sixth grade comes across a word that is strange in form or meaning, it is usually best not to pronounce it for him or tell him the meaning of it, if he has been taught how to solve it himself. Solving the word himself not only gives him practice in using phonics and other word-recognition skills, but also reinforces his feeling of being an independent reader. As soon as he has been taught to use the dictionary, be sure he has a junior dictionary [4] to use when other word-recognition skills fail, or when he wants to check on the accuracy of his analysis. It is so easy to say to a child who asks you the meaning of a word, "Look it up in the dictionary." But have you ever watched a child fuss and fumble over a word he is trying to look up?

There's a real skill in using the dictionary. It is usually not taught until about the fourth grade. Actually, three skills are needed—skill in locating the word in the dictionary, skill in pronouncing it, and skill in getting its meaning.

Skill in locating the word requires knowledge of the alphabet. If the child has learned the alphabet in four sections, as described on page 112, then he knows that *d* will be in the first quarter of the dictionary and will turn at once to that section. Since he knows the sequence of the letters, he will easily find *d*. For further guidance he will look at the guide lines at the top of each page. These will enable him to locate quickly the page on which the word appears. Teachers sometimes have children run races in finding a given word. Those who use these location skills usually win.

If the child has heard, but not read, the word he is looking up, its spelling may cause him some trouble. He may have to try several possible spellings before he finally locates it.

After he has located the word, he may have difficulty in pronouncing it. Here he needs an understanding of the diacritical marks, which are usually found at the bottom of each page, and are explained at the beginning of the dictionary. He also needs to understand how words are divided into syllables, and what the accent marks mean. A child can get excellent practice in using the dictionary by making his own vocabulary-spelling file: a card for each word, which he must divide correctly into syllables.

The third skill is in getting the meaning of the word from the information given. This is a discouraging process when the child has to use an adult dictionary. A simplified dictionary such as the *Thorndike-Barnhart Junior Dictionary* is much better to begin with, since the definitions are stated in words that the child can understand. As he notices how many meanings a word may have, the child will soon realize that he must choose the meaning that fits the context.

When used to the fullest extent, dictionary study can be a liberal education. There is a wealth of fascinating facts in the back pages alone. And the main body embraces words and meanings that have evolved through the centuries as people have used and refined (and misused) the language. Children aged ten and eleven are often fascinated by the dictionary; some ask for a dictionary as a birthday gift.

STUDY-TYPE SKILLS

Study-type skills are usually considered to include the use of tables of contents, indexes, headings, italicized inserts, and other guides to sources of information, and the reading of maps, graphs, and tables. These are skills that children of this age need, and enjoy learning.

As soon as the child has had classroom instruction and practice on a given skill, the parents can give him occasions to use it at home. If he has to find information on a certain topic, let him use the table of contents or index of a book to locate it. If he wants to know whether a given chapter contains information that he needs, suggest that he skim over the chapter, noting especially the headings and italicized words, and the first sentence of each paragraph. If he has had lessons on reading maps, let him figure out the route for your next auto trip. The next time you have to get information about planes or trains, give him addition practice in reading tables. These practical applications not only give the child additional practice but also convince him that school learning is useful.

Parents can often supply source material for the intensive study of a question or topic. These facilities for independent learning include newspapers, news weeklies and other magazines, almanacs, atlases, and other materials that adults use to keep abreast of the times. Children's weeklies such as *My Weekly Reader* and the publications issued by Scholastic Magazines help to bridge the gap between children's reading and adult reading. In school, children should be given instruction in how to select and use these sources of information. At home, they can obtain additional practice and guidance.

Discussion of selected television and radio programs can greatly enrich the child's background in the fields of social studies, science and, to a lesser extent at present, literature. National educational television can make a significant contribution to the enrichment of children's school experience.

READING FOR MEANING

It is fascinating to sit down with a child in these grades and see just how he reads. After introducing him to the selection so that he becomes interested in it and has some purpose in reading it, we let him read it silently. Then ask him to reread it orally, a few sentences at a time, and to express his thoughts as he reads. Then ask him a number of pertinent questions about word meanings, main ideas, details, antecedents and consequences, inferences, generalizations, and the author's intent or purpose. In this way both the adult and the child can learn a great deal about the way he reads—whether he merely skims the surface and picks up separate facts without stopping to interpret or organize them, or whether he moves easily from specifics to generalizations and from literal to applied meanings and evaluations; [5] whether he confuses the author's point of view with his own views and prejudices, or whether his response to reading material is objective rather than personal or emotional.

These skills of interpretation, critical reading, and the making of generalizations should be taught in school. The teacher may direct pupils' attention to the ways in which different authors make their writing effective. "How does the author make you feel as he did about the South Seas? How does he use sights and sounds and odors to create the impression? How does the author capture your attention in the first paragraph? How does he show you that the characters have changed during the course of the story?"—questions like these help the pupils to become sensitive to the elements of effective writing. A greater awareness of the differences between good and poor writing will improve their own writing as well as heightening their enjoyment of reading.

At home, the parents can use more informal discussions of books that they and the children have read to increase the children's literary sensitivity and sharpen their critical judgment.[6]

Books may be read on different levels. For example, *Huckleberry Finn* may be read as a story of a boy's adventures, as an account of life on the Mississippi, as a study in character interpretation, or as an account of the conflict between the social groups represents by Huck Finn's father and by Aunt Polly. Questions such as "What kind of person was Johnny Tremain? Why did he say ... ? What would make him feel and act this way?" evoke a deeper understanding of fictional characters and point up their influence on the reader's own life.

At home, children have freedom to select the books that appeal to them at a given time, that illumine their present or past experiences, that meet an immediate emotional need. The child may not get out of a book what we or certain literary critics think he should get. But we defeat our purpose if we force our interpretation upon the child. Let him interpret the book in the light of his past experiences and in accord with his present needs. Then it makes sense to him; it clarifies his experiences and helps him to understand a little more of his expanding world. In his imagination he can experiment with life without fear of the consequences. In his mind's eye he can try out various ways of handling a given situation, and see more clearly what makes a good life. If he trusts us enough to share some of his insights with us, we must be careful not to discourage his explorations into the realm of the unknown and the spiritual; we must refrain from expressing our own disillusionment or indifference.

In their readings in the social studies children should gain an understanding of other places, times, and people. This kind of reading is in harmony with their desire for independence and for freedom to move beyond the family circle. It is a joy for them to read stories and books that take them into other lands and, nowadays, into outer space. If the social purpose of social studies is to be realized, pupils need to see beyond the detailed facts of geography and history, and come to an understanding of the way people have struggled, and are struggling, to achieve a better life.

For children in the intermediate grades history should come largely in the form of biography. It should be centered on people—not only on the few who have achieved prominence but also on the unknown multitudes: their work, their play, their aspirations, and their collective influence. When history and geography become personalized so that the pupils put themselves in the place of people who are confronted by problems, then they can grasp significances that are not to be gained by memorizing dates, names, and principles. Children of these ages have a creative approach to problems; they are eager to explore new concepts.

To obtain this deep appreciation of times, places, and people, children need much supplementary reading. Fortunately there are many books that children of this age can read independently. Here are some that have been recommended for their understanding of other peoples, of early explorations, of family life.

Easy books include:

Clark, Ann Nolan. *In My Mother's House*. A description of Indian life.
———. *Secret of the Andes*.
Handforth, Thomas. *Mei Li*.
McCloskey, Robert. *Blueberries for Sal*.
———. *One Morning in Maine*.
Politi, Leo. *Juanita*.

For more able readers:

Bleeker, Sonia. *The Cherokee: Indians of the Mountains*.
———. *ThePueblo Indians: Farmers of the Rio Grande*.
Brink, Carol Ryrie. *Caddie Woodlawn*.
Burns, William. *A World Full of Homes*.
———. *America Begins*.

Dalgliesh, Alice. *America Builds Homes.*
Seredy, Kate. *The Good Master.*

Boys enjoy exciting stories of discovery:

Daugherty, James. *Landing of the Pilgrims.*
————. *Of Courage Undaunted.*
Janeway, Elizabeth. *The Vikings.*
Jennings, John. *Clipper Ship Days.*
Neuberger, Richard. *Lewis and Clark Expedition.*
Sperry, Armstrong. *Voyages of Christopher Columbus.*

These and many other books related to the social studies help children to bring a deeper understanding to their reading in the content field.

At home, it is natural for children of these ages to share their parents' interest in the daily newspaper and current magazines. They are already becoming aware of the values to be found in newspaper and magazine reading, and are already growing more selective about the parts they read. Discussion of certain headlines, news reports, and articles stimulates them to think as they read, reflect about what they have read, and relate the ideas they gain from various sources.

Children in the intermediate grades usually look forward eagerly to their science periods. As in the case of social studies, the home can do much to enrich the child's school instruction. Popular science books and magazines both raise and answer questions. Television programs offer glimpses of the adult world of science and of explorations into outer space. Science is news; many references to new discoveries are published in the daily papers. Parents can help children to organize and relate the knowledge they gain from these scattered sources.

From these sources and from classroom experiments pupils acquire the background and mental content that are necessary for comprehending science material. For example, geography and science may be combined in the study of the precipitation on the western and eastern slopes of the Rocky Mountains. Pupils read the rainfall maps and perform an experiment in the science laboratory to answer such questions as:

Which are the prevailing winds laden with moisture?
Why do the winds blow?
Why do they blow from the west?
Why does condensation take place?

INDIVIDUAL DIFFERENCES

Two children in the same family can be quite different in their reading development. Since they have the same parents and have been brought up in the same environment, we expect them to be similar. But they were really *not* brought up in the same environment. Even the physical environment is somewhat different for each one, and the psychological environment may be radically different. The family may have been in a better financial position when the second child was born. The parents may have profited by their experience in bringing up the first child. Different people outside the family may have come in contact with the second child. Many other factors may have made the environment different for the second child than it was for the first. Heredity, too, may have favored one child over the other with respect to mental ability and emotional stability. The only thing to do is to accept these differences and help each child develop his potentialities.

Parents can be glad they are not fifth-grade teachers who have to cope with forty children, some of whom are nonreaders and some of whom have high school reading ability—not to mention still greater differences in personality and background.

How does a teacher with such a variegated class individualize reading instruction? There are many ways of doing this; parents can apply some of them at home.

If the teacher is working with the class as a whole, he may ask different kinds of questions. To Johnny, who is having difficulty in getting the barest meaning from the assignments, the teacher may put a simple factual questions: "Who was President of the United States during the Civil War?" Of Clarence, a superior reader, the teacher may ask a question that requires him to find the antecedents and consequences of a certain event. Similarly, the teacher will vary his assignments in accordance with abilities and needs.

If the students are reading books they have selected, or doing a written assignment, the teacher may take this opportunity to help several of them individually.

If some children are deficient in basic reading skills, the teacher may group them according to their types of difficulty, and give them the instruction and practice they need. A child's difficulty in reading may be aggravated by the attitude of his classmates. A twelve-year-old boy in the sixth grade who was able to read only on the fourth-grade level was ridiculed by his classmates. Their laughter was particularly disturbing to him because he had an unrealistic ambition to become a doctor. He tried to conceal his poor reading ability by reporting higher marks than he really obtained and by taking many books from the library which he could not and did not read. His mother's attitude was scornful rather than sympathetic.

If the subject that is being taught lends itself to division into several topics, the children may choose the topic that interests them most and read to prepare a report on it. Whenever pupils divide themselves in this fashion, each group contains some good readers and some poor readers; the teacher tries to see to it that there is enough reading material on each of the various levels of difficulty so that all the children can make an appropriate contribution.

With the help of the librarian, the teacher also tries to provide a wide range of material for free reading, and to guide individuals in their choices.

Occasionally the teacher asks pupils who, regardless of their ability, are reading well, to describe and discuss their reading and study methods. A pupil may be able to describe effective reading methods to his classmates more clearly than the teacher can.

Finally, the teacher encourages pupils to keep a record of their reading progress. "Nothing succeeds like observed success."

At home, too, in discussing books that the children have read, the parent can vary the questions according to the child's special reading needs and abilities. He can also give the child the practice that is prescribed by the teacher to help him over a specific difficulty, and can provide supplementary leisure reading on the child's independent reading level, whatever that may be.

For exceptional children, an individual approach is certainly needed. Those who are visually handicapped may need other avenues of learning—listening and talking may help them more than reading. All exceptional children need exceptional interest and motivation—though even these cannot overcome lack of basic skills.

The reluctant reader—the child who can read but doesn't—may have one or more of several different attitudes: apathy—"I don't like to read"; a feeling of inadequacy—"I can't read"; or resistance—"I won't read." The approach to a child of this sort should be governed by the attitude. Apathy may be overcome by means of attractive, interesting reading material: for example, stories about the child himself or about other children of his age. A feeling of inadequacy is best dispelled by an experience of success in reading. To combat resistance, it is useful to know something about its origins—whether it stems from parental pressure or parental neglect, from a hopeless sibling rivalry, or some other actual or fancied cause. If one can determine this, one may be able to remove the cause or help the child accept the situation and succeed in spite of it.

SPECIAL HELP FOR READING DIFFICULTIES

When a child appears to lag behind other children of his age in reading, parents begin to worry. They tend to relieve their worry by taking action, often prematurely. In the primary grades, these differences in reading progress should be dealt with by the concerted action of teacher and parent. To refer a child to a clinic at this stage may do more harm than good; it may give the child the impression that something must be very wrong with him and that his parents want to change him.

During the intermediate grades referral to a reading clinic, laboratory, or center may be helpful, depending upon the nature of the reading difficulty and the kind of service that is offered.

Some of these reading centers are part of the public school system, some are privately operated, and a few are connected with mental hygiene or guidance clinics. However, they should all have the same aim: to help each child develop his reading potentialities.

The usual procedure is first to assess the child's potentialities and determine the causes of his reading difficulties. Accordingly, parents are often asked to furnish information about the child's early development and other data that might have a bearing on the reading problem. Information is also obtained from school records, social agencies, and other sources. The initial interview with the child is important in aiding the clinician to understand his attitude toward the situation and to establish a friendly relationship with him.

Appropriate procedures are then used, sometimes with individual children and sometimes with small groups. The worker starts where the child is in his reading development, and builds on his present interests, learning ability, and proficiency.

The role of the parent is to cooperate with the clinic and with the school. Concerted action is necessary. The child himself is a part of the team; he should share, with parents, teachers, and special technicians, the responsibility for developing his reading potentialities.

SUMMARY OF READING OBJECTIVES AND WAYS TO REALIZE THEM

Quick word recognition	Review as necessary skills that have been learned
Increasing word knowledge —key words in each field	Study each new key word when it is introduced Make vocabulary cards or compile a picture dictionary of these words
Location of information skills	Practice using card catalogue, table of contents, index, headings, italics, and other sources and signals
Proficiency in writing a report	Make a tentative outline Find sources Examine sources for accurate, relevant material Select important ideas on the topic Take notes Organize facts Write report, present it in an interesting way
Special skills—reading maps, graphs, tables	Instruction and practice at school, and practice outside school

Wide voluntary reading	{ Read supplementary books in connection with each subject and with outside interests and hobbies
Reading for meaning—recognition of the author's purpose, interpretation of literature on deeper levels, critical thinking	{ Raise thought questions before reading and while reading; look for clues to deeper interpretation; relate to one's own knowledge and experience

It is the child who must take the initiative in improving his reading during the intermediate grades. But teachers and parents can still guide his learning and provide him with instructional material. They can help him to improve his speech; develop his reading vocabulary; use context clues and other word-recognition skills more effectively; locate sources of information; read maps, tables, and graphs; and interpret, organize, and apply what he reads. We are concerned that the child's reading have increasing personal significance for him during these years.

QUESTIONS AND ANSWERS

1. *What can parents do to provide a good home background for the reading development of their children in the intermediate grades?*

Continue the same general procedures that they used in earlier years:

(1) Enjoy reading themselves.

(2) Read aloud stories and other selections that are enjoyable to both parent and child.

(3) Listen to children read or tell about what they have read, when they come home proud of any newly acquired ability or knowledge.

(4) Bring home books that are especially interesting and suitable to the children.

(5) Take the children with you when you go to the library to read.

(6) Don't force reading upon them, but lead them up the path to better reading.

(7) Show them ways in which they can improve, rather than criticize them for lack of improvement.

(8) Capitalize on the children's interests as incentives to read. A TV program or an overnight camping trip may serve as an occasion to introduce books on this subject.

2. *How does television affect children's reading?*

From many studies of this question Paul Witty [7] concludes that about one-third of our children read less than they did before television came in to usurp reading time. The solution is to take positive action—to see that children learn to read well and have continuous opportunity and encouragement to do so.

3. *Is it better for children to read anything than to read nothing?*

This question has generated more heat than light. The most reasonable answer is that we have to start where the child is and gradually help him to climb the ladder of better reading. Some of us are so reluctant to start where children are that one is reminded of the story of the traveler who asked a native the way to Carnavan. The old fellow replied, "If I was going to Carnavan, I wouldn't start from here." On the road to better reading, it would be fine if we could start at a high point of literary quality, but we have to start where the child or adolescent is. We find out what qualities he enjoys in the books he is reading, and try to provide better books that have the swift action, adventure, humor, romance, or heroism that attracts him. Thus he might start with adventure comics, move on to science fiction, Stevenson's *Treasure Island* and *Kidnapped*, and eventually take on a book like *Moby-Dick*. Every child, no matter what his reading ability, can choose to read excellent books on his level.

4. *How can we divert children from reading "trash"?*

We sometimes forget how many insignificant "series books" we ourselves once read with the greatest satisfaction. Some persons of literary stature have testified that "The Rover Boys" or "The Little Colonel" series made a real contribution to the development of their reading interests. Undoubtedly these books meet a need that some children have at a certain stage of their development. In time they usually get tired of them and turn to more mature books. There is, however, a pernicious kind of trash that should be avoided at all age levels. These books give a distorted picture of life, depict sheer violence and brutality, and disparage the good, the true, and the beautiful.

Good teen-age literature helps to bridge the gap between children's books and the classics. Children whose lives have been placid and uneventful cannot suddenly come to appreciate the struggle and despair, the doubt and death and tragedy that are found in great literature. As they grow emotionally they become increasingly capable of seeing the world as it is viewed by great artists.

5. *How can a parent encourage a child to widen his reading interests?*

Many parents are concerned because their child's reading interests are narrow. Gifted children often read intensively in one field. In their case, intensive reading should not be discouraged, but they should be helped to see the connections between their specialty and other areas of knowledge.

David, for example, had an absorbing interest in the conservation of natural resources. He read everything he could find on the subject. So accurate and thorough was his knowledge of conservation that the teacher let him teach this unit to the class in social studies. He brought his pictures and charts and presented his store of information. He even made up a test to give at the end of the unit. The class was interested and appreciative.

The teacher helped David see connections between conservation and other subjects, and interested him in the conservation of human resources. This took him into the realm of literature, especially the personal-social type of novel and short story. The parents agreed to promote these broader interests at home by giving David access to selected books and encouraging him to talk about his reading.

6. *Can a child read too much?*

Few parents worry about this. Today's world is so full of a number of things besides reading that few children read excessively. However, an occasional parent or child may overemphasize reading. For a few individuals reading becomes an escape from the responsibilities and disappointments of life. Wisely chosen books that deal realistically with problems of human relations may give insights that can be applied to their own lives.

7. *What are some ways to encourage voluntary reading and make it a lifetime habit?*

Reading interest often stems from other interests. Trips to exciting places, nature walks, hobbies, special projects—all may require reading that opens new vistas and leads on to more reading.

Friends are influential. You are lucky if your child's friends enjoy reading and share their reading interests with one another. Membership in teen-age book clubs may convince the child that reading is approved by his peers.

By promoting discussions of current events and books at home, you may raise questions that can be answered only by further reading.

Children should be encouraged to make trips to the library or bookmobile. If the child cannot go himself, the parent can bring home books that accord with the child's interests and reading ability. These should be neither too hard nor too easy—books that the child can read independently with pleasure.

Give the child carefully chosen books on various occasions, along with other things that he especially wants.

Subscribe to a children's magazine or a teen-age magazine or book club. Most children are thrilled to get things through the mail. They enjoy building a library that is their very own.

8. *What kinds of summer reading programs are possible?*

Before the end of school it would be a good idea to ask the teacher about the child's present reading ability, the kinds of books he can read independently, and the kinds of experiences he needs. Parents should welcome a frank appraisal of their child's reading. It would be helpful if the teacher were to furnish a list of suitable books in various fields that are easy enough for the child to read with enjoyment. This kind of reading would build up the child's confidence, increase his fluency, and broaden his vocabulary.

Summer trips enlarge the child's background of experience, and this enlargement facilitates meaningful reading and speaking.

If there is a public library in the vicinity, children should be encouraged to make use of it in their vacation time.

If there is no library, the school might arrange to circulate books through its library, or even give each child five or six suitable books that he could take home as his own summer library.

To prevent books from being crowded out of the vacation schedule, it is helpful to have a planned time for reading. The child should select the time of day that he would prefer to set aside as "reading time." However, the schedule should not become a fetish. Exceptions should be made if other valuable activities occasionally become available in the reading time.

9. *Why do not all the children in a grade have the same reader?*

Sometimes they do, but they go through it at different rates. When the good readers have convinced the teacher by their superior performance that they have mastered the basic skills that are taught in that particular grade, they turn to other books, which they can read independently.

Sometimes there are three groups of readers in a class. One group is reading above their grade level, another group is reading about on their grade level, and the third group is reading below grade. For these three groups different books are provided. No one book would be challenging enough for the best readers and simple enough for the poorest readers.

Multilevel reading material provides for a wide range of reading ability. The Reading Laboratories, developed by Don Parker and published by Science Research Associates, consist of a graded series of boxes. Each Laboratory includes pamphlets on six or seven levels of difficulty. The articles are highly interesting; there are questions to test the pupils' reading abilities; and the system of scoring and score recording on each lesson stimulates pupils to do better next time. As soon as they can read well on their present level, they progress to the next higher set of pamphlets. Both teachers and pupils are enthusiastic about these "Reading Laboratories," which are being used by millions of children.

10. *What do reading scores mean?*

Scores on reading tests may be misleading. A test says that a child is reading on the fifth-grade level. You give him a fifth-grade book and he stumbles through it, comprehending little. What was wrong with the test? In the first place, some children are clever at guessing the right answers to multiple-choice questions; they do not really comprehend the selection. Second, the test score may reflect the child's frustration level—that is, the level at which his reading ability breaks down—not his independent reading level. Third, some children, especially those who have eye defects or a short attention span, can do quite well on a short test but not on a sustained reading task. Fourth, reading tests measure only a limited number of reading skills, perhaps not the one that is required for the book you handed the alleged fifth-grade reader.

Thus reading tests give only a general idea of how well a child reads as compared with other children of his age and grade. If he has high mental ability and a home background that encourages reading, you can expect his score to be higher than the average. If he is generally slow in learning and immature for his age, his score will probably be below average.

The best way to find out how well he reads is to ask him to read different kinds of material, beginning with easy selections and going on to more difficult ones. As he reads aloud a paragraph or two, you can note any difficulty that he may have in word recognition, phrasing, or expression. After he has read a passage silently, you can see how well he answers questions that indicate his comprehension of the passage.

In this way a teacher or parent can find out exactly how a child reads. At the same time, he can show him how to read the passage more effectively. This procedure will also indicate what kinds of books you can suggest for his independent reading.

11. *Why should a child be promoted to the next grade when he isn't reading up to his present grade level?*

If the child is big for his age, if he has a younger brother or sister who would be in the same grade with him if he were left back, if he hasn't got along very well with his present teacher, and if the teacher in the next higher grade is skillful in providing for individual differences, then it would probably be better to promote the child even though he is reading below his grade level.

If none of these conditions prevail, and both the child and the parent believe that another year in the same grade would help him to gain the reading skills in which he is deficient, then it would probably be wise for him to remain in that grade for another year or at least another semester. If a child is pushed into a grade that is above his present ability, he may feel like a drowning man, unable to keep his head above water.

12. *How can we help to speed up our child's learning so that he will be promoted with his class and be up to grade level in the fall?*

First, we should learn more about the child. Does he seem to be trying as hard as he can? Is he worried about being behind the other children in his class? What are his reading difficulties? Has he had special instruction in reading during the year? How much did he profit by it? What are his summer plans? Would going to summer school deprive him of outdoor play and social activities that he needs for his best development?

The answers to these and other questions would help us to determine (1) whether the child should try to improve his reading, and (2) if so, what summer plan would be best for him.

If the child has a naturally slow rate of learning and is maturing slowly, putting pressure on him might have an unfavorable effect on his total development. It would be better for him to have a healthful, happy summer and read as many easy, interesting books as possible. This would increase his vocabulary and fluency, and prepare him to profit by the reading instruction in whichever grade he enters next fall.

If the child's unsatisfactory performance in reading is due to poor previous instruction, frequent absences, or an emotional disturbance, a summer program in a reading center should help him to recognize his deficiencies, assess his present ability, and make progress, perhaps up to the next grade level.

13. *How does comparing a child with other children affect his reading?*

Instead of stimulating a child to read better, invidious comparisons may set him back. If the brother or cousin has higher general ability, we are setting an impossible goal. Moreover, comparisons may give the poor reader the impression that we care more for the other child than we do for him. One boy sensed that his parents felt this way; he said, "They really don't care for me—only that I be a credit to them."

Comparing the child with Uncle Jim or with Father in his younger days may have a variety of effects. If Dad, who is now a successful businessman, didn't learn to read, why should the child bother? If the child is fond of Uncle Jim, who is also a poor reader, the comparison may confirm his idea of himself as a poor reader. If an adult whom the child dislikes is held up as a model reader, the child will not want to emulate this quality.

Children usually resent comparisons. We should help each child to establish individual standards that he can achieve with satisfaction and without undue competition.

SEVEN

Reading Development During Adolescence

AN ADOLESCENT boy made this comment: "Parents pay a lot of attention to their children during the early years, but neglect them more and more as they grow up." This tendency is due partly to the adolescent's apparent rejection of parental authority and supervision and partly to the parent's feeling of inadequacy to guide an adolescent's learning.

The home loses much of its influence as the peer group comes to be a decisive arbiter. For example, in the matter of speech, a word sounds right to an adolescent if it is used by the clique or gang, and wrong if it is not. School and neighborhood associates compete with parents and teachers as authorities on preferred usage. Similarly, values, standards, and purposes are shaped by the dominant attitudes of the group. Only a very mature youngster dares to be different.

In his schoolwork as well as in his social relations, the junior and senior high school student is growing away from his parents. He is becoming more and more independent. It is much harder for parents to help him with his homework. They are unfamiliar with many of the books and assignments that he brings home.

As the child moves from elementary into junior high school, the required reading becomes more voluminous and more complex. His textbook assignments are longer, he has more reference reading to do, more facts to organize more abstract concepts to comprehend, more need for critical and interpretative reading skills.

In his survey of the junior high school, James B. Conant [1] stated that students need at least sixth-grade reading ability to succeed in high school.

Reading instruction should be continued throughout the high school years; it is especially needed in the seventh and eighth grades. These are the strategic years in which to perfect the basic word-recognition and comprehension skills, and to develop the more complex techniques of interpretation, critical reading, and application.

CHARACTERISTICS OF TEEN-AGERS

In the early adolescent period, between the ages of twelve and fifteen, youngsters are sorting out and revising their childhood values and traits of behavior. Reading should make an important contribution to their personal development. In order to do so, reading must compete with many other attractions: TV, disc-jockey shows, social dancing, clubs, sports, and other preferred leisure activities. A tenth-grade girl described one possible way of putting books on an equal footing:

My parents have always encouraged me to read. They have built a library of classics, . . . beautifully bound. In spite of the encouragement of teachers and my parents, I have read a small number of books. I find it hard to get interested enough to read a good book, the main reasons being that I don't have much time and I'd rather do other things than read. Once I do get into a good book, however, I can hardly keep away from it.

This year I explained my problem to my dad who solved it very quickly. He said I had to read at least one book a week before I could go to any of my club meetings after school. Every week he assigns me a certain book to read, usually a classic or a good novel. This week I am reading *The Moonstone*, which is proving very interesting.

Despite the competition of other activities, many teen-agers maintain a lively interest in voluntary reading. The following composition, entitled "Future Readers of America," by a gifted high school girl bespeaks a remarkable degree of maturity:

In this scientific, well educated world of today, good reading ability and background are essential parts of a youngster's schooling, both elementary and higher. Without the ability to read and comprehend easily, how can a young person be expected to understand newspaper editorials and keep up on current events? How can anyone poor in reading expect to successfully complete high school and enter the competitive college race, when so much depends on the ability and ease with which words are read and used? The answers to both these questions illustrate the fact that reading is an important part of a child's life; it is up to us, the future parents, to prepare to instill an interest in literature in our own children and those of others.

During the last year, I read an article by a mother of two teen-age sons who, since her boys could read, has set aside a certain time in the evening for a "reading hour." During this time, her whole family puts away whatever each member is doing and reads various books and articles together or separately; how much better this must be for children than to be wasting time on cowboy programs or cartoons! If I am ever fortunate enough to have my own family, a "reading hour" will certainly be part of each day, for an hour a day would instill good reading habits in almost any child.

In my own future home, there will be plenty of good reading material where youngsters can reach it, and the titles will not all be of children's books. When I was nine, Mother gave me *Tale of Two Cities* for Christmas; I read one chapter, became thoroughly bored, and put it back on the shelf. This incident repeated itself three more times, about once every two years, and finally six years after receiving the book, I was able to see through Dickens' longwindedness to the warmly emotional plot and magnificent characters. When I commented on how long it had taken me to read her gift, Mother confided that her parents had done the same thing and that it had taken her almost as long to enjoy *Tale of Two Cities!* This same thing has happened with other classics; just having the books around made them seem like old friends and encouraged me to finally read and understand them.

Besides preparing to interest future children, there are certain things I and others of my age can do now to "inspire" young readers. I leave my own dusty store of Terhune, Nancy Drew, the Alcott series, and other well-loved children's classics to any neighborhood child who wants to use them; one third-grader even wrote a book report on *Little Women* which won a prize at school. This is not a particularly exciting or amazing feat, but it feels good to know that it was my book which supplied all the enthusiastic enjoyment shown in the report!

Another method which I have unconsciously used to stimulate my younger brother's interest is taking part in my parents' discussions of books. It made me feel very grown up to see David's wide eyes when I coyly mentioned one of my books, so when *he* began to join in, it became an all-out battle to see who could read the best and the most books!

With more and more stress being put upon reading and English skills in schools, it seems reasonable that a child's grade-school teachers will give him most of his background in reading; but the fact remains that it is in the youngster's home life that he gets a good part of his interest.

Today and in the future, I shall try my best to introduce as many young readers as possible to the wonderful world of books.

As we have already suggested, the adolescent is extremely sensitive to the opinion of his peers. If his gang scoffs at the bookworm, he may suppress his genuine interest in reading. On the other hand, the enthusiasm of his friends may stimulate him to do more voluntary reading. In the words of another tenth-grade girl:

Most all of my friends read a lot, and their interest in certain books often rubs off on me. When one of my friends has read a good book, his enthusiasm often causes my reading it also. I notice I do the same thing and recommend a great many books to my friends.[2]

Sometimes a small group of popular boys or girls can overcome their classmates' indifference or hostility to reading by taking a firm stand for intellectual interests. They may form a Great Books Club, meet regularly to do dramatized readings of one-act plays, or select stories to read to children in a recreation center or hospital.

The adolescent's exuberant urge for independence tends to subside by the senior year of high school. At first, adolescents crave only the freedom of staying up late, choosing their own clothes, going places without adults. As they grow older they become more aware of the responsibility that accompanies freedom.[3] They read more serious books: descriptions of various careers, true-to-life stories, and biographies of people who have faced life's problems courageously. In their reading they seek answers to their questions of *who they are, where they are going,* and *why*.[4]

In addition to these common characteristics, we find all sorts of individual differences in ability, interests, achievement, attitudes, and values. All of these factors influence an adolescent's response to reading. They determine what he reads, how he reads, and why he reads.

READING DEVELOPMENT DURING HIGH SCHOOL YEARS, AND WAYS OF ACHIEVING IT

For some children, the junior high school period is a kind of renaissance. They enter this new era in their school life hopefully. They should have all the help they need in mastering these reading skills that will be their chief tools of learning:

Location of information skills
{ Real problems to solve
{ Reports to write

Word-recognition skills
  Context clues
  Prefixes, suffixes, and roots
  Rapid recognition of word
    meaning; fewer clues
    needed
{ Exercises prepared by students
{ Practice in solving unfamiliar
{   words by appropriate methods,
{   using a minimum number of
{   clues

Vocabulary building
  Precise and vivid usage
  Semantic interpretation
{ Preliminary or subsequent study
{   of words in selections read
{ Collecting synonyms and homonyms
{ Interesting word origins
{ Interpretation of symbols

Ability to organize and
communicate ideas gained
from reading
{ Discussion of books
{ Practice in making written and
{   oral outlines and summaries

Ability to interpret
  Read critically
  Draw sound conclusions
  Make generalizations
{ Instruction and practice in finding
{   and interpreting clues to character,
{   plot
{ Material that requires this kind
{   of reading
{ Stating purpose for reading

Increased appreciation
{ Orientation to the selection
{ Discussion of characters,
{   motives, etc.

Expanding interests
{ Individual reading plans
{ Conferences with teacher
{ Publicizing of books

Concern for quality
{ Comparing books of different
{   quality
{ Development of criteria

Increasing fluency, adjusting
rate to purpose and motives
{ Time limits
{ Exercises in reading for
{   different purposes

Appropriate methods for
different subjects and kinds
of material
  Pleasure in precision
{ Demonstrations and instruction
{   in how to read effectively
{   in each subject

Location of Information Skills

During the high school years the student develops his ability to write reports on various topics. This requires searching more widely than he did in the lower grades for sources of information. Parents can sometimes help by giving him access to references that are not in the school library. They may also help the student to select information that is pertinent to the topic and to evaluate its relevancy, accuracy, and adequacy. By discussing the topic with members of his family, the student may get a sense of the structure of his materials and a better idea of how to organize his report and present it interestingly. Of course, all these skills should be taught in school, but they may be developed by the interest and cooperation of the parents.

Clues from Context

Although the child has long been using context clues to get word meanings, he will continue to use them all his life; he should become more and more expert in recognizing subtle indications of character, of motives, and of cause-and-effect sequences.

During the high school years, the student will probably get more instruction and practice in recognizing and interpreting context clues. (McCullough gives examples of a variety of context clues.[5]) He will become more adept at using various clues to meaning. He will look carefully at pictures and diagrams. Well-chosen charts and illustrations make certain meanings much clearer than any verbal explanation could do. For example, how could you describe a space ship as clearly as a color photograph would do, with a man beside it to give an idea of its relative size? In some instances, a picture *is* worth a thousand words. For more abstract ideas, a diagram may be still better; it can focus on essential principles and relationships, ignoring the irrelevant details that might be present in a photograph.

A second common context clue is furnished by the reader's experience. Some city children would have no difficulty in supplying the word *delicatessen* in the sentence: "Cooked food is sold in a _____ store." Any reader who was familiar with the ways of pickpockets from reading *Oliver Twist* would have a fairly clear idea of the meaning of *deftness* in the sentence: "He removed the watch with the *deftness* of a pickpocket."

Synonyms give specific clues: "He had never been so gay; he was simply buoyant."

Sometimes the meaning of a word is given in a summary statement: "She was *disheveled* in appearance. Her hair was dirty and uncombed. Her dress was torn and stained and falling off one shoulder."

A mood or situation that is first described may then be crystallized in a single word whose meaning thus becomes plain: "The day was dull—the air was oppressive. This dreary landscape cast a *melancholy* spell over him."

In textbooks, a definition frequently explains the unknown word: "The land was dry and sandy; it was a *desert*."

A familiar expression may suggest a clue: "As *famished* as a bear" suggests the more familiar "As hungry as a bear."

Of course, getting the meaning from context is not always so easy as in the example we have given. Quite often, no context clues are to be found. However, all readers need a battery of skills for searching the text itself for possible meanings of unfamiliar words.

Literary Interpretation

When you read a story you would probably enjoy it more if you looked for the subtle clues that the author gives to help you understand the characters, and anticipate developments in the plot. Students are taught to do this in school. It makes reading more meaningful and enjoyable to them.

The teacher may demonstrate the process of clue recognition and interpretation with the entire class as they read a story together. They may go through the process together a number of times. Then the students read a story at home and the next day in class discuss the clues they have found and the interpretations they have given to them. After they have learned how to do so, and have discovered the interest and depth it adds to their reading, they will continue to read in this way on their own.

Some clues make clear the physical appearance of the characters and the setting. These may comprise a direct description like this: "The cook squatted in the bottom and looked with both eyes at the six inches of gunwale which separated him from the ocean. His sleeves were rolled over his fat forearms, and the two flaps of his unbuttoned vest dangled as he bent to bail out the boat." Or a few significant details: "In the wan light, the faces of the men must have been gray. Their eyes must have glinted in strange ways as they gazed steadily astern."

Or the clue may lie in the character's own speech or action: "The cook had said: 'There's a house of refuge just north of the Mosquito Inlet Light, and as soon as they see us, they'll come off in their boat and pick us up.' 'As soon as who sees us?' said the correspondent." The three preceding quotations were from Stephen Crane's "The Open Boat."

Appearance may also be implied by a suggestive observation: "At the very sight of her, children would stop their merry chatter and freeze in their places."

Similarly, feelings, moods, motives, and intentions may be inferred from the character's statements, tones of voice, actions, reactions, and the responses they evoke from others. Figures of speech, subtle shades of meaning, irony, sarcasm—all these literary devices point to meanings.

The setting and mood of a story may be inferred from its opening sentences: "None of them knew the color of the sky. Their eyes glanced level, and were fastened upon the waves that swept toward them" (Stephen Crane, "The Open Boat").

The title may contain a clue: "The Phantom of Buck Hill Caves," "The Spell of the Yukon."

Appreciation of humor sometimes requires recognition of double meanings, as in Mercutio's words describing his fatal wound: " 'Tis not so deep as a well, nor so wide as a church door, but 'tis enough, 'twill serve. Ask for me tomorrow and you shall find me a grave man." A word may be given an unexpected or absurd meaning by the turn of a phrase. A situation may be so outrageously exaggerated that it becomes hilarious. Cumulative detail may make a character appear more and more ludicrous.

Inferences about a character's appearance, personality, and changes in personality are based on the cumulative effect of separate clues scattered throughout the story. For example, the change in Silas

Marner that is brought about by the presence of the little child may
be inferred from statements such as the following:

"Gold—his own gold—brought back to him as mysteriously as it had
been taken away! . . . He leaned forward at last, and stretched forth
his hand; but instead of the hard coin with the familiar resisting outline,
his fingers encountered soft warm curls."

"Presently she slipped from his knee and began to toddle about, but
with a pretty stagger that made Silas jump up and follow her lest she
should fall against anything that would hurt her."

These few examples suggest how much students need to learn
about the subtle aspects of interpretation. To be sure, a few youngsters need no help in learning to read with keen appreciation. But
most students profit by class instruction in recognizing and interpreting the clues from which inferences may be drawn.[6]

Thus the reader enters into the thoughts and feelings of the characters, follows the interaction of characters and events, and pictures the whole story in his imagination. Good readers do this. They
prefer reading to television because it gives them a chance to use
their imagination.

To do successful interpretation of this kind independently, the
reader should choose books that are appropriate to his reading ability and emotional maturity. Some fifteen- and sixteen-year-olds can
bring real understanding to books like *Silas Marner, A Tale of Two
Cities, Winter Wheat*. Others would gain more from books like
Johnny Tremain, Hill Doctor, and *To Tell Your Love*. Still others
can read with pleasure and profit simpler books such as *Two Logs
Crossing, Going on Sixteen, Escape on Skis*. The child gains nothing
by floundering about in books that are beyond his reading capacity
or emotional readiness. When he has acquired skill on an initially
appropriate level, the individual should raise the quality and broaden
the scope of his reading interests.

The child's response to a book indicates whether he is ready for it.
Parents sometimes choose books the child lacks the capacity to
understand or enjoy, or expect a depth of interpretation of which he
is not capable. Children, too, in their anxiety to please the parent or
gain prestige among their peers, choose books that they had better
leave until later.

Increased awareness of the many factors involved in interpretation enables parents to help children apply and enhance what they have learned in school. In discussing a book with the child or in reading aloud in a family group, parents can increase both their own enjoyment and that of their children by paying attention to plot and character clues, figures of speech, and subtle humor, and by stopping occasionally to reflect upon a word or a phrase or to trace a sequence of cumulative impressions.

Parents further strengthen teachers' instruction in literature by helping adolescents go beyond a knowledge of "who did what and when." In their conversation with the children they can consider such questions as these: What was the author's purpose in writing the book? What was its thesis? Do you agree with it? What kind of philosophy—materialistic or idealistic—does the author emphasize? Do the characters do what they do because of their deep-seated personality traits, or are their actions unpredictable and subject to blind chance? Comparing a classic with a modern book is especially useful in bringing out certain unchanging elements in human nature, and the way writers depict them in different situations.

The teacher will usually give students a list of recommended books from which they may choose. Students like this degree of freedom. There is something in adolescents that resists required reading. One youngster advised: "If I wanted to stimulate a young person's reading, I would have his teachers encourage reading and make as many good books on his level as possible available. In his family I would never try to force reading on him. I would have his parents encourage reading, but leave it completely up to the individual to decide to read."

However, some young people admit that they are now glad someone made them read certain books. "After the first few chapters," they say, "we became interested and were glad we read it."

Thinking While Reading

In these days when there is so much propaganda in circulation, our young people must learn to recognize a writer's intent so that they will not accept blindly whatever they read or hear. The process of learning to think while reading begins in the first grade and continues throughout high school. The teacher must ask searching questions and use other means to teach students to distinguish between fact and opinion, to test the accuracy of statements, and to appraise the soundness of an author's inferences, conclusions, and generalizations.

Recognizing the Author's Intent—The importance of knowing something about the author and his intent was brought out clearly in an experiment in which high school students were asked to read a parody by Mark Twain of a sentimental overblown style of writing. The students did not know the author's name, and did not think about what his purpose might have been in writing the paragraph. Practically all of them took it seriously, not realizing that it was satirical.

To avoid such misinterpretations and to encourage critical reading, teachers give students practice in recognizing the author's intent. They ask such questions as these: Is he trying to inform, amuse, persuade, prejudice, or otherwise influence the reader? Or is he neutral, maintaining a take-it-or-leave-it attitude toward the reader? Putting the onus on the reader, is there likely to be anything in the reader's background and attitudes that might lead him to interpret the facts incorrectly, or remember only those details that support his point of view?

Thinking About Words—In secondary school, word study attains new importance. One teacher played the overture of an opera over and over while the students wrote on the board all the words the music suggested to them. One boy said, "I never want to hear that overture again, but that was when words first became fascinating to me." Other teachers ask students to think of substitutes for a given word such as *said*—words that have different shades of meaning—and use these words in sentences or in a short story.

Students also learn that there are various levels of abstraction; one begins with a concrete object in a specific situation, and then becomes more and more general: for example, a Newton Pippin→apple→fruit→food. They observe how, as the level of abstraction increases, readers bring an increasing number of different meanings to the word *democracy*, for example, or *security*. High school students find this kind of semantic analysis fascinating. They also enjoy looking for the symbolic meaning that lies behind a word or phrase. They like to pick out signal words and phrases such as *but, moreover, on the other hand,* that give clues to organization.

Some classes write word autobiographies in which they assume the role of the word: telling its history, how it originated, what its original meaning was, how the meaning changed, how it is used today. They may find or draw pictures that show its use or meaning, and write sentences illustrating its use. Parents should not be surprised if their teen-agers begin to cut up magazines to find pictures that aptly illustrate the word meanings they are studying. We should encourage their enthusiasm and aid them in seeing more deeply into words.

Interpreting Sayings—Another kind of experience that promotes thinking while reading involves the interpretation of sayings and proverbs. For example, the saying, "Trifles make perfection but perfection is no trifle." When asked to interpret this saying, in his own words, one eighth-grade pupil wrote: "To me this means doing little or trifling things makes one perfect, but after you are perfect, there is nothing little or trifling about that."

When asked to interpret the saying, "The secret of happiness is not doing what one likes but liking what one has to do," another eighth-grade student wrote: "To me this means to find happiness, one cannot do what he likes all the time, but when he has something to do that he does not like, it will make him a lot happier if he learns to like what he has to do."

Thinking to Solve Problems—Thinking is stimulated if there is a problem to be solved, a situation to be handled, a practice to be improved. Thinking does not take place in a vacuum. That is why the most skillful teachers, in presenting a problem whose solution requires reading, make the situation vivid and personal, and raise questions that will help to clarify difficulties.

In history, for example, one teacher used the "you-were-there" technique. The students read concrete descriptions of an event, and imagined that they themselves were participating in it—how they felt, what they were thinking, what they thought should be done, and what they thought would follow if it were done. Then they consulted reliable sources to find out what actually happened in consequence of the event. The best approach to thoughtful reading is guidance in finding solutions to real problems.

Examining Sources—Critical reading is essential to the writing of reports or themes. After the student has located sources on the topic, he must examine them critically, asking such questions as these:

Will it serve my purpose?
Is it an original document or someone's comment on a document?
Is it sufficiently specific?
Is it up to date?
Is the author an authority on the subject?
Is his intent to inform or to persuade?
Does he discriminate between fact and opinion?

When students are reading different books on a topic, they will often find differences of opinion. Exercises such as the following help them to distinguish between fact and opinion. Are these statements facts or opinions?

The New York Central railroad trains are never on time.
The train this morning was ten minutes late.
California is the most beautiful state in the union.

Students learn to look for clues that indicate statements of opinion rather than fact:

It is believed . . .
According to authorities . . .

Students also learn that the value of an opinion depends on the degree to which it can be substantiated, on the amount and accuracy of the information on which it is based.

Detecting Propaganda—High school students enjoy a unit on propaganda analysis. They start with advertisements and TV commercials. They may reject the criteria on which a judgment is made: "Everyone uses Sunrise cereal." Or they may question the validity of generalized statements. "No young person can succeed without a college education." They detect bias that stems from the omission of facts on the opposite side of the argument, words that are quoted out of context, words that purport to be factual but carry an emotional charge, half-truths, exaggerated statements, and similar devices used with intent to influence the reader.

From the study of propaganda, teachers move into the interpretation of more subtle literary devices: metaphors, irony, satire, parody, and others.

Finding Applications—When students read critically and creatively, their purpose is not merely to find out what happened and what the people did, but why it happened and why they did it.

Many students are content to read superficially and thoughtlessly unless they are challenged. They can be challenged by thought-provoking questions:

1. Can you think of similar situations today?
2. Will the solutions you've read about be applicable today? Why or why not?
3. What results of that past event still persist today?
4. Does the description you have read give us any understanding of the ways people act today?
5. What motives might have prompted the peoples' action at that time?
6. How is this event related to what went before and came after?
7. What additional information do you need? Where can you find it?

These are some of the ways in which teachers systematically help students to read critically and think about what they read.

The Role of Parents—Parents may informally guide their children's thinking in similar ways. If Jeanie comes home with a history assignment, Mother or Father may talk with her about it before she begins to read. They may be able to recall incidents or details that make the time and place seem less remote. They may help her to see the event as a problem that people of that time had to solve. This will encourage her to speculate about what happened, and then read eagerly to see whether she was right. After she has read the selection, she may want to discuss it with her parents in order to add their experience to hers for its interpretation.

This approach is quite different from the one we usually use in helping a child with his homework. It is more like two adults discuss-

ing a topic in which both are interested. Both enjoy the experience
and learn from it.

EXPANDING READING INTERESTS AND APPRECIATIONS

Reading contributes to the adolescent's expanding world, as do selected programs on television. Both take him far afield in time and
space. In the following account, a gifted fifteen-year-old girl describes her expanding reading interests:

This morning, I finished Dickens' immortal novel, *Tale of Two Cities*.
As I cried over Carton's heart-rending last thoughts, I began to think of
how terrible it would be not to be able to take pleasure in such great
works as those of Dickens, Poe, Shakespeare, and others. I think that the
gift of ease, enjoyment, and interest in good reading material is one of
the greatest that schools and parents can bestow on young people, and I
am thankful for some very understanding persons who helped me along
the "royal road to literature."

Mother influenced my interests in literature. Of course I went through
the horse story stage and, later, the teen-age romances, but since the age
of seven I have, for many years, been reading and enjoying historical
novels. Mother taught history before she was married, and the only books
I ever received for Christmas were about Queen Elizabeth, King Louis,
or some similar topic!

The point at which I was doing the most reading was about five or six
years ago. During the spring and fall I would be sick with asthma most
of the time and often would read fifteen or twenty books a week. These,
of course, were mostly children's books, but here I became acquainted
with classics such as *David Copperfield, Secret Garden,* and the entire
Alcott series.

Only this year have I started picking up the works of Schweitzer,
Shakespeare, and other great minds, and I do not thoroughly understand
this thought-provoking literature as of yet. But I hope and feel sure that
the interest and understanding will grow with time and that I can look
forward to enjoying good reading material for the rest of my life.

Parents and teachers may expect teen-agers to grow in their
ability to make deeper interpretations of books and to show increased
skill in finding clues to character and plot that make voluntary reading more creative and rewarding. They may also expect them to
show increased ability to grasp the author's pattern of thought as

they read, to make a creative summary, and to read fast when skimming is appropriate.

INCREASING INDEPENDENCE

During the senior high school years students should take more responsibility for their own improvement in reading. Some teachers let each student choose a topic on which he wants to read intensively. From time to time the teacher will have a conference with the student to discuss the books he has read and to suggest others along similar lines.

When special reading groups are formed, juniors and seniors often join them voluntarily. They are eager to take advantage of opportunities to improve their reading. This represents admirable growth in self-direction. They no longer depend on parents or teachers to make them do what they ought to do.

PERSONAL DEVELOPMENT THROUGH READING DURING ADOLESCENCE

Why do we read? Do not most of the objectives as stated represent means to personal development? Through reading, the adolescent may identify himself with heroes he would like to emulate, with persons who have admirable character traits and exemplify them in action. He compares his own character as he sees it with that of persons in fiction or biography who were courageous and resourceful in difficult situations.

By changing the ways in which young people perceive reality, books may influence their vocational aims, help to shape their philosophy of life, give them insights into their own lives and the lives of others, and develop in them a sense of destiny. After children have mastered the mechanics of reading, it becomes a thinking-feeling-responding process.

The degree to which a book influences a child or young person depends on his need at the time, the intensity with which he identifies himself with the characters, and his ability to place himself in the situations they are facing. Readers extract from a book what they need at a particular time. This is not always exactly what the author intended to communicate or what parents and teachers thought the individual should get out of the reading. Efficient readers who have to cover a large amount of reading material use a method of judicious selection; they extract from books, newspapers, and magazines ideas that are pertinent to the problems with which they are concerned.

We cannot measure the exact extent to which reading changes young people in this flexible, unstable period of their lives. However, we do have many introspective reports in which high school students describe how books and articles have influenced their points of view, attitudes, and behavior. They tell how books have helped them to find goals and persist in their efforts to attain them, have made them more understanding of their parents and brothers and sisters, have helped them clarify their religious perplexities, and have led them to think about life decisions and commitments.

EFFECTIVE INSTRUCTION

In junior high school you may expect your child to be given instruction in the reading of every subject. When he enters the class in science, English, or social studies, the teacher will want to find out how well he can read the text or reference books that are to be used. The student will read a selection, write a summary, answer specific questions, and define the key words and concepts. By scoring and discussing their answers, the students learn what kind and degree of comprehension the subject requires—and where they fall short. They are then receptive to instruction in the reading skills in which they are deficient.

The teacher will also demonstrate effective study approaches to each type of assignment. The students will practice each one until they have acquired sufficient proficiency. Then they will know how to select and use the best reading method for each day's study.

The key words and concepts in each subject require special instruction. The teacher will bring as much meaning and interest as possible to each new word as it is introduced. Students will share their experiences with the word, find pictures that illustrate its meaning, and use it in their conversation. They may make individual dictionaries or a class dictionary of the new words they have learned.

At home parents can encourage their children to talk about the interesting ideas they have gained in each subject, to see relationships among them, and to find applications for them in their own lives. They can help children tremendously by enriching the meanings of new words; they can describe their own experiences, show the children pictures, take them on trips to historic places, and give them access to selected radio and TV programs. With suggestions from the teacher, parents can make available additional reading material that will enrich the subject for an able reader, or develop the specific skills and abilities that another child may need. Enrichment of the single basal reader or textbook by many supplementary books is common practice today in the teaching of all subjects.

Books should be easily available. We often pick up a book that is lying around, when we would not bother to get the book from the library. Youngsters do likewise. They may also prefer buying a paperback book at the corner drugstore or stationery store to going to the library. Although the number of high-quality paperbacks is increasing, they are still in the minority among the lurid volumes on display in most stores.

In English classes, teachers are putting increasing emphasis on the deeper interpretation of literature. One boy expressed appreciation of his freshman English teacher's approach to reading: "Sure I knew how to read when I was his pupil. But he taught me to read for meaning and the idea in the story, not just the story itself."

Occasionally the class may undertake a word-by-word analysis; they compile all the possible meanings of a word and decide which is the most exact. Sometimes it takes a sentence or a paragraph to clarify the meaning of a single word. To determine an author's full and precise meaning, one needs to understand his overt or hidden intention, know something of his life and times, and assess his attitude toward himself, his reader, and his subject.

The questions that the teacher asks about chapters in history or the social studies should accord with his main purpose in teaching the subject. It is generally agreed that the main purpose in these subjects is to help the pupil understand his world and assess his relation to its diverse population, in order that he may become a more effective participant in it.

In accord with this purpose, the questions the teacher asks about the student's reading are not all of a simple factual nature. Many of them are designed to bring out relationships, sequences of events, conditions that gave rise to important moments or periods of history;

in short, the student should consider how the present grew out of the past, and what changes and trends should be encouraged in the future. Such questions as the following might serve these purposes:

What conditions led up to Paul Revere's Ride?

What countries have lost their colonies in far corners of the world in recent times? What were the reasons behind their desire for independence? What problems has this independence created, for example, in the Congo? Home discussions of similar questions would help children read history more effectively.

Parents may encourage supplementary reading that is related to the period of history their children are currently studying. For example, one advanced class, in studying the American Revolution, read Carl Van Doren's *Mutiny in January* and *Secret History of the American Revolution*, Kenneth Roberts's *Oliver Wiswell*, and Esther Forbes's *Paul Revere*. Another group used the Reader's Guide to locate the facts about Woodrow Wilson's philosophy as seen in articles published in the 1920's and in articles published in the 1940's. This was preliminary to writing their own estimate of Wilson's ideas.

Able learners are especially happy when they have a wealth of reading material, freedom of choice, and opportunity to discuss the ideas they have gained from reading. The ideas they bring to family discussions are often as stimulating to the adults as to the other young people. Parents can keep in touch not only with what is going on in the school but also, to some extent, with what is going on in the world, by sharing their children's school interests.

In addition to giving instruction in the reading of every subject, your school may offer special courses in reading. These may take many forms. One type of program is called individualized reading. The teacher, usually with the help of the librarian, provides books for every member of the class. These are suitable to various degrees of reading ability and appealing to varied interests. Each student chooses the book he wants, reads it independently, and writes a book review of it. During this free reading time the teacher has ten-minute conferences with individuals who need help. The period of silent reading is followed by a class discussion of the books the students have read. Thus the students are getting experience in reading, speaking, listening. But this should not be the whole reading program. Group instruction, special practice for those who need it, and help in reading the various school subjects should also be included.

Another form of reading program uses what has been called multi-level material. This idea was first developed in its present effective form by Don Parker; the materials are published by Science Research Associates, Chicago. A preliminary test is given to determine on which level the individual should begin. Then he starts reading interesting short articles on this level. After reading each article he answers a series of comprehension questions, scores himself on the answers by using a scoring key, makes a graph showing his progress day by day, and notes the skills in which he needs to improve. Teachers, students, and parents have been most enthusiastic about this multilevel material that is used in many schools as part of the total reading program.

You may also have heard of reading programs that use various kinds of machines, designed chiefly to increase speed in reading. Some students, especially those who have already acquired a good vocabulary and fair comprehension skills, but have slipped into unnecessarily slow habits of reading, are enthusiastic about these machines. One type of machine flashes a phrase on a screen for a small fraction of a second; the reader is expected to recognize its meaning. Another type simply forces the student to read faster by means of a lever or bar that moves down over the page at a rate slightly faster than his present reading rate. There has been no conclusive evidence that these machines are, in general, any more effective than psychologically sound instruction that does not involve machines.

The best type of reading class is one in which the reading abilities of the students are continuously studied, and a combination of practice and instruction is given to meet the needs thus indicated. Some of this instruction and practice will be given to the whole class, some to small groups, and some to individuals.

READING PROBLEMS AND WHAT TO DO ABOUT THEM

The course of improvement in reading does not always run smoothly. Sixteen-year-old Jim described the ups and downs in his reading development as follows:

I was about four years old when my mother tried to teach me to read. She would take a card and write a word on it and then say it. This took a very long time and after a while I became very tired of reading.

The school entered was a country school and I did not care much about it, but in the second grade I began to read more and more and to like to read very much.

In about the sixth grade I read a great deal about airplanes and each year I read more and more about airplanes. When I go to the school library I always get a book about airplanes, but I wish the library had more books about them.

In the eighth grade at junior high I lost interest in reading. Instead of reading I watched TV and radio. As summer came on, most of the stories on TV were reruns and I lost interest in them.

Now, in the tenth grade, I have to do a lot of reading, but it is not for pleasure; it is for school. So far this year I have read only a few short stories.

Here was a boy of average ability whose early dislike of reading was owing to inappropriate home instruction that was begun before he was ready to learn to read. In subsequent years, his reading interest seemed to be left to chance; the home did not support the school by making suitable books available and by giving him approval for reading them.

The Reluctant Reader

Perhaps the child who annoys his parents the most is the reluctant reader who can read but won't. The parents realize that he is missing the enriching experience of wide and thoughtful reading.

It would be well for the parents to explore the possible reasons for this indifference or resistance to reading. The child may have accepted at face value the philosophy of life presented by the mass media. This is represented by such slogans as "Take it easy," "Dream your troubles away," "Pleasure up," and many other invitations to indolence. This philosophy is inimical to serious reading, which requires effort.

A lackadaisical school atmosphere may lead certain students to accept or even prefer mediocrity. This kind of anti-intellectual attitude is more effectively countered by example than by exhortation.

If the individual's background of experience is limited, he has little to bring to a book. He cannot get much meaning out of it because he cannot put much meaning into it.

Adolescents are normally more or less rebellious. We sometimes create resistance to reading by just plain nagging. It is better to set a goal for the child to strive toward. Children and young people try to live up to the expectations of others. "Because my mother and father took it for granted that I would enjoy good books, I read with an intent to like them," one girl said, and added, "and I really did." However, the goals set must be reasonable; we must not expect full steam ahead all the time.

Another reason for resistance to reading may lie in the child's personal relations. Hostility toward a parent or teacher may cause a child to resist learning anything that person advocates.

Voluntary reading may be crowded out by too many distractions in the home or by the pressure of too much required homework. Recognizing this, one French school left one school night each week free of homework, with the understanding that the students would use the evening to read books of their own choice.

Previous experience with reading is a potent factor. If the individual has found no rewards in his previous reading, he has no incentive to continue this boring and futile experience. From this standpoint, the recommendation of appropriate books is most important.

Of course, if the child's reluctance to reading is extreme, even careful personal recommendation of books is likely to be ineffectual. However, one mother got through to her reluctant teen-age son by carefully choosing one or two books that seemed to be in line with his interests, and merely leaving them lying around, without making any reference to them. After pursuing these tactics for several weeks she was rewarded one day when he picked up one of the books and, of his own accord, began reading it. This experience proved to be the entering wedge. He read other books by the same author and gradually widened his reading interests. When he found that reading was a satisfying personal experience, he became willing to put forth effort; he realized that reading involves work as well as pleasure.

Children whose homes are well stocked with books, magazines, and reference material, and whose families discuss current events and the books they have read and often recommend books and articles to one another, usually read wisely and well.

If a young person can read but doesn't, there's a reason. We can usually discover it and start him forward on the royal road to reading.

Difficulty with Spelling and Writing

Occasionally a child or adolescent who reads with fairly good comprehension is very poor in writing and spelling. One boy had no concept of words as composed of letters, and no understanding of the relationships between letters and sounds. After some training in phonics, he now tends to spell words the way they sound; he writes *ate* instead of *eight*, and sometimes adds an extra *e* to a word. He still copies words wrong from the board. He seems to see them wrong. This tendency may be caused by defects of vision that should be diagnosed and corrected, or by confusion in the brain areas that are involved in perception. At present he has become really concerned about his spelling and writing, and wants help. Some boys who have this kind of difficulty have been greatly helped by the kinesthetic or tracing method described by Fernald.[7] It is important to recognize competency and approve the good spelling and writing that children do; we should not constantly call attention to their errors.

Retardation Due to Immaturity

General immaturity may be associated with reading difficulty. A bright boy whose father was an architect had a home environment that presented rich opportunities for acquiring word meanings and fluent speech. Tests showed a marked difference between the boy's verbal ability and his nonverbal or quantitative ability. At eleven years of age he was reading at the third-grade level. His school had placed him in the sixth grade. Physically he was only as mature as a nine-year-old. Although he was six years old when he entered school, he was probably very immature for his age and did not respond to formal beginning reading instruction.

The parents were relieved to know that the boy's present retardation in reading seemed to be due to slow maturation and early failure to learn. They were glad to cooperate in a program of improvement that began with building a basic vocabulary, acquiring word-recognition skills, and reading many books far below his present grade level.

Slow Rate of Comprehension

Slowness in reading is one of the most commonly recognized difficulties. This tendency may be part of a temperamental lethargy. The mother of one fourteen-year-old boy said that he began to have difficulty with reading in the fifth grade. Her chief concern is the amount of time it takes him to master his lessons—much longer than his younger brothers and sisters have to spend. He is very conscientious and does a good deal of homework under the parents' supervision. Both parents fear that he will not be able to keep up with the pace of a private preparatory school unless he can read faster than he has been able to do thus far.

The boy is overweight. He has poor motor coordination and does not participate in sports. Nevertheless, he seems to be quite well accepted by his peers. To all appearances, he accepts his difficulties philosophically and does not seem to be overconcerned about his academic problems or his younger brother's ability to complete his homework faster than he does. He likes to help with the household chores and the cooking. He is exceedingly polite for a boy of his age.

According to his mother, he does not read as much as he should during his free time. His comprehension is up to par but his word attack is poor. His favorite subject, in which he obtained an average of 95, is mathematics; his poorest subject is spelling. He was placed in a remedial reading class in the fifth grade.

This boy's reading difficulty may be explained in many ways. He may have had poor instruction in beginning reading. A lethargic temperament has already been suggested. Feminine interests, though often associated with reading interest, may in this case be causing conflict with the counterdesire to establish masculinity. Inner conflict tends to distract attention from reading.

In this case, as in many others, general immaturity seems to be affecting reading performance. And the parents, instead of encouraging initiative and responsibility, seem to be fostering dependency by helping the boy so much with his homework and assuming so much responsibility for his reading. It is also possible that environmental conditions during the boy's infancy and preschool years may have established attitudes of apathy and passivity.

Improvement may occur when the boy modifies his self-concept and when his parents and teachers begin to expect him to assume more responsibility for his own learning. If he then receives instruction in the reading techniques in which he is deficient, these changes should pave the way to better reading and more effective study.

Unevenness in Abilities

Sometimes we meet students of high school age who are proficient in science but poor in reading. One understanding father described this difficulty in the following letter to the director of a reading center:

My wife spoke with your secretary concerning our 15-year-old son who will be entering his second year of high school in the fall, and she advised that we write you full particulars concerning same.

In the spring he took the entrance exam for a private preparatory school, and while he excelled in math, receiving a 97 percentile in math, and a 96 percentile in theoretical math, he only got a 23 percentile in spelling, and a 27 percentile in reading.

We have been aware of this deficiency in reading, and hate to have him approach college level without help. We thought remedial reading would be the answer. He never reads unless it is a book on science or math.

Spelling words which he studies he can get perfectly without too much effort but words he is not familiar with, he is at a loss at trying to spell. We felt that if his reading scope were enlarged, his spelling would benefit, also.

He finished this year with very creditable marks; 98 in science, 97 in math, 95 in Spanish, 95 in English, and an 85 in history. The latter, I am sure, he read as little as possible.

Even though his present high grades are good, we feel he must have help in his weakest point as it will be a hindrance to him in college.

I would appreciate your opinion and help in this matter, and would be very happy if he could take work in reading in your center in the fall.

Early Retardation in Reading

Adolescents sometimes have a history of poor health and unfortunate early school experiences. Such is the case with Paul. During his first five years he suffered from poor health—spasms, diarrhea, digestive disturbances, and foot defects that required him to wear specially fitted shoes.

In the first grade he had an elderly teacher who was actually cruel in her treatment of some of the children. Though she seemed to like Paul, she expressed her fondness for him roughly and he was terrified of her. During this year and the next, he did not learn to read, and his reading has remained a problem ever since.

In Junior high school he was placed in a class of slow learners because he was reading at only third-grade level. In this class he did average work, but made no friends because he had few interests in common with these children. In the ninth grade, he had been transferred to an average group where he has made friends, joined clubs, and engaged in sports, even though his foot defects are still uncorrected.

Though his older brother is a good reader, versatile, well liked, and very good in sports, Paul does not seem to regard him as a threat. In fact, he is protective and kind toward Paul.

Since Paul has the potential ability to read well, and since the social and emotional factors are favorable, it would appear that what he needs is instruction and practice in reading to make up for what he lost in the earlier years. The Science Research Elementary Reading laboratory might be very useful in helping Paul.

MULTIPLE CAUSES OF READING DIFFICULTY

Reading difficulties have many causes. But some adolescents have all the cards stacked against them and need all the understanding and help we can give them. For example, a fifteen-year-old boy of average intelligence, was "born blue"; that is, he suffered a serious oxygen deprivation, which usually affects the brain cells that are connected with speech and reading. To revive him, the doctor administered an injection, which injured a nerve and made one leg shorter than the other. He had so much pain as a baby that he used to bang his head against the wall.

All through his childhood he had headaches and throat infections. He walked at eleven months, but did not talk much until he was two and a half. He had special difficulty in pronouncing f and r. His family thought this was cute. In the first grade, he said he wasn't going to school any more because people laughed at him because of his mispronunciations. His speech defect continued to make him terribly self-conscious. In the fifth grade he went to a speech class, but still has trouble with his *r*'s. He has always been poor in reading and spelling.

Despite all these handicaps, this boy is now studying and trying to do better. It is hard for him to concentrate, and it takes him a long time to do his homework. He does some reading, but his mother feels that the books he reads are either childish or quite beyond him. He makes friends and behaves in school. Through his pain he has maintained a sense of humor, although his frustration occasionally breaks out in fits of temper. School takes most of his time and he has no special interests, not even drawing, which he used to enjoy.

Home conditions are unfavorable. He fights with his sister and calls her a "stupid idiot." She retaliates with similar disparaging remarks. He shares a room with his grandmother and they hate each other. A change in environment is clearly indicated.

Through wise and sympathetic counseling, this boy might gain a more hopeful and more realistic self-concept. When he has clearly recognized and accepted both his strengths and his weaknesses, he should be helped to focus on the things he *can* do.

As handicapped children grow toward adulthood, they become increasingly anxious about the future. They wonder what is to become of them. If they find a suitable vocational goal, they will put forth much effort in preparing for it. If they know what reading is required for their chosen work, they are often willing to start on a childish level and progress step by step as fast and as far as they are able. Parents should accept a realistic goal and give the child the opportunities, encouragement, and special help that he needs to make progress toward it. A boy of this kind needs individual reading instruction that begins where he is. His physical and emotional distractions should be reduced, and he should receive genuine approval for the progress that he makes. Under these conditions he will gradually attain his reading potentialities.

A negative attitude toward a child may not only aggravate a reading difficulty; it may even cause one. The mother of a thirteen-year-old boy constantly expressed her fears for the boy's future, and stated that regardless of how hard she worked to support him, he did not appreciate it. Both the mother and the older sister tried to help him with his reading, but he was so stupid, according to the mother, that they lost patience with him. The boy seemed to be satisfied, she said, to go through junior high school accumulating report cards full of F's, just as he did in the lower grades. She said he was irresponsible and lazy at home; he refused to help around the house, and was constantly bickering with his older sister. The mother's plan was to get him through the ninth grade so that he could enter the auto mechanics course in a nearby senior high school, but she was afraid he was "too dumb to make it."

Since we tend to believe what we hear others say about us, it is no wonder that this boy thought of himself as stupid, dumb, lazy, irresponsible. If he were given suitable tasks in which he could succeed, if people expected him to do *his* best, and consistently made reasonable demands upon him, the chances are that he would put forth the effort to learn to read. His efforts would be fruitful if he received instruction from a skillful teacher or clinician.

Parents may not be aware of certain home conditions that are contributing to a child's reading difficulty. For example, the mother of a thirteen-year-old boy mentioned the following:

His father has very little use for him and seldom associates with him. The boy has to go elsewhere for adult male companionship.

His older brother is an excellent student and very ambitious. He goes to high school and holds down two jobs besides. The mother is very proud of him. This brother has always called the boy stupid because he has not been able to do his schoolwork. The mother has put a stop to this.

The mother is very much concerned about the boy's reading, and is anxious to get help from a reading clinic.

All these conditions conspire to build up feelings of inferiority in the boy: he lacks a normal relationship with his father; his mother is anxious and overconcerned; and he cannot possibly compete with his brother who is so much more able, and so very superior.

Somewhat similar family conditions account, in part, for the reading difficulties of a thirteen-year-old girl:

She has a twin brother who is capable and enthusiastic and reads well; he gives her much competition. She was retained in the first grade while the brother was promoted. The mother has always given the brother more opportunities for doing things.

The girl doesn't want to do a thing unless she can do it perfectly.

School conditions are also unfavorable. In the primary grades, her school was overcrowded, and operated on a part-time schedule. Consequently she missed out on basic reading instruction. Since she has not acquired word-recognition skills, she cannot do independent reading. She fears tests; her usual poor performance intensifies her feeling of inadequacy. If she were given the instruction that she missed during the primary grades, so that she could recognize words readily, her confidence would increase. She would then be able to do the wide voluntary reading that she needs to increase her information, vocabulary, and fluency.

Many school conditions may contribute to an adolescent's reading difficulties. Parents frequently mention the hazards of overcrowded classrooms, schools on part-time sessions, and a curriculum in which, as one mother said, "children were not supposed to do anything unless they wanted to. They just weren't challenged." Certainly such conditions create reading problems that are likely to accumulate as the child goes through elementary school and enters high school. Then the child who was not much concerned about his reading in elementary school begins to see its personal importance, and wants to improve.

Each reading problem is unique. There is no blanket rule that can be applied to all children, except one: Parents and teachers must maintain a sensitivity to the individual child—his capacity for learning, his present stage of development, his self-concept, his relationships with the important people in his life, his feelings, and the meaning that a given situation has for him.

QUESTIONS AND ANSWERS

1. *How can a parent encourage an adolescent's love of reading?*
The surest method is by setting a good example. Love of reading is caught from persons who genuinely enjoy reading, who care deeply about it, and who are convinced of its importance. Such persons talk about the books they read, argue about them, read excerpts from them, and recommend suitable books to their children.

If the child is resistant to reading, or passing through a peak of resentment toward adult authority, it may be better just to leave the book lying around.

A sound selection is tremendously important. Nothing is worse than to arouse a child's interest in a book that turns out to be boring or disgusting to him. Such an experience confirms his opinion that "reading is for the birds."

2. *If a child is interested in nothing but sports or mechanical things, how can a parent or teacher interest him in reading?*

Though interest in sports is not always related to interest in *reading about* sports, sports stories and biographies of sports heroes may be an entering wedge.

A group of boys interested in auto mechanics developed their language skills in connection with the renovation of old cars. Each boy did the job first, and then described the procedure in his own words, down to the last step in cleaning a carburetor. A careless write-up was no more acceptable than a careless job; it had to be technically accurate, correct as to spelling and grammar, and clearly expressed. Weekly spelling quizzes tested their ability to spell and define words like *centrifugal, chassis,* and *differential.* Reading became interesting and meaningful to these boys when it dealt with experiences that were familiar to them and began with descriptions that employed their own vocabulary and sentence structure. This principle can be applied to any kind of experience reading.

3. *Is failure in reading related to behavior problems and juvenile delinquency?*

It would be absurd to claim that all poor readers become juvenile delinquents. Some cope with their sense of failure in nonaggressive ways: by becoming indifferent or apathetic, by daydreaming that they are successful, by getting satisfaction from sports, music, or something else that they can do well.

But judges in juvenile courts have found that about three-fourths of those who were brought before them were two or more years retarded in reading. Some were practically nonreaders. The child who fails to learn to read and thus gets little satisfaction from school is likely to play truant. In his hours out of school, he may join gangs of older boys and thus get into trouble.

Improvement in reading often produces improvement in behavior. For example, Dave's bad behavior made his mother sick with worry. He was by far the worst reader in his tenth grade. After six weeks in a special reading class Dave "caught on"—he discovered that he could learn to read. He calmed down in class because he was too busy reading to think of ways of causing trouble.

With some children, emotional problems underlie both reading and delinquency. They may need counseling or psychotherapy. However, individual help in reading often has a beneficial effect. It changes children's attitudes toward themselves, and improves their relationships with parents and teachers.

4. *How may reading help adolescents with their personal problems?*

We can give them access to books and other reading materials that deal with adolescent problems and thus aid them in achieving their developmental tasks. Studies have shown that young people do read about the problems that are of concern to them.

As they read novels, short stories, and biographies that describe numerous incidents in which the central characters experience some of the conflicts, uncertainties, and anxieties that beset most adolescents, they can attain insight into their own behavior and build up their self-confidence and self-assurance. Such books will also aid them in their efforts to achieve personal and social adjustment. For example, broken families are common today, and the adolescent suffers from this painful situation. *Divided Heart,* by Mina Lewiton, has a wholesome approach to this problem that may help some young persons understand and accept a situation of this kind in their own lives. In *Going on Sixteen,* by Betty Cavanna, Julie was not accepted socially by her high-school peers until she had won a school-wide poster contest. *Your High School Days,* by M. F. Detjen, helps students to understand some common school problems. *Teen Days,* by Frances Strain, discusses hygiene, sex, entertainment, jobs, love, and marriage. In *Senior Year,* by Anne Emery, the problem of going steady crops up. Each book of *Teen-Age Tales,* published by D. C. Heath, contains many short stories in which adolescents achieve satisfactory solutions of their problems. By supplying books like these that deal with choosing one's vocation and way of life, dating, courtship, marriage, family life, broken homes, manners, and good grooming, we can help adolescents in achieving their developmental tasks.

5. *What advice about reading have teen-agers given to teachers?*

Take more time with individual students and gain more understanding of them; find out why they make mistakes and help them. One youngster said, "The teacher never helps you. She just says, 'You ought to know that.'"

Divide the class into subgroups. This makes it possible for the teacher to help the students who have special difficulties; the student has more confidence when he is in a small group.

Give more instruction in creative and critical reading.

Give practice in writing as well as reading—for example, writing book reviews or making radio script out of a story.

"Teach us, don't just test us."

Don't embarrass students about their reading before other people.

Stimulate them to read better books; don't let them keep reading the same type of book too long.

Give them a list of recommended books from which they may choose.

Set a good example; children imitate adults who display enthusiasm for reading and appreciation of literature.

Have conferences with the parents; working together, teachers and parents can help a child improve his reading.

6. *What are some of the common reading difficulties and dissatisfactions that teen-agers recognize?*

They wish to read faster, but have not learned the art of skimming.

They have a meager vocabulary. "My worst reading difficulty," one boy said, "is not understanding words. Now I am reading the newspaper for a half-hour every night."

They wish that they had learned more words and read more worth-while books when they were younger. As one said: "When I was little I used to have lots of time to sit around and read a book. But now there are movies to go to, TV to watch, comic books to read. You just don't seem to have the time to sit down and read a good book."

They do not have time to read what they want; they cannot enjoy a book because they have to rush through it.

They are bored with the books they are given to read.

They resent being deprived of activities they do well, such as sports, because their reading is poor.

They are embarrassed when they have to read before the class; one boy said, "When I begin to read in front of a group, I get embarrassed and then begin to stutter and fumble around with words."

Emotional problems may interfere with their reading: "The thing that is most difficult for me, I think, is when I have something on my mind that is bothering me. Then I can't seem to get my mind on what I am reading."

7. *How do parental values affect adolescents' reading?*

Your children's reading ability and reading interests are strongly affected by the value you and your neighbors place upon reading and other intellectual interests in the home. Are your values showing? Which is prominent in your home—the up-to-the-minute kitchen, the colorful tile bathroom, the two-car garage, the television set, or the library with its book-strewn tables? Reading is fostered in an atmosphere of ideas, and ideas grow out of values and interests.

Selected Books, Pamphlets, and Bulletins on Reading for Parents *

Books

Artley, A. Sterl. *Your Child Learns To Read*. Chicago: Scott, Foresman & Company, 1953. 255 pp. An authoritative book explaining the reading process and how it is taught.

Bond, Guy L., and Eva Bond Wagner. *Child Growth in Reading*. Chicago: Lyons & Carnahan, 1955. 431 pp. A simple description of how reading is taught, with illustrations of pages from basal readers.

Duff, Annis. *Longer Flight: A Family Grows Up with Books*. New York: The Viking Press, Inc., 1955. 269 pp. A rich and inspiring account of the intelligent use of books in a family. An appendix contains lists of recommended books, phonograph records, and sources of obtaining prints for a family art collection.

Duker, Sam, and Thomas Nally. *The Truth About Your Child's Reading*. New York: Crown Publishers, Inc., 1956. 181 pp. A thorough refutation of Rudolf Flesch's point of view.

Fenner, Phyllis. *The Proof of the Pudding: What Children Read*. New York: The John Day Co., 1957. 246 pp. Tells about the best books of all times, why children like them, and the age when they usually read them. It also suggests good books to read aloud.

Frank, Josette. *Your Child's Reading Today*. New York: Doubleday & Company, Inc., 1954. 328 pp. Sound suggestions and guide to children's reading.

Henderson, Ellen C. *You Can Teach a Child That Reading Can Be Fun*. A Guide for Parents and Teachers. New York: Exposition Press, 1956. 172 pp. A "do it yourself" book that attempts to provide solutions to individual difficulties children are experiencing from reading readiness to "teaching yourself to read aloud."

Hymes, James L., Jr. *Before the Child Reads*. Evanston, Illinois: Row, Peterson & Company, 1958. 96 pp. Readable and clear presentation of child growth in relation to how a child learns to read.

Judd, Romie Dustin. *Setting the Stage for Johnny To Read*. New York:

* Prepared with the assistance of Mrs. Charles W. Wegener.

Pageant Press, 1955. 101 pp. An engagingly personal but simply
stated explanation of reading-readiness factors and techniques and
methods of beginning reading.

Larrick, Nancy. *A Parent's Guide to Children's Reading.* Garden City,
New York: Doubleday & Company, Inc., 1958 (also New York:
Pocket Books, Inc., 1958). 283 pp. Criteria for selecting books
for children together with excellent annotated references of a large
variety of books for children of different ages, ability, and interests.

McEathron, Margaret. *Your Child Can Learn To Read.* Grosset & Dunlap,
1956. 92 pp. Designed to be used by mothers without teaching experience to help their own children with reading problems.
Combines sight and sound method.

Monroe, Marion. *Growing into Reading.* Chicago: Scott, Foresman &
Company, 1951. 274 pp. The most detailed treatment of children's
prereading and early reading experiences, with many illustrative
exercises.

The Reading Teacher, Vol. 7, pp. 193–219, April, 1954. An issue on
parents' concern with their children's reading, which discusses a
number of common problems.

Tooze, Ruth. *Your Children Want To Read.* Englewood Cliffs, N.J.:
Prentice-Hall, Inc., 1957. 222 pp. Shows how parents and teacher
may work together to foster children's growth in reading, and how
the child's everyday experiences can be enriched through search
for information in books.

Van Atta, Frieda E. *How To Help Your Child in Reading, Writing and
Arithmetic.* New York: Random House, 1959. 374 pp. A book
planned for the use of parents in helping children with their
schoolwork from kindergarten through eighth grade. Contains
many sample exercises.

Pamphlets and Bulletins

Association for Childhood Education International.
        Reading. Washington 5, D.C.: The Association, 1956. 32 pp.
        Combines basic theories about reading and some fresh viewpoints
        with practical suggestions in accord with the theory.

Auerbach, Aline B. *How To Give Your Child a Good Start.* New York
28: The Child Study Association of America, 1961. 31 pp. Considers common physical and psychological problems of bringing
up children and suggests sensible solutions to them.

Casey, Sally L. *Ways You Can Help Your Child with Reading.* Row,

Peterson & Company, 1950. 26 pp. A booklet with excellent suggestions for some of the things a parent can safely do in the home to help the child to read well.

Cooke, Dorothy E. *The First "R" Reading.* Bureau of Elementary Curriculum Department. Albany, N.Y.: The State Education Department, 1955. 40 pp. A very small, attractive, illustrated booklet, with important ideas on every page, very simply stated.

Department of Elementary School Principals, National School Public Relations Association, National Congress of Parents and Teachers. *Happy Journey.* Washington, D.C.: National Education Association, 1953. 32 pp. An excellent approach to school on the part of both parent and child is described in concrete detail.

————. *How To Help Your Child Learn: A Handbook for Parents of Children in Kindergarten Through Grade 6.* Washington, D.C.: National Education Association, 1960. 40 pp. An entertaining introductory page or two precede a number of specific, sound suggestions as to how parents can help a child with reading, arithmethic, and other major aspects of his school program.

————. *Janie Learns To Read: A Handbook for Parents Whose Child Will Soon Learn To Read.* Washington, D.C.: National Education Association, 1954. 40 pp. Written in story form, this pamphlet also includes the right emphases on important things for parents to do at home and for teachers to do in school.

————. *Sailing into Reading: How Your Child Learns To Read in the Elementary School.* Washington, D.C.: National Education Association, 1956. 40 pp. Invites parent interest through pictures and attention-getting devices that carry sound comments about the process of learning to read, and some things the parents can do, such as watch the child's health, be sympathetic and understanding, make suitable books available.

Dolch, Edward W. *Helping Your Child with Reading.* Champaign, Illinois: The Garrard Press, 1956. 24 pp. An attractively written, psychologically sound, clearly and interestingly stated simple handbook on reading for parents.

Good Ways of Helping Your Child in Reading. Inglewood, California: Board of Education, Inglewood Unified School District, 1957. 4 pp. A leaflet written for parents who want suggestions for what can be done in the home to ensure that children will read widely and wisely.

How Does Your Child Learn To Read? Warren, Ohio: The Warren City Schools, 1954. 4 pp. A small pamphlet that answers parents' questions about how the child's first teachers go about the task of teaching him to read.

MacDougall, Ursula Cooke. *If Your Child Has Reading Difficulties.* New York: The Dalton School, 1952. 63 pp. A clearly written, authoritative explanation of the factors that cause reading problems and what can be done about them by the school and by reading specialists.

Mackintosh, Helen K. *How Children Learn To Read.* Bulletin 1952, No. 7, U.S. Department of Health, Education and Welfare, Washington 25, D.C. 120 pp. A concise, informative, and simple description of the teacher's part in the reading experience of children and the ways in which parents can help. Part of the bulletin deals with skills in the mechanics of reading. It explains to parents why and how methods of teaching beginning reading have changed.

McKee, Paul. *A Primer for Parents: How Your Child Learns To Read.* New York: Houghton Mifflin Company, 1957. 32 pp. By means of code that parents must decipher, the author puts parents in the place of the first grader. In describing the child's reading process, he emphasizes practice with letter forms, with beginning sounds, and with context clues and "phonic clues."

Public Schools, Montclair, New Jersey. *How Parents Can Help Their Children with Reading.* Montclair, New Jersey: The Division of Instruction and Guidance, Montclair Public Schools, 1952. 12 pp. An attractive booklet briefly explains new teaching methods so that parents can avoid confusing the child by using an approach that is unlike that presented by his teacher.

Reading in the Chicago Public Schools. Chicago: Curriculum Department of the Public Schools, 1955. 12 pp. A brochure that explains in simple detail how reading skills are taught in the Chicago Public Schools.

Stauffer, Russell G., comp. and ed. *What Parents Can Do To Help Their Children in Reading,* Vol. 1. Reading Clinic, University of Delaware. Proceedings of the first annual Parent Conference on Reading, December 1950. 49 pp. School people and university professors tell what they think parents should know about children's language development.

Van Riper, C. *Helping Children Talk Better.* Chicago 10, Illinois: Science Research Associates, Inc., 1951. 49 pp. Suggestions for furthering speech development and preventing or correcting speech defects.

Van Roekel, G. H. *Preparing Your Child for First Steps in Reading*. Professional Series Bulletin No. 6, East Lansing, Michigan: Bureau of Research and Service, School of Education, Michigan State University, 1955. 20 pp. Written from the parents' viewpoint, this booklet gives brief practical suggestions about attitudes, development of speech, reading together, choice of books, and other prereading experiences.

Witty, Paul. *Helping Children Read Better*. Chicago: Science Research Associates, Inc., 1950. 49 pp. A comprehensive coverage of important facts about children's reading from preschool through high school, admirably condensed into pamphlet form.

APPENDIX B

Children's Reading Materials *

BOOKS TO READ TO PRESCHOOL CHILDREN

Anglund, Joan Walsh. *A Friend is Someone Who Likes You*. Harcourt, 1959. $1.95. Explaining that a friend may be a boy, a girl, a cat, a mouse, and so on, this charming little book with enchanting illustrations contains many happy surprises on the subject of friendship for small children.

Austin, Margot. *Margot Austin's Churchmouse Stories*. Dutton, 1956. $3.95. Children are enchanted with the silly escapades of Peter Churchmouse, Gabriel, the cat, who took to Peter's poetry, and Trumpet, a little dog. This omnibus volume contains new full-color pictures as well as all of the pictures and text of the five beloved stories by this author-artist.

Bannister, Constance. *A Child's Grace*. Dutton, 1948. $2.50. The simple text of the well-known Grace by Ernest Claxton and on every page an appealing photograph depicting a child's everyday experiences from Grace before breakfast to restful sleep at night and linking that life to God's love.

Borg, Inga. *Parrak—the White Reindeer*. Warne, 1959. $2.50. Attractive illustrations and realistic text depict the life of a Lapland reindeer as he grows from a calf to leader of his herd.

Brewton, Sarah Westbrook, comp. *Birthday Candles Burning Bright*. Macmillan, 1960. $3.50. Bearing the subtitle "A Treasury of Birthday Poetry," this collection by outstanding authors about birthdays and growing up offers a variety of appealing poems for reading aloud.

Brown, Margaret Wise. *The Big Red Barn*. W. R. Scott, 1956. $2.25. For the child who is interested in farm animals; other books by Brown.

Coatsworth, Elizabeth. *Hide and Seek*. Pantheon, 1956. $2.00. A mother and her small son enjoy a game together. Charming verse and illustrations enhance this lovely book, ideal for reading aloud.

* Bibliography prepared by Louise James, District Librarian, Palm Springs Unified Schools, Palm Springs, California. The very familiar, favorite children's classics are, in general, not included in this list.

Cook, Bernadine. *The Little Fish That Got Away.* W. R. Scott, 1956. $2.25. An appealing little "fish story"; good to read aloud.

Cooney, Barbara. *Chanticleer and the Fox.* Crowell, 1958. $3.00. A distinguished picture-book adaptation of the familiar fable of the vain cock and cunning fox of Chaucer's *Canterbury Tales.* Handsome woodcut illustrations in color and in black and white depict the medieval background.

De Regniers, Beatrice Schenk. *The Snow Party.* Pantheon, 1959. $2.75. An old man and his wife lived alone with their chickens in Dakota. The woman's wish to have some people visit them came true when a snowstorm struck and 84 adults, 17 children, 7 babies, and a number of animals were stranded at the couple's home. The gay happenings spiced with humor make a delightful read-aloud story for small children.

Ets, Marie Hall. *Play with Me.* Viking, 1955, $2.50. A little girl finds out for herself how to make friends with the birds and animals of the meadow. Charming illustrations.

Felt, Sue. *Hello—Goodbye.* Doubleday, 1960. $2.50. When the family moves to a new home, Lucy, who had had the experience of moving, explains the "Hello—Goodbye" procedure to her little sister Candace. A pleasant and simple story.

Fischer, Hans. *Puss in Boots.* Harcourt, 1959. $3.00. This is a beautiful, humorous, and distinguished adaptation of Charles Perrault's famous fairy tale about the miraculous cat who provided his master with a castle and a princess for a bride.

Freeman, Don. *Cyrano the Crow.* Viking, 1960. $2.75. Cyrano, who was both talkative and talented, took pride in being different from other crows until he learned the valuable lesson of just being himself.

Gág, Wanda. *Millions of Cats.* Coward, 1928. $2.50. This classic tale of the little old man who went to search for one cat and returned with "millions and billions and trillions of cats" is a universal favorite with young children. Engaging black-and-white illustrations.

Geisel, Theodor Seuss. *And To Think That I Saw It on Mulberry Street.* Vanguard, 1937. $2.50. A delightful nonsense story told in ryhme. A small boy sees a plain horse and cart and lets his imagination run wild until the vehicle becomes a circus bandwagon drawn by an elephant and giraffes. Bright, colored, perfectly matched illustrations.

Grimm, Jakob Ludwig Karl, and Grimm, Wilhelm Karl. *The Shoemaker and the Elves*. Scribner, 1960. $2.95. This new version of the long-time favorite among fairy tales has sprightly illustrations. The elves have real personalities, and the shoemaker and his wife show amusing facial expressions.

Hoberman, Mary Ann. *Hello and Good-by*. Little, 1959. $2.50. Delightful and humorous verses about such ideas as a bus for a birthday present, a bug in a puddle, and the people in Backward Town.

Johnson, Crockett. *Ellen's Lion*. Harper, 1959. $1.99. Twelve entertaining stories about Ellen and her stuffed lion who can never speak when the child does and who keeps his "cool voice of reason" when Ellen wanders into fantasy.

Langstaff, John. *The Swapping Boy*. Harcourt, 1960. $2.95. A pleasantly illustrated retelling of the old Appalachian Mountain trading song. The repetitious refrain and nonsensical humor are appealing to young children.

Lifton, Betty Jean. *Kap the Kappa*. Morrow, 1960. $2.75. Kap, a mischievous little water elf, must keep water in a shallow bowl on his head to stay alive. This is the fact that reveals Kap's true nature to the townspeople after he has been disguised as a human boy. Lovely brush-painted black ink illustrations.

McGinley, Phyllis. *Lucy McLockett*. Lippincott, 1959. $3.00. Told in rhyme, this is a delicately illustrated story of a little girl who lost her first tooth and then began to lose other things—including her mother. An entertaining read-aloud book that realistically portrays typical behavior in small children.

Marokvia, Mireille. *Nanette, a French Goat*. Lippincott, 1960. $3.00. Nanette, a goat with a real personality, is bought by a French family whose youngest child needs goat's milk. As could be expected, she is mischievous and gets into trouble but eventually becomes a great heroine. Illustrations are unmistakably French.

Martin, Patricia Miles. *Happy Piper and the Goat*. Lothrop, 1960. $2.75. Happy's mother, who feels he already has too many pets, refuses to let him add a stray goat to his collection. However, through the aid of a neighbor artist and the goat itself, a happy solution is reached. A warm and understanding story.

Milne, A. A. *When We Were Very Young*. Dutton, 1924. New edition, redesigned by Warren Chappell, 1961. $2.95. Dutton Lifetime binding $2.86. Verses written for Milne's small son, Christopher Robin, which, for their nonsense, nice whimsy, and unexpected surprises furnish immeasurable joy to children.

Potter, Beatrix. *Tale of Peter Rabbit*. Warne, n.d. $1.50. A classic and charming tale of the famous rabbits—Flopsy, Mopsy, Cotton Tail, and Peter Rabbit himself, who disobeys his mother's warning and visits Mr. McGregor's garden.

Proysen, Alf. *Little Old Mrs. Pepperpot*. Obolensky, 1959. $2.50. A dozen amusing and clever stories about an unusual little old woman who would shrink to the size of a pepperpot and then return to her normal size. Good bedtime reading!

Seignobosc, Françoise. *Jeanne-Marie at the Fair*. Scribner, 1959. $2.75. Another of the author's appealing stories of a little French girl and her pet sheep, Patapon. This time Jeanne-Marie goes to the fair and leaves Patapon at home. How the pet joins her makes a suspense story for the small listener.

Stover, JoAnn. *If Everybody Did*. McKay, 1960. $2.95. Depicts in an exaggerated and humorous manner what would happen "if everybody did things like slam the door, stomp and roar, squeeze the cat," and so on.

Titus, Eve. *Anatole and the Robot*. Whittlesey, 1960. $2.50. Another amusing and colorful picture book about the magnificent French mouse. This time he is concerned with the problem of automation, and finds that even a cheese-tasting robot is no substitute for an expert.

Walker, David E. *The Fat Cat Pimpernel*. A. S. Barnes, 1960. $2.50. Pimpernel, who has repeatedly failed to catch Bertram Blackbird, finally becomes Bertram's protector and friend. An imaginative, different, and humorous cat story with handsome illustrations.

Ward, Lynd Kendall. *The Biggest Bear*. Houghton, 1952. $2.75. This classic picture book, a Caldecott Medal winner, has strong, forceful illustrations and an outstanding text. How Johnny acquires a bear and later solves the problem of what to do with the animal makes an engaging story.

Williams, Gweneira Maureen. *Timid Timothy*. W. R. Scott, 1944. $2.50. An engaging story of a little kitten who learned to be brave. In fact, he became so brave his mother warned him about getting into trouble.

PICTURE BOOKS FOR PRESCHOOL CHILDREN

Alain. *The Elephant and the Flea*. Whittlesey, 1956. $2.00. A humorous picture book about a big animal that tries to get rid of a tiny flea.

Anglund, Joan Walsh. *In a Pumpkin Shell*. Harcourt, 1960. $2.95. A delightful and enchanting ABC book of Mother Goose rhymes. Illustrations are most appropriate.

Ardizzone, Edward. *Johnny the Clockmaker*. Walck, 1960. $3.00. Johnny's family do not accept too seriously his ability to make things, but his friend Suzannah and the blacksmith are very encouraging. Everybody praises him, however, when the grandfather clock he builds actually works. The balloon captions enhance the attractive illustrations.

Bright, Robert. *My Hopping Bunny*. Doubleday, 1960. $2.00. Interestingly illustrated in red and black. Adventure of a little boy and his extraordinary bunny. Humorous and exciting fantasy.

Brown, Myra. *First Night Away from Home*. Watts, 1960. $2.50. A realistic account of a little boy's overnight visit to a friend's house.

Galdone, Paul, illus. *Old Mother Hubbard and Her Dog*. Whittlesey, 1960. $2.25. A fresh and handsome edition of the old nursery rhyme. Pictures the "poor dog" story page by page, with each illustration enhanced by a single line of text.

Gramatky, Hardie. *Homer and the Circus Train*. Putnam, 1957. $2.75. Homer, a bright new caboose, becomes a hero when he saves a truckload of circus animals on an exciting down-the-mountain ride. Appealing and colorful pictures.

Gregor, Arthur. *1–2–3–4–5*. Lippincott, 1956. $2.50. This enchanting counting book is illustrated with pleasing photographs.

Grimm, Jakob Ludwig Karl, and Grimm, Wilhelm Karl. *The Wolf and the Seven Little Kids*. Harcourt, 1959. $3.75. A skillful interpretation of the beloved tale. The rich, glowing illustrations in vivid color by Felix Hoffman give a splendid blending of realism and fantasy.

Hall, Julia Rosalys. *Animal Hide and Seek*. Lothrop, 1958. $2.50. An entertaining little book in which the child can play his own game of hide-and-seek with the bright colored animals from page to page. Text consists of few words.

Ipcar, Dahlov. *Brown Cow Farm*. Doubleday, 1959. $2.50. An excellent picture book for the preschool child. The interesting illustrations and simple text give an introduction to the cycle of farm life and will also stimulate interest in learning to count, to add, and to multiply.

Joslin, Sesyle. *What Do You Say, Dear?* W. R. Scott, 1958. $2.75. A clever little book on etiquette for the young child. Absurd situations such as "being introduced to a baby elephant, bumping into a crocodile, being rescued from a dragon," afford instruction in proper behavior. Humorous illustrations by Maurice Sendak.

Krauss, Ruth. *Open House for Butterflies*. Harper, 1960. $1.84. More "good and useful things to know," by the author of *A Hole Is To Dig*. Humorous and childlike illustrations.

Leaf, Munro. *The Wishing Pool*. Lippincott, 1960. $2.75. Three easy-to-read stories about imaginative children in a pool. They make wishes about things they'd like to see happen—a knightly rescue, a Western rodeo, and a jet flight to the North Pole. Simple, humorous nonsense.

Lionni, Leo. *Little Blue and Little Yellow*. Obolensky, 1959. $2.95. An unusual and engaging picture book in which the author tells of little blue and little yellow, who hugged each other until they were green. A simple and effective approach to color mixing that should encourage creative play in the mixing of other colors.

McCloskey, Robert. *Make Way for Ducklings*. Viking, 1941. $3.00. This classic tells the unusual and irresistible story of Mr. and Mrs. Mallard and their eight children who live on an island in the Charles River and march across the streets of Boston.

Matsuno, Masako. *A Pair of Red Clogs*. World Pub., 1960. $3.00. A beautifully illustrated picture book in bright, gay colors about a little Japanese girl who cracked her new red clogs and almost performed a trick to obtain another pair.

Merrill, Jean. *Emily Emerson's Moon*. Little, 1960. $2.75. Emily Emerson's father offered her "the moon, or a piece of milky way or even the sun." In spite of her brother's teasing, she really received the moon, and in a wonderful way! A delightful story.

Miles, Betty. *Having a Friend*. Knopf, 1959. $2.25. A delightful and simple little book about Sara who played alone and watched other children play together. Then she met Ann and formed a first friendship. For more mature pre-primary children.

Minarik, Else Holmelund. *Father Bear Comes Home*. Harper, 1959. $2.00. A simple I-Can-Read book about an ingenuous little bear and his amusing experiences—especially with the hiccups.

Munari, Bruno. *ABC*. World Pub., 1960. $3.50. A fascinating alphabet book. The bold black letters, colorful illustrations, and brief identifying text constitute an ingenious work of art.

Politi, Leo. *Moy Moy*. Scribner, 1960. $2.95. A warm family story of a little Chinese girl who lives above a store on Chanking Street in Los Angeles. Depicts the celebration of the Chinese New Year with the lion dance and the dragon parade.

Slobodkin, Esphyr. *The Clock*. Abelard, 1956. $2.50. A simple but impressive story about how people depended upon the old clock in the church steeple.

Slobodkin, Louis. *One Is Good, but Two Are Better*. Vanguard, 1956. $2.50. A picture book showing how much more fun two children can have together than one alone.

Tresselt, Alvin. *Timothy Robbins Climbs a Mountain*. Lothrop, 1960. $2.75. Timothy Robbins and his small friend hike up a twisting path to the top of the mountain where they have lunch and make a pleasant discovery. A good nature-study approach and beautiful illustrations.

Trez, Denise. *The Butterfly Chase*. World Pub., 1960. $3.00. A little French boy goes with his best friend, his grandfather, to search for an elusive butterfly with the colors of the French flag: red, white, and blue. Pictures and text are filled with action and gaiety.

SUPPLEMENTARY READING IN PRIMARY GRADES

Andersen, Hans Christian. *The Emperor's New Clothes*. Harcourt, 1959. $3.00. Erik Blegvad, a Danish translator-illustrator, has portrayed with humor and charm the beloved fairy tale of the foolish emperor and his vain desire for fine clothes.

Anderson, Clarence Williams. *Blaze and the Mountain Lion*. Macmillan, 1959. $2.50. Another effectively illustrated book of universal appeal about Billy and his pony Blaze. In this story Billy lassos and saves a calf from a mountain lion. Has appeal to children beyond the picture-book age who are slow readers.

Anderson, Poul. *Yong Kee of Korea*. W. R. Scott, 1959. $2.75. Yong Kee wants to be old enough to accompany his father into the hills to cut grass for fuel and to go with him to trade in the city. How he proves his ability to assume responsibilities makes a good story and vividly describes the Korean way of life.

Ayer, Jacqueline. *Nu Dang and His Kite*. Harcourt, 1959. $2.75. A little boy of Thailand is very fond of his elaborate orange-and-red kite. When it slips away from him on a windy day, he goes up the river inquiring if anyone has found it. Stylized pictures in exotic colors.

Bannon, Laura Mae. *Hop-High, the Goat*. Bobbs, 1960. $3.25. A little Indian girl is confident that her mischievous little goat, Hop-High, can become the leader of her father's sheep herd. How Hop-High proves himself to the little girl's delight makes a warm and convincing story and gives an authentic account of contemporary Navajo life.

Belting, Natalie M. *Cat Tales*. Holt, 1959. $3.00. Sixteen folktales about cats. Stories are taken from the literature of Africa, Ceylon, the Netherlands, Egypt, Romania, Russia, and other countries.

Branley, Franklyn M. *Book of Moon Rockets for You.* Crowell, 1959. $3.00. A simplified and informative book for the young scientifically inclined child. Facts are presented through a brief text accompanied by instructive illustrations.

Brown, Marcia. *Tamarindo.* Scribner, 1960. $2.95. An engaging story of a lost donkey and a riotous search by four small boys around the village of Sicily. Colorful and appropriate illustrations.

Bulla, Clyde Robert. *Three-Dollar Mule.* Crowell, 1960. $3.00. Unexpectedly Don becomes the owner of a supposedly mean mule—instead of the horse he wanted for his birthday. Named Sinbad by Don's sister, the ingenious little mule lives up to his reputation by getting into various scrapes, and it looks as if Don will have to part with the animal. Then Sinbad saves Don's life. Good for independent reading and will interest older slow readers.

Campbell, Elizabeth A. *Nails to Nickles.* Little, 1960. $3.00. An artistic, factual, and highly interesting story of our American coins. Begins with the fascinating part money has played in our history and ends with informative descriptions of individual coins. An excellent supplementary book for the history collection!

Carlson, Natalie Savage. *Family Under the Bridge.* Harper, 1958. $2.95. Some French children living under a bridge change the life of old Armand, a hobo. This outstanding story will appeal to better readers of the upper primary level.

Caudill, Rebecca. *Higgins and the Great Big Scare.* Holt, 1960. $2.95. This simple but effective story tells how Henny helps a frightened puppy overcome his "great big scare." Shows kindness and understanding toward a pet and a good relationship between small children and an older girl.

Chute, Marchette. *Around and About.* Dutton, 1957. $2.95. An enchanting collection of rhymes expressing the small child's thoughts and feelings, ranging around and about the everyday world and the enchanting land of make-believe. Illustrated with silhouettes by the author.

Clark, Ann Nolan. *Blue Canyon Horse.* Viking, 1954. $2.75. A little Indian's beloved mare runs away from the Utah canyon pasture and joins a wild herd. In the spring, however, the mare returns with her colt. An outstanding animal story.

Dalgliesh, Alice. *Adam and the Golden Cock.* Scribner, 1959. $2.50. This Revolutionary War story has handsome format with black, white, and gold illustrations by Leonard Weisgard. Adam dreams of the weather vane on the church steeple and asks advice about helping his friend Paul whose father is a Tory; however, he makes his own decisions. Good solution to a conflict in friendship.

Ets, Marie Hall. *Nine Days to Christmas*. Viking, 1959. $3.25. Ceci, a little five-year-old girl who lives in Mexico City has her own posada, nine days before Christmas. Simple pictures in few colors against a gray background portray the authentic atmosphere of the setting.

Floethe, Louise Lee. *The Cowboy on the Ranch*. Scribner, 1959. $2.75. Describes the seasonal tasks of the cowboy on a large ranch. Beautiful format, large print, and factual text.

———. *The Indian and His Pueblo*. Scribner, 1959. $2.75. An informative and colorful account of the life of the Rio Grande Indians of yesteryears and modern times.

Gallant, Kathryn. *Flute Player of Beppu*. Coward, 1960. $2.75. A young, shy Japanese boy's chief desire was to learn to make such magical music as that played by the village flute player. When the musician lost his instrument, the boy found it, faced a real decision, and gained the chance to fulfill his dream. Distinguished pictures by Kurt Weise.

Gannett, Ruth Stiles. *My Father's Dragon*. Random House, 1948. $2.95. An original and humorous story of a little boy who rescues a baby dragon from fierce animals on Wild Island.

Goudey, Alice E. *Houses From the Sea*. Scribner, 1959. $2.95. An outstanding and scientifically accurate picture book in lovely pastel colors. Brief rhythmic text points out how shells are houses for sea animals.

Graham, Helen Holland. *Little Don Pedro*. Abelard, 1959. $2.95. Pedro, who is small for his age, despairs at playing with bigger boys who call him a " 'fraidy cat." Yet he saves his small sister from a bull, and really proves his courage. The story is filled with the warmth and color of Mexico.

Grimm, Jakob Ludwig Karl, and Grimm, Wilhelm Karl. *The Sleeping Beauty*. Harcourt, 1960. $3.50. A distinctive picture book of rare beauty that portrays vividly and effectively the enchanting fairy tale.

Haviland, Virginia. *Favorite Fairy Tales Told in England*. Little, 1959. $2.75. An effective version with handsome format. Contents are: Jack and the Beanstalk, Johnny-Cake, Tom Thumb, Molly Whuppie, Dick Whittington and His Cat, and Cap O'Rushes.

Haywood, Carolyn. *Eddie Makes Music*. Morrow, 1957. $2.95. Another amusing book about Eddie Wilson and his antics. How Eddie becomes a vocalist for the newly formed school orchestra is as funny as his experiences in earlier books.

Hoffman, Gloria. *Primitivo and His Dog.* Dutton, 1949. $3.75. Simple text and photographs tell the story of a little boy and his dog in the silver-mining town of Taxco. A book which promotes sympathetic understanding of the children of Mexico and the home life of a worker family.

Iwamatsu, Jun. *Crow Boy.* Viking, 1955. $2.75. A shy little boy attending school in a Japanese village is not accepted by his classmates until he displays his own special talent. Slight text with remarkable Oriental illustrations.

Krasilovsky, Phyllis. *Benny's Flag.* World Pub., 1960. $2.50. The true story of a little Indian boy's flag design "based on his love of the stars, and forget-me-nots and blue sky of his homeland," which was chosen as the official Alaskan flag. Portrays the industry and people of the country.

Lattimore, Eleanor Frances. *The Youngest Artist.* Morrow, 1959. $2.75. A delightful story of Eliza who lived in the artistic atmosphere of historic Charleston and became an artist in her own right.

McClung, Robert M. *Buzztail: the Story of a Rattlesnake.* Morrow, 1958. $2.50. An informative, factual, and readable account of the characteristics, habits and behavior of a rattlesnake. Clarifies some mistaken concepts about the reptile and will be of special interest to young would-be naturalists.

Merrill, Jean. *Shan's Lucky Knife.* W. R. Scott, 1960. $3.00. A modern retelling of a Burmese folk story. Relates how Shan, a country boy, turns the tables on a greedy trickster from the city of Rangoon. Gay and colorful pictures of river life and street bazaars.

Milne, A. A. *Winnie-the-Pooh.* Dutton, 1926. New edition, redesigned by Warren Chappell, 1961. $2.95. Dutton Lifetime binding $2.86. Pooh, Christopher Robin, Rabbit, Piglet, Kanga, and Roo are among the most treasured characters of story land. (Also, available, combined with *The House at Pooh Corner* in one volume together with nine new full-color illustrations by E. H. Shepard, *THE WORLD OF POOH.*)

Quigley, Lillian. *The Blind Men and the Elephant.* Scribner, 1959. $2.95. A retelling of the familiar account of six blind men who each felt a different part of the elephant and expressed diverse views of what the animal was like. Stylized illustrations are well suited to the Indian setting.

Reeves, James. *Prefabulous Animiles.* Dutton, 1960. $2.50. Nonsense verse by a skilled poet that may open the door of poetry to many children. Edward Ardizzone's drawings match perfectly the strange and wonderful animals in Mr. Reeves's menagerie.

Rey, Margaret. *Curious George Flies a Kite*. Houghton, 1958. $2.75. Another of the author's stories of popular appeal. The text and gay illustrations further portray the determined little monkey's knack for getting into and out of predicaments.

Russell, Solveig Paulson. *A Is for Apple and Why*. Abingdon, 1959. $2.00. Shows that the story of our alphabet is also the story of many people in many lands, as well as the story of the growth of language, trade, nations, and literature. Illustrated in purple and gold.

Sucksdorff, Astrid Bergman. *Chendru: The Boy and The Tiger*. Harcourt, 1960. $3.25. Attractive color photographs depict the friendship of a boy of the Indian jungle with a tiger.

Untermeyer, Louis. *The Golden Treasury of Poetry*. Golden Press, 1959. $4.95. Joan Walsh Anglund's gentle and delicate illustrations greatly enhance this well-selected collection of four hundred poems. Poets represented range from Chaucer to Ogden Nash.

BOOKS THAT HELP BOYS AND GIRLS
UNDERSTAND THEMSELVES AND OTHERS' BEHAVIOR
AND THAT FOSTER BETTER RELATIONSHIPS

Elementary

Alcott, Louisa. *Little Women*. Little, 1868. $3.00. Meg, Beth, Jo, and Amy March, "little women" of the past century, face the same problems in growing up as girls of today.

Allen, Elizabeth. *The In-Between*. Dutton, 1959. $2.75. 15-year-old Lynn, too young for college, faces the special problems of the superior high school graduate who is an impatient, frustrated "in-between."

Behn, Harry. *The Two Uncles of Pablo*. Harcourt, 1959. $3.00. An unusual and well-written account of how Pablo goes with his happy, disreputable Uncle Silvan to live in the city. There the boy meets another rich but sad uncle whom he learns does not get along with Uncle Silvan. Through Pablo's understanding of both men, he helps to solve their problem. Good characterization.

Bragdon, Elspeth. *That Jud!* Viking, 1957. $2.50. An orphan whose father has died at sea has many problems and is constantly in trouble until he gets a real chance to prove his true character to the people of the Maine village.

Chase, Mary. *Loretta Mason Potts*. Lippincott, 1958. $3.50. This modern fairy story of a "bad girl" who did not want to live with her real mother is told with humor and understanding. Portrays good relationships.

Chauncy, Nan. *Devil's Hill*. Watts, 1960. $2.95. How two Tasmanian boys, Sam and Badge, become good friends after Sam comes to accept the primitive manner in which Badge's family live. An adventurous and exciting story.

Cleary, Beverly. *Beezus and Ramona*. Morrow, 1955. $2.50. This humorous story of well-behaved Beezus and her mischievous little sister depicts excellent family relationships. May have significance in helping older children to be more understanding of younger members of the family.

Clewes, Dorothy. *The Runaway*. Coward, 1957. $2.50. Penny's experiences in running away gives a child's reaction to having to adjust from city to rural living.

De Jong, Meindert. *House of Sixty Fathers*. Harper, 1956. $2.50. Portrays the adventures and courage of a small Chinese boy separated from his parents during the Japanese invasion and his temporary adoption by American soldiers.

Dodge, Mary Mapes. *The Silver Skates*. Scribner, 1958. $3.50. Authentic history and customs of the Dutch people are depicted in this classic story of two children who win silver skates.

Embry, Margaret. *Kid Sister*. Holiday, 1958. $2.50. When Zib brought home a baby rat the already strained relationship between the boy and his two sisters wasn't improved. Then a congenial elderly aunt came to visit, and things began to straighten out. A humorous family story.

Estes, Eleanor. *The Hundred Dresses*. Harcourt, 1944. $2.75. When Wanda Petronski's schoolmates teased her about wearing the same old faded, blue dress, she replied that she had a hundred dresses. After Wanda moved away, the children learned the truth. A simple and touching story of problems in human relationships faced by one who is different.

————. *Pinky Pye*. Harcourt, 1958. $3.00. The interesting Pyes of *Ginger Pye* acquire a new family member, an unusually talented black kitten. A humorous and sincere story of family relations and devotion to pets.

Felsen, Henry Gregor. *Bertie Comes Through*. Dutton, 1957. $2.95. Overweight, fifteen-year-old Bertie compensates for his lack of sports ability by a display of school loyalty and good sportsman-

ship that brings him recognition and high esteem among his classmates.

Friedman, Frieda. *A Sundae with Judy*. Morrow, 1949. $2.50. A group
of neighborhood children in New York City, representing all races
and creeds, put on a show and earn money to help a poor family.
Good intercultural relationships.

Fritz, Jean. *Brady*. Coward, 1960. $3.00. In 1836, during a raging slavery
controversy, a Pennsylvania boy with an inclination to talk too
much and think too little became deeply involved when his min-
ister father was endangered. During the crisis he acted with sin-
cerity and good judgment and won high family recognition.

Garthwaite, Marion. *Mario, a Mexican Boy's Adventures*. Doubleday,
1960. $2.75. An eleven-year-old Mexican boy, the victim of un-
fortunate circumstances, is compelled to cross the border with
wetbacks to pick cotton in the Imperial Valley of California.
Vividly and sensitively portrays his loneliness, fears, and language
difficulty in a strange country.

Gates, Doris. *Blue Willow*. Viking, 1940. $2.50. Ten-year-old Janey,
whose father was a migrant laborer in the California cotton fields,
longed for a real and permanent home. Janey's courage and the
sacrifice of her most cherished possession in the attempt to attain
her aim make an appealing story.

George, Jean. *My Side of the Mountain*. Dutton, 1959. $3.00. The story
of young Sam Gribley's year of complete self-sufficiency spent in
the Catskill Mountains. Especially good for nature-loving or ad-
venturous youngsters.

Gilbert, Nan. *Champions Don't Cry*. Harper, 1960. $2.95. Striving to
become a tennis champion, impetuous thirteen-year-old Sally
learns the importance of self-discipline and stability.

Gray, Elizabeth Janet. *The Cheerful Heart*. Viking, 1959. $3.00. When
Tomi's family return to Tokyo at the end of the war, they face
many adjustments. Their home has been destroyed, and they must
live in a small, inconvenient house. Yet Tomi always sees the
bright side of the situation. Depicts Japanese life and true understanding of a universal eleven-year-old girl.

Hall, Natalie. *The World in a City Block*. Viking, 1960. $2.50. An easy-
to-read account of a young boy who runs a bakery route in New
York City and learns much about the Old World backgrounds of
his customers. Should stimulate intercultural understanding.

Hark, Mildred, and McQueen, Noel. *A Home for Penny*. Watts, 1960.
$2.95. Self-reliant Penny experienced hope and disappointment as

other children were selected from the orphanage to live with families. However, after facing her own problems honestly, she finally and surprisingly won her own home. A humorous and heart-warming story.

Harry, Robert Reese. *Elephant Boy of Burma*. Random House, 1960. $2.95. This story of a twelve-year-old boy's efforts to train an elephant for work vividly portrays life in a Burmese village. Stimulates appreciation of a different way of life.

Hayes, Florence. *Skid*. Houghton, 1948. $2.50. A Georgia Negro boy adjusts to his new Connecticut environment and wins acceptance through his baseball-playing ability. The problem of race relations in interspersed with elements of humor.

Howard, Elizabeth. *Courage of Bethea*. Morrow, 1959. $2.95. A moving story of a pretty, lively, and intelligent orphan girl who lived in Ohio a hundred years ago. Her problem with a neurotic aunt, her relationship with her kind uncle, her adjustment to new situations, and her courage make lively reading.

Hunt, Mabel Leigh. *Ladycake Farm*. Lippincott, 1952. $2.50. Depicts the Negro Freed family's adjustments in moving to a new country community where some of their neighbors are prejudiced against "coloreds." Honest and sincere treatment of the interracial problem with a good lesson in democracy.

Krumgold, Joseph. *Onion John*. Crowell, 1959. $3.00. This 1960 Newbery Award winner depicts the unique and genuine relationship of a twelve-year-old boy with the town's character. The book will perhaps create a sympathetic and more understanding tolerance for those who may deviate from the norm in standards of behavior but who nevertheless constitute an element of our society.

Lansing, Elizabeth Carleton. *Liza of the Hundredfold*. Crowell, 1960. $2.95. Liza Mather, whose mother had died, disliked being a girl and having to do women's work. She was irresponsible and negligent until a tragedy occurred. Then she proved she could think and act as well as a boy. A sympathetic and candid account of a twelve-year-old's problems.

Molloy, Anne Stearns. *Blanche of the Blueberry Barrens*. Hastings, 1959. $2.95. Ten-year-old Blanche faced humiliation, loneliness, and fear all because she was too young to participate in the summer berry-raking activities. However, in assuming her duties as housekeeper and baby sitter she proved her usefulness and won the approval of her family.

O'Dell, Scott. *Island of the Blue Dolphins*. Houghton, 1960. $2.75. This

1961 Newbery Award winner is the story of an Indian girl who in the 1800's spent eighteen years alone on a lonely island off the coast of California. Portrays a genuine picture of courage and self-reliance.

Penney, Grace Jackson. *Moki*. Houghton, 1960. $2.75. A little Indian girl resents the fact that she's deprived of many things "because she is a girl or is too young." In attempting to grow up prematurely she makes many mistakes but finally proves herself through unselfishness. Excellent background of Indian lore and customs.

Simpson, Dorothy. *A Matter of Pride*. Lippincott, 1959. $2.95. Janie, who misunderstands her new teacher, is too proud to explain that she is barefooted because she has no money to buy shoes. Instead she wears her mother's best shoes to school until things erupt and an understanding is reached.

Sindall, Marjorie A. *Matey*. St. Martin's, 1960. $3.25. Thirteen-year-old Britannica Stubbins faces a real adjustment when she moves from the city to inherited property in the country. Thus, she makes disdainful efforts to win acceptance by schoolmates and neighbors and creates other problems.

Stolz, Mary Slattery. *A Dog on Barkham Street*. Harper, 1960. $2.50. Edward was confronted with two pressing problems: how to convince his parents that he was sufficiently responsible to own a dog and how to free himself of the constant bullying of the boy next door. His hobo uncle and a collie traveling companion provide the answer to both. A warm and natural account of a preadolescent's maturing experiences.

Vance, Marguerite. *Willie Joe and His Small Change*. Dutton, 1959. $2.50. As the only enterprising member of his lazy, ne'er-do-well family, Willie Joe shocks them all by peddling vegetables in his native Tennessee so that he can go to Annapolis some day.

Van Stockum, Hilda. *Friendly Gables*. Viking, 1960. $2.75. A story about the Mitchells, an "irrepressible American family, transplanted to Canada." Their gay attitude toward life, their friendships, and wonderful family relationship make engaging reading.

Wilson, Hazel. *Jerry's Charge Account*. Little, 1960. $3.00. Jerry's scheme for a charge account, a secret from his family, caused him worry and trouble before the affair was settled. A humorous, suspenseful and true-to-life family story with a hidden lesson.

Yates, Elizabeth. *Amos Fortune; Free Man*. Dutton, 1950. $2.50. The moving story of a slave who made the democratic ideal come true and achieved recognition as a free man and a worthwhile citizen. A Newbery Award winner.

Junior High School

Allan, Mabel Esther. *Black Forest Summer*. Vanguard, 1959. $3.00.
Three English girls, orphaned by the death of their mother,
reluctantly spend a summer with their uncle's family in Freiburg,
Germany. Through the kindness of relatives the girls overcome
prejudices and find solutions to pressing problems.

Archibald, Joseph. *First Base Hustler*. Macrae Smith, 1960. $2.95. Amiable
Eddie Jarman, just out of high school, is hired by the Redbirds, is
given a disappointing assignment, and is released after an injury.
How he overcomes bitterness and goes on in major-league baseball
makes a convincing and realistic story.

Barnes, Nancy. *The Wonderful Year*. Messner, 1946. $2.75. When Ellen
left her Kansas home for a fruit-farming ranch in Colorado, she
did not anticipate a wonderful year. Kate Seredy's pictures add to
the story of Ellen's miraculous change into a young lady.

Benary-Isbert, Margot. *Long Way Home*. Harcourt, 1959. $3.00. An
East German boy fleeing from his country for political reasons
comes to live in California. Portrays realistic adjustments of young
people to various problems and ways of living.

Bolton, Carole. *Christy*. Morrow, 1960. $2.95. A story, somewhat humor-
ous and serious, of a sixteen-year-old girl who becomes infatuated
with an older man. A satisfactory description of Christy's problem
encountered in growing up.

Booth, Esma. *Kalena*. Longmans, 1958. $3.00. A teen-age African girl
of the Belgian Congo fights for an education, marries the man of
her own choice, and launches her career as a professional writer.
An effective portrayal of the conflicts between native traditions
and ways of Western civilization devoid of emphasis on inter-
racial problems.

Buck, Pearl S. *The Man Who Changed China*. Random House, 1953.
$1.95. This simply written book covers more than the life of a
great leader. It creates an appreciation for the greatness of Chinese
culture and the people's struggle for self-government.

Carson, John F. *The Coach Nobody Liked*. Farrar, Straus, 1960. $2.95. Sid
Hawkes submits to his father, a domineering ex-champion basket-
ball player, and sacrifices scholastic recognition for athletic attainment. Coach Hugh Hanson stresses character building above
winning games and proves to Sid's father the true value of competitive sports.

Cavanna, Betty. *Accent on April*. Morrow, 1960. $2.95. Portrays fifteen-year-old Kathy McCall's sudden change in attitude toward her family. Particularly depicts the problem of an adolescent brother-sister relationship.

————. *Scarlet Sail*. Morrow, 1959. $2.95. During an interesting summer at Cape Cod fifteen-year-old Andrea comes to accept her new stepfather and changes in her life as a result of her widowed mother's remarriage. Shows perception into adolescent anxieties and emotions.

Cleary, Beverly. *The Luckiest Girl*. Morrow, 1958. $2.95. After leaving her comfortable Oregon home, for a year's visit in California, a teenage girl learns from the Michie family many ways to be herself and acquires confidence and strength through the experience. Good mother-daughter relationship.

Cosgrove, Marjorie C. *Discovering Yourself*. Science Research, 1957. $1.40. Well-presented advice on understanding oneself and getting along with family and friends. Encourages self-rating through charts and questions.

Dahl, Borghild Margarethe. *The Daughter*. Dutton, 1956. $3.00. Set in Norway in the 1860's, this story gives a sensitive account of how a fifteen-year-old girl rebels against the strict manner in which she is reared but eventually acquires a true set of values of her own.

Decker, Duane Walter. *Third-Base Rookie*. Morrow, 1959. $2.95. Struggling to overcome a bad reputation, young Vic Scalzi faces many unjust accusations and personal conflicts before he is actually accepted by the Blue Sox baseball team.

Duncan, Lois. *The Middle Sister*. Dodd, 1960. $3.00. Tall and plain Ruth Porter feels inferior to her two attractive and talented sisters whom she envies and loves. The relationship of the sisters and Ruth's struggle to succeed in finding her "own niche in life" offer a worthwhile message to teen-age girls who may feel the need of competing with a younger or older sister.

Fedder, Ruth. *You: The Person You Want To Be*. Whittlesey, 1957. $3.50. Discusses the origin of immature behavior, points out ways of solving normal adolescent conflicts, and gives suggestions on personality adjustments that lead to maturity.

Felsen, Henry Gregor. *Street Rod*. Random House, 1953. $2.50. Immature Ricky Madison feels that he can assert his independence and gain acceptance of school friends only by owning a car and leading the hot-rod gang. His inability to turn down a fateful challenge brings the book to a provocative climax. Good family counseling!

Gorsline, Douglas Warner. *Farm Boy*. Viking, 1950. $2.75. John Warner finds true freedom through self-discipline, hard work, and his relationship with Uncle Gene. Good characterization and vivid portrayal of farm life.

Hahn, Emily. *Francie*. Watts, 1951. $2.50. Through her year's experience in an English school, a self-centered American girl makes personal adjustments and acquires an appreciation for the people and their culture.

Hayes, Florence. *Joe-Pole, New American*. Houghton, 1952. $3.00. Joe Pulaski longed to be accepted as a real American despite his odd clothes, his Polish parents, and his background. How he became "Joe, New American," is a warm and understanding story.

Hutchinson, Dorothy Dwight. *That Summer by the Sea*. Lothrop, 1960. $3.00. During a summer spent on a New England seaport estate, teen-age Tena resolves personal problems of her own through her efforts in helping her brother's unfortunate and insecure young friend. A well-written and sometimes humorous story.

Jacobs, Emma. *Chance To Belong*. Holt, 1953. $2.75. A Czechoslovakian boy adjusts to life in the United States and struggles to continue his education. Depicts Old World traditions and ideas as opposed to those of the United States today.

Johnson, Annabel and Edgar. *Torrie*. Harper, 1960. $2.75. Traveling to California in a covered wagon during the 1840's fourteen-year-old Torrie Andrews, spoiled and selfish, learns to appreciate true character values of others. Good description of the youthful maturing process.

Kipling, Rudyard. *Captains Courageous*. Grosset, 1954. $2.50. The son of a wealthy American falls off the deck of an Atlantic liner, is picked up by a fishing schooner, and learns a lot about growing up.

Lewiton, Mina. *The Divided Heart*. McKay, 1947. $3.50. Shows genuine understanding and sympathy for young people who must face problems presented by parental divorce.

Means, Florence Crannell. *Borrowed Brother*. Houghton, 1958. $3.00. Jan, an only child, spends one month with a large family in a mountain home and learns much about herself and her "borrowed brother."

Olson, Gene. *The Bucket of Thunderbolts*. Dodd, 1959. $2.75. Though not outstanding, this book on sports-car racing does deal effectively with prejudices, human relationships, and racing safety.

Person, Tom. *The Rebellion of Ran Chatham*. Longmans, 1957. $2.75. At sixteen Ran Chatham feels he has all the knowledge he needs, resists his father's advice, and runs away from home. However, after some unusual experiences and an unexpected lesson, he returns to school a "sadder and wiser young man."

Ringwood, Gwen Pharis. *Younger Brother*. Longmans, 1959. $3.50. A sensitive and perceptive account of a fourteen-year-old Canadian ranch boy's struggle to overcome grief and loneliness, to assume adult responsibilities and to grow toward manhood.

Sherburne, Zoa. *Evening Star*. Morrow, 1960. $2.95. Sixteen-year-old Nancy Hillis fears that having to help maintain a pseudo-Indian atmosphere at her parents' island summer resort off the coast of Washington may make an adverse impression on a young boy guest. Portrays adolescent problems and deals with family relationships.

Simon, Charlie May. *The Sun and the Birch*. Dutton, 1960. $3.50. By depicting the contrasting early lives of Crown Prince Akihito and Crown Princess Michiko, the author describes their marriage as a "product and symbol of changing Japan." The book will help young people to appreciate and understand Japanese life and customs.

Sterling, Dorothy. *Mary Jane*. Doubleday, 1959. $2.75. Entering the newly integrated Wilson Junior High, a school in the deep South, presents many problems for a Negro teen-ager. However, she slowly begins to form friendships and compatible relationships with classmates.

Stolz, Mary Slattery. *The Beautiful Friend, and Other Stories*. Harper, 1960. $2.75. These nine well-written short stories formerly published in *Seventeen, Ladies Home Journal* and *McCall's* reveal the author's understanding of teen-age problems and emotions.

Vetter, Marjorie, and Vitray, Laura. *Questions Girls Ask*. Dutton, 1959. $2.95. Useful and sensible information for girls on emotional maturity, family relationships, school adjustments, social developments and ethics. Written in an informal and readable style.

Westerveld, Virginia. *Getting Along in the Teen-Age World*. Putnam, 1957. $2.50. This book written in simple and readable language that will appeal to teen-agers, gives wise counseling on family relationships, friendships, and dating.

High School

Ahern, Nell Giles. *Teen-Age Living*. Houghton, 1960. $3.95. A frank and informal text on adolescent interests and problems. Covers such subjects as dating, home and social relationships, personal appearance, attitudes toward sex and personality development.

Allan, Mabel Esther. *Stranger in Skye*. Criterion Books, 1958. $3.50. Seventeen-year-old Elizabeth anticipating entrance to Oxford in the fall learns that because of an eye condition she must forgo all study during the summer. However, an understanding older brother opens the way for new experiences that lead Elizabeth to a wholesome romance and the solution to personal problems.

Baker, Laura Nelson. *The Special Year*. Knopf, 1959. $2.95. A well-written story of seventeen-year-old Scott Wagnor who in his senior year of high school experiences disappointment and loss. Yet he gains an awareness of his own potentialities and better understanding of himself and others.

Bockner, Ruth. *Growing Your Own Way: An Informal Guide for Teen-Agers*. Abelard, 1959. $3.50. A readable book with a personal approach. The author, a psychologist, offers worth-while counseling for adolescents.

Bossard, James Herbert Seward and Ball, Eleanor Stoker. *The Girl That You Marry*. Macrae Smith, 1960. $3.00. This frank, factual, and informative book will serve as a guide to help young men understand the opposite sex. Discusses various problems and adjustments in attaining a happy marriage.

Bothwell, Jean. *The Silver Mango Tree*. Harcourt, 1960. $3.25. Barbara Tennant, an American girl in India, is an unhappy and resentful adolescent. She comes to the States for schooling but returns to India to face complications and problems that help her attain maturity.

Buck, Pearl. *The Good Earth*. Day, 1949. $4.00. Through the absorbing story of a Chinese landowner, Wang Lung, and his family the reader gains an understanding of Chinese people and their way of life.

Craig, Margaret. *Now That I'm Sixteen*. Crowell, 1959. $2.75. Beth makes the highest grades scholastically but the lowest score in personality rating—that is, until she begins dating Chip Endicott. Then she gains a new perspective into her relationships with family and friends.

Crane, Stephen. *The Red Badge of Courage*. Appleton, 1926. $3.25. This psychological classic tells of a sensitive boy of Civil War days who knew both cowardice and courage. A perceptive study into teen-age emotional reactions for mature readers.

Cronin, Archibald Joseph. *Green Years*. Little, 1944. $3.75. Young Robert

Shannon, an orphan, goes to live with his grandparents in a small Scottish industrial city where he becomes more tolerant of nationality and religious differences, learns to appreciate his eccentric grandfather, and starts his medical career.

Daly, Maureen. *Seventeenth Summer*. Dodd, 1942. $3.25. This wholesome story of family life and boy-girl relationship in a small-town setting is superbly written and has universal appeal to teen-age girls.

Durell, Ann. *My Heart's in the Highlands*. Doubleday, 1958. $2.95. Jill Brown attends St. Andrews University in Scotland where she overcomes a feeling of disappointment and unhappiness, adjusts to European standards and traditions, becomes aware of her tactlessness and snobbishness, and learns the meaning of genuine love.

Emery, Anne. *Going Steady*. Westminster, 1950. $2.75. Scott and Sally want to marry when they graduate from high school; however, after wisely considering the future, they decide to wait until they have finished college. Sound approach to family relationships and early marriage problems.

Felsen, Henry Gregor. *Crash Club*. Random House, 1958. $2.95. The author of *Hot Rod* and *Street Rod* reveals a genuine understanding of teen-agers and their adjustments in this story of a boy whose car meant "more to him than anything else."

Gault, William Campbell. *Drag Strip*. Dutton, 1959. $2.75. Two boys from different economic, racial, and social backgrounds cooperatively work to obtain an abandoned airport to serve as a county-supervised drag strip. Emphasizes democratic action and good human relations.

Hawthorne, Nathaniel. *The Scarlet Letter*. Dodd, 1948. $3.25. This classical and psychological romance set in the early days of the Massachusetts Colony deals with the universal subject of one particular sin as it affects four different individuals. Provocative reading for mature high school students, with many implications for penetrating character analyses.

Hersey, John Richard. *A Bell for Adano*. Knopf, 1944. $3.50. This forceful novel reveals an American Army major's sympathy and understanding toward the people of Adano who consider the restoration of their town bell to be of supreme importance.

Hill, Marjorie Yourd. *Look for the Stars*. Crowell, 1956. $3.00. Sixteen-year-old Marta Mitrovic, a German DP, is self-conscious of her clothes and foreign accent when she enters a Wisconsin school, but eventually she gains acceptance as well as self-understanding. An objective and honest approach to a refugee girl's adjustments.

Howard, Robert West, ed. *This Is the South*. Rand McNally, 1959. $6.00. Written by outstanding authorities on the South, this book provides a new understanding of this section of the country and its citizenry. Avoiding such issues as the Civil War and integration, the aim is to acquaint the reader with the South's social and environmental forces, past, present, and future.

Huggins, Alice Margaret. *Red Chair Waits*. Westminster, 1948. $2.75. After Shu-lan's training in a Western-style school, she can not accept a traditionally arranged marriage. How she copes with the problem and fights her own way to happiness makes an interesting story that affords a better understanding of modern China.

Lawrence, Mildred. *The Shining Moment*. Harcourt, 1960. $3.00. Attractive and popular Janey Kirsten, temporarily scarred as the result of a car accident, postpones college for a year. During this time she overcomes self-pity, engages in community work, and experiences true inner growth.

Lewis, Elizabeth. *To Beat a Tiger, One Needs a Brother's Help*. Holt, 1956. $2.95. Young refugees in Japanese-occupied Shanghai, left without families, must stick together in order to survive. Creates sympathetic understanding for unfortunates struggling against odds.

Lorenz, Clarissa. *Junket to Japan*. Little, 1960. $3.50. A first-preson, partly fictionalized account of a young American exchange student's experiences in living with a traditional Buddhist family in Japan. Fosters an understanding and appreciation for the country's old and new culture.

Maugham, William Somerset. *Of Human Bondage*. Doubleday, 1936. $4.50. A sensitive and perceptive portrayal of the experiences of a crippled youth who must cope with self-torture, the cruelty of schoolmates, and feelings against a selfish and hypocritical uncle before he finds a way of life.

Menninger, William Clair. *Blueprint for Teen-Age Living*. Sterling, 1958. $2.95. Through well-selected excerpts from *Life Adjustment Booklets*, the writer stresses emotional growth, personality development, philosophy toward life, honesty, and other topics of concern to youth.

Parton, Margaret. *The Leaf and the Flame*. Knopf, 1959. $3.95. An American author writes of life in India—events, personalities and spiritual beliefs—in a manner that should stimulate better understanding.

Paton, Alan. *Cry, the Beloved Country*. Scribner, 1948. $3.50. Set in

South Africa, this novel deals effectively with human suffering and misunderstanding caused by racial prejudice. Will interest the more mature readers.

Pike, Esther, ed. *Who Is My Neighbor?* Seabury, 1960. $3.50. Fourteen short articles written by persons of varying faiths who have been eminent in work with the physically handicapped, the mentally ill, alcoholics, underprivileged, the segregated, and others who need help and understanding.

Pitkin, Dorothy. *Wiser Than Winter*. Pantheon, 1960. $3.50. While Kit's parents are abroad, she remains on the family farm in Virginia and attends her junior year in high school. During the year she renews a friendship, befriends a Hungarian refugee, and faces problems and conflicts that help her attain self-understanding and maturity.

Scholz, Jackson Volney. *The Football Rebels*. Morrow, 1960. $2.95. This somewhat humorous and fast-moving sports story shows how Clint Martin successfully overcomes disappointments and prejudices after he fails to make the Midwestern University football team.

Scott, Judith. *Patterns for Personality*. Macrae Smith, 1951. $2.50. Sound counseling for teen-age girls on family adjustments, school life, making friends, dating, planning for a career, and marriage.

Stolz, Mary. *Because of Madeline*. Harper, 1957. $2.75. Madeline, endowed with brains but lacking in social background, attends an exclusive school where she learns to conform to changes in simpler dress but in other ways retains her individuality. A realistic and vivid portrayal of social relationships as well as human values.

Thomas, Elizabeth Marshall. *The Harmless People*. Knopf, 1959. $4.75. A highly interesting book about the primitive bushmen of the Kalahari Desert. The author, who lived among the people for years, depicts their way of life in a manner that should help young people understand their culture and their problems.

Walker, Mildred. *Winter Wheat*. Harcourt, 1944. $2.50. While overcoming the disappointment of her first love, Ellen acquires an understanding of her Russian mother and New England father and finds a way to be of real service in the community. One of the better teen-age novels.

Wibberley, Leonard Patrick O'Connor. *The Hands of Cormac Joyce*. Putnam, 1960. $2.95. This novelette set on a small island off the coast of Ireland tells how Jackie, the son of Cormac Joyce, learns during a storm that "it is not the strength in one's hands but the strength inside that counts."

GUIDES TO CHILDREN'S READING FOR PARENTS AND TEACHERS

Adams, Bess Porter. *About Books and Children.* Holt, 1953. $7.50.

Arbuthnot, May Hill. *Children and Books.* Scott, 1957. $6.00.

Baker, Augusta. *Stories, a List of Stories To Tell and Read Aloud.* New York Public Library, 1958. $1.00.

Eaton, Anne Thaxter. *Treasure for the Taking.* Viking, 1957. $4.00.

Fenner, Phyllis Reid. *Proof of the Pudding: What Children Read.* Day, 1957. $4.50.

———. *Something Shared: Children and Books.* Day, 1959. $4.50.

Frailberg, Selma. *The Magic Years.* Scribner, 1959. $3.95.

Gates, Doris. *Helping Children Discover Books.* Science Research, 1956. $.60.

Hanna, Geneva, and McAllister, Mariana. *Books, Young People and Reading Guidance.* Harper, 1960. $3.50.

Hazard, Paul. *Books, Children and Men.* Horn Book, Inc., 1947. $3.50.

Heaton, Margaret. *Reading Ladders for Human Relations.* American Council on Education, 1955. $1.75.

Johnson, Edna; Sickels, Evelyn; and Sayers, Frances Clarke. *Anthology of Children's Literature.* Houghton, 1960. $10.50.

Larrick, Nancy. *Parent's Guide to Children's Reading.* Doubleday, 1958. $2.95.

———. *A Teacher's Guide to Children's Books.* Merrill, 1960. $4.95.

Montgomery, Elizabeth Rider. *Story Behind Great Books.* Dodd, 1946. $3.00.

———. *Story Behind Modern Books.* Dodd, 1949. $3.00.

Munson, Amelia H. *An Ample Field: Books and Young People,* A.L.A., 1950. $3.00.

Norvell, George. *What Boys and Girls Like To Read.* Silver Burdett, 1958. $4.75.

Roos, Jean Carolyn. *Patterns in Reading.* A.L.A., 1954. $2.00.

Smith, Lillian Helena. *Unreluctant Years: A Critical Approach to Children's Literature.* A.L.A., 1953. $4.50.

Strang, Ruth May, and others. *Gateways to Readable Books.* Wilson, 1958. $3.00.

Tooze, Ruth. *Your Children Want To Read.* Prentice-Hall, 1958. $6.00.

Walker, Elinor. *Book Bait.* A.L.A., 1957. $1.25.

REFERENCES USED IN COMPILING THE BIBLIOGRAPHY

Adventuring with Books: A Reading List for the Elementary Grades. National Council of Teachers of English, 1960. 189 pp.

A.L.A. *A Basic Book Collection for Elementary Grades.* 7th ed., A.L.A., 1960. 136 pp.

A.L.A. *A Basic Book Collection for Junior High Schools.* 3rd ed., A.L.A., 1960. 136 pp.

A.L.A. *A Basic Book Collection for High Schools.* 6th ed., A.L.A., 1957. 186 pp.

A.L.A. *Booklist: A Guide to Current Books.* January, 1959, to April, 1961 issues.

Books for the Teen Age. New York Public Library, 1960. 50 pp.

Books on Exhibit: First Collection of Books for Young Adults. Exhibit provided by E. G. Wood and R. B. Kent, Mount Kisco, New York.

Books on Exhibit: the 1960–61 Collection of Elementary and Junior High Library Books. Exhibit provided by E. G. Wood and R. B. Kent, Mount Kisco, New York.

Bulletin of the Children's Book Center. University of Chicago. January, 1959, to April, 1961 issues.

Catalog of 3300 of the Best Books for Children, Including Adult Books for Young People. Compiled in the offices of Library Journal/Junior Libraries by Mary C. Turner. Bowker, 1960. 207 pp.

Children's Catalog. 9th ed. Wilson, 1956 (with the 1957–1959 and the 1960 supplements).

Standard Catalog for High School Libraries. 7th ed. Wilson, 1957. 948 pp. (with the 1958–1960 and the 1961 supplements).

Your Reading: A List for Junior High Schools. National Council of Teachers of English, 1960. 109 pp.

References

Chapter One

[1] Witty, Paul. "Public Is Misled on Meaning of Reading," *The Nation's Schools*, Vol. 56: (July 1955), pp. 35–40.

Espy, Herbert G. "What Specialists Tell Us About Improving the Teaching of the Three R's," *The Nation's Schools*, Vol. 54: (November 1954), pp. 52–55.

[2] Conant, James Bryant. *Recommendations for Education in the Junior High School Years*, p. 21. Educational Testing Service, 20 Nassau Street, Princeton, New Jersey, 1960.

[3] Witty, Paul. *Helping Children Read Better*. Chicago: Science Research Associates, 1950.

[4] Studholme, Janice. "Changes in Attitudes of Mothers of Retarded Readers During Group Guidance Sessions," pp. 84–85. Unpublished Doctoral Project, Teachers College, Columbia University, New York, 1961.

[5] *Ibid.* pp. 98–100.

[6] Sprout, Janet E. "Using Tape Recordings of Reading Lessons with Parents," *Reading for Effective Living*, International Reading Association Conference Proceedings, Vol. 3, 1958, J. Allen Figurel, Editor. Published and distributed by Scholastic Magazines, 33 West Forty-second Street, New York 36, N.Y.

[7] Wollner, Mary H. B. "What Parents Should Know About the Retarded Reader," *Education*, Vol. 78: (September 1957), pp. 14–21.

Chapter Two

[1] Glasgow, Ellen. *The Woman Within*, pp. 24–25. New York: Harcourt, Brace and Company, 1954.

[2] Repplier, Agnes. *Eight Decades*, p. 4. Boston: Houghton Mifflin Company, 1937.

[3] In all the quotation from children's compositions, the original wording and spelling are retained for the additional insights they may yield with respect to the individual's language development.

[4] The technical term *percentile* will be used to make the individual's reading status precise. A percentile is the point on a distribution of scores at which an individual stands. For example, a percentile of 50 means that 50 per cent of the other pupils tested made higher scores, and 50 per cent made lower scores. A percentile of 4 means that 96 per cent of the other pupils tested made higher scores, and only 4 per cent made lower scores. A percentile of 95 represents high reading ability for an individual of a given age and grade—only 5 per cent made higher scores than he did, while 95 per cent made lower scores. A child of average mental ability may be expected to read at about the 50 percentile. This way of reporting scores is often used; parents need to be familiar with its meaning.

[5] Repplier, *op. cit.*, p. 4.

[6] Strang, Ruth and Paul J. Eagan. "Teen-Age Readers," pp. 10–12, *National Parent-Teacher*, Vol. 55: (June 1961), p. 10.

[7] Strang, Ruth. *The Adolescent Views Himself*, Chapters 7 and 13. New York: McGraw-Hill Book Company, 1957.

[8] Witty, Paul. *School Children and Television: Summary of the results of ten yearly studies of children's television viewing in the Chicago Metropolitan Area.* Television Information Office, 666 Fifth Avenue, New York 19, N.Y., 1960.

Chapter Three

[1] Arbuthnot, May Hill. "Fostering Personal Development Through Reading Literature," *Reading for Effective Living*, p. 60. International Reading Association Conference Proceedings, Vol. 3, 1958.

[2] Watson, J. Madison. *Independent Fourth Reader*, p. 58. New York: A. S. Barnes & Co., published in 1872.

[3] Strang, Ruth, Constance McCullough, and Arthur Traxler. *The Improvement of Reading* (Third Edition), p. 433. New York: McGraw-Hill Book Company, Inc., 1961.

[4] Olson, Willard C. "Seeking, Self-Selection, and Pacing in the Use of Books by Children," *The Packet*, Vol. 3: (Spring 1952), pp. 3–10.

[5] Strang, Ruth. *An Introduction to Child Study* (Fourth Edition), p. 49. New York: The Macmillan Company, 1959.

[6] Holmes, Jack A. "Personality Characteristics of the Disabled Reader," *Journal of Developmental Reading*, Vol. 4: (Winter 1961), pp. 111–122.

[7] *Ibid.*

[8] National Education Association of the United States. *Your Child's Intelligence.* Washington 6, D.C.: National Education Association.

Chapter Four

1 McCarthy, Dorothea. "Language Disorders and Parent-Child Relationships," *Journal of Speech and Hearing Disorders,* Vol. 19: (December 1954) p. 519.

2 Overstreet, Bonaro W. "The Role of the Home," *Development in and Through Reading.* The Sixtieth Yearbook of the National Society for the Study of Education, Part I, Paul Witty, Chairman, Chapter V. Chicago: The University of Chicago Press, 1961.

3 Wibberley, Leonard. "Father's Adventures in Reading Aloud," Children's Book Section, *The New York Times Book Review* (November 13, 1960), p. 1.

4 McKee, Paul. *A Primer for Parents.* New York: Houghton Mifflin Company, 1957.

5 " 'Tis Time He Should Begin to Read," *Carnegie Corporation of New York Quarterly,* Vol. 9: (April 1961), pp. 1–3.

6 McCarthy, Dorothea, *op. cit.,* p. 520.

Chapter Five

1 Dolch Basic Vocabulary cards. Champaign, Illinois: Garrand Press.

2 One test frequently used is The Metropolitan Reading Readiness Test published by the World Book Company, Yonkers-on-Hudson, New York.

3 Oppenheim, June. "Teaching Reading as a Thinking Process," *The Reading Teacher,* Vol. 13: (February 1960), pp. 188–193.

4 Stauffer, Russell G. "Productive Reading-Thinking at the First Grade Level," *The Reading Teacher,* Vol. 13: (February 1960), pp. 183–186.

5 Strang, Ruth. "Question: What Is the Place of Oral Reading in the Total Reading Program?" *The Instructor,* Vol. 70: (May 1961), p. 49.

6 Arbuthnot, May Hill. "Fostering Personal Development Through Reading: 1. In the Primary Grades," *Reading for Effective Living,* International Reading Association Conference Proceedings, Vol. 3, 1958, edited by Allen Figurel. Scholastic Magazines, 33 West Forty-second Street, New York 36, N.Y., c. 1958.

7 Strang, Ruth, and Eagan, Paul J. "Teen-Age Readers," *National Parent-Teacher,* Vol. 55: (June 1961), pp. 10–12.

Chapter Six

[1] Mearns, Hughes. *Creative Power,* New York: Dover Publications, Inc., 1958, pp. 36–37.

[2] Van Riper, C. *Helping Children Talk Better,* Chicago: Science Research Associates, 1951, p. 46.

[3] Elfert, William. "An Exploration of Sixth-Grade Pupils' Acquisition of Word Meanings Through Classroom Instruction." Unpublished doctoral project, Teachers College, Columbia University, New York, 1960.

[4] Thorndike, E. L., and Barnhart, Clarence L. *Thorndike-Barnhart Junior Dictionary.* Chicago: Scott, Foresman and Company, 1952.

[5] Pickarz, Josephine A. "Getting Meaning from Reading," *Elementary School Journal,* Vol. 56: (March 1956), pp. 306–309.

[6] McCullough, Constance M. "Reading in the Intermediate Grades," *Development Through Reading,* Chapter XVI. The Sixtieth Yearbook of the National Society for the Study of Education, Part I, Paul A. Witty, Chairman. Chicago: The University of Chicago Press, 1961.

[7] Witty, Paul. "Answers to Questions about Reading," *National Parent-Teacher,* Vol. 49: (September 1955), pp. 10–13.

Chapter Seven

[1] Conant, James B. *Education in the Junior High School,* Princeton, New Jersey: Educational Testing Service, 1960, p. 21.

[2] Strang, Ruth and Eagan, Paul J. "Teen-Age Readers," *National Parent-Teacher,* Vol. 55: (June 1961).

[3] Strang, Ruth. *The Adolescent Views Himself,* New York: McGraw-Hill Book Company, 1957, pp. 145–147.

[4] Burton, Dwight L. *Literature Study in the High Schools.* New York: Henry Holt and Company, Inc., 1959.

[5] McCullough, Constance M. "Context Aids in Reading," *The Reading Teacher,* Vol. 11: (April 1958), pp. 225–229.

[6] *Reading Grades 7·8·9.* Curriculum Bulletin No. 11. Board of Education, New York City, 1959.

[7] Fernald, Grace. *Remedial Techniques in the Basic School Subjects.* New York: McGraw-Hill Book Company, Inc., 1943.

Index